GERMANY IN TRANSITION

Published in cooperation with
The Robert Bosch Foundation
Alumni Association
and The Robert Bosch Foundation, GmbH

OTHER VOLUMES IN THIS SERIES
SPONSORED BY THE BOSCH FOUNDATION

**Dimensions of German Unification:
Economic, Social, and Legal Analyses,**
eds. A. Bradley Shingleton, Marian J. Gibbon, and Kathryn S. Mack

Germany at the Crossroads: Foreign and Domestic Policy Issues,
eds. Gale A. Mattox and A. Bradley Shingleton

Germany Through American Eyes: Foreign Policy and Domestic Issues,
eds. Gale A. Mattox and John H. Vaughan, Jr.

GERMANY IN TRANSITION

A Unified Nation's Search For Identity

EDITED BY

Gale A. Mattox, Geoffrey D. Oliver, and Jonathan B. Tucker

Westview Press
A Member of the Perseus Books Group

Copyright © 1999 by Westview Press, A Member of the Perseus Books Group

Published in 1999 in the United States of America by Westview Press, 5500 Central Avenue, Boulder, Colorado 80301-2877, and in the United Kingdom by Westview Press, 12 Hid's Copse Road, Cumnor Hill, Oxford OX2 9JJ

Library of Congress Cataloging-in-Publication Data
Germany in transition : a unified nation's search for identity /
    edited by Gale A. Mattox, Geoffrey D. Oliver, Johnathan B. Tucker.
    p. cm.
    Includes bibliographical references and index.
    ISBN 0-8133-9150-4 (hc.). — ISBN 0-8133-9151-2 (pbk.)
    1. Germany—Foreign relation—1990- 2. Germany—Economic
policy—1990- 3. Germany—Ethnic relations. 4. Germany—Economic
integration. 5. Germany (East)—Economic Integration. I. Mattox,
Gale A. II. Oliver, Geoffrey D. III. Tucker, Jonathan B.
DD290.3.G474 1999
943.087'9—dc21   98-54301
                                                                            CIP

The paper used in this publication meets the requirements of the American National Standard for Permanence of Paper for Printed Library Materials Z39.48-1984.

10   9   8   7   6   5   4   3   2   1

To the Memory of Gerd Wagner (1942–1997) and the many others
whose work has strengthened and contributed to U.S.-German relations

* * *

Gerd Wagner (1942–1997) was a staunch advocate of close relations between Germany and the United States throughout his long and distinguished career as a diplomat in the German Foreign Service. He was born in Wallern and received his doctorate from the University of Munich. His first posting in Belgrade was followed by postings in Beirut, Bonn, Washington, and again Bonn where from 1991 to 1994 he directed the office for U.S. relations. From 1994 to 1997 he returned to the German embassy in Washington as the Minister for Political Affairs. During his tours in Washington and Bonn, his support for the Robert Bosch Foundation Alumni Association and its goal of improving and enhancing U.S.-German understanding was substantial. In 1997 he was posted to Bosnia where he perished in a helicopter accident while on a UN mission in the Balkans in pursuit of peace for the region.

Contents

Foreword

Over the past fourteen years, the Robert Bosch Foundation has invited fifteen highly qualified young Americans for a nine-month stay in Germany. As a result of this success, the Foundation made the decision to extend the program to twenty participants in 1998. The fellows have educational backgrounds and professional experience in law, business, public administration, and international relations. Their stay in Germany draws on their professional expertise and interests and allows them to acquire practical experience in the German federal and state government, business, and media.

Whereas many of the Robert Bosch Fellows during the first five years of the program focused on issues of security policy and the Atlantic Alliance, since 1989 the fellows have shown a special interest in the challenges confronting unified Germany and have frequently selected internships in the new federal states. Increasingly, they also have become involved in issues of environment, immigration policy, education, health care policy, and a range of societal issues—areas that offer opportunities for fruitful and often new interaction between the United States and Germany.

The nearly 200 former fellows constitute a notable group, many pursuing successful careers not only in the United States but also in Germany, Europe, and elsewhere around the globe. Many have remained personally and professionally involved with promoting and improving German-American relations. They and their German counterparts have learned from one another and the program has benefited both sides of the Atlantic relationship.

Through the fellowship program, the Robert Bosch Foundation has demonstrated its appreciation to the American people, who have magnanimously helped the Germans to overcome two dictatorships and to return to the community of free and democratic nations. The Foundation commitment to pursuing and improving strong German-American ties has been serious and successful.

Thanks are owed to the editors of this book, Gale A. Mattox, Geoffrey D. Oliver, and Jonathan B. Tucker, for publishing the fourth volume of essays by Robert Bosch Fellows. I also thank past co-editors of this series—

Gale A. Mattox, John H. Vaughan, A. Bradley Shingleton, Marian Gibbon, and Kathryn S. Mack—and commend your attention to the three earlier volumes. I am also grateful to the Fellowship Selection Committee for its hard work under the excellent chairmanship of John Reilly, president of the Chicago Council on Foreign Relations.

Without the personal engagement of the officials of the Robert Bosch Foundation and CDS International in New York under the leadership of Wolfgang Linz, the Fellowship Program would not have been implemented successfully. To all of them, in particular Dr. Peter Theiner and Jacqueline von Saldern, I extend my sincere thanks. Finally, I am grateful for the work of the Robert Bosch Foundation Alumni Association, which was founded by the alumni and is staffed solely through the substantial volunteer efforts of alumni dedicated to furthering the cause of German-American relations.

Dr. Ulrich Bopp
Robert Bosch Foundation

Preface

In many ways, the mid-1990s was a period of consolidation in Germany. After the dramatic changes introduced by unification in 1990, Germans appeared to settle into a new consensus by the middle of the decade. Domestically, there were few bold new initiatives, as attention focused instead on fine-tuning existing measures. The Kohl cabinet appeared tired and uninspired, and the media began to speculate openly about the possibility of a new generation of political leaders assuming power in coming years. In foreign relations, attention turned to reform of NATO and the European Union and the need to integrate east European countries into the existing European and transatlantic institutions. But the fundamental lack of agreement about the nature and role of each organization made change agonizingly slow. Economic conditions stagnated, with sluggish growth and high unemployment and the continued need for substantial government expenditures in eastern Germany. The budget pressures associated with the drive toward monetary union at the end of the decade robbed the government of control over economic planning.

As is so often the case, however, appearances may be deceiving. This period witnessed important developments which indicate that significant and deep-rooted changes are occurring in Germany. The influx of refugees early in the decade has led Germans to reconsider the nature of their society and the role of minorities and immigrants in that society. Unification has forced Germany to reconsider its foreign relations and its role in international organizations. Domestic budgetary pressures and global economic developments have fostered calls for greater reliance on market forces in the economy. Most of these developments have been evolutionary rather than revolutionary; their origins lie in the distant past and they are still far from complete. These developments nevertheless indicate how Germany has been developing and in what direction it will evolve in the future.

This book is divided into five parts. The first part, introduced by Gale A. Mattox, covers selected topics in German foreign relations, including relations with Europe. The second section, which contains an introduction by Geoffrey D. Oliver, includes chapters concerning Germany's current economic condition and economic reform. The third part, also introduced by Geoffrey Oliver, presents selected topics in the recent development of eastern Germany. The final part, with an introduction by Jonathan B. Tucker, addresses recent social developments in Germany relating to minority rights.

The Robert Bosch Foundation selects between fifteen and twenty fellows each year on the basis of professional background and experience. Each fellow spends nine months in Germany working at both the national and local levels in his or her field of expertise. Each fellow is required to produce an essay on a topic of his or her choice. This book contains updated and expanded versions of selected papers submitted to the Robert Bosch Foundation between 1994 and 1996 as well as addresses given by noted public officials and observers of Germany.

The objective of the Robert Bosch Alumni Association in publishing this volume is to reinforce and further the purposes outlined in the association by-laws, which include:

- providing a continuing education for former Bosch Fellows on current German and European social, political, and cultural issues;
- supplying a forum for maintaining personal and professional contacts with German counterparts;
- creating and fostering contact and communication among successive groups of Bosch Fellows; and
- encouraging and fostering any other such activity that promotes the long-term improvement of German-U.S. relations.

The editors thank the authors for their diligent work on their chapters. The task was complicated by the press of time and the continuing evolution of the subject matter of their chapters, but they admirably met the challenge. Each of them has brought an important and unique insight to their topic which contributes to mutual understanding in their chosen fields. We trust that their chapters also will contribute to the readers' understanding and appreciation of the challenges confronting Germany during its transition to a unified nation.

In dedicating *Germany in Transition* in memory of Dr. Gerd Wagner and to the many others whose work continues to strengthen German-American relations, we acknowledge, on behalf of all former and future fellows, the enormous and generous contribution they have made to mutual understanding between our two countries.

Gale A. Mattox
Geoffrey D. Oliver
Jonathan B. Tucker

Acknowledgments

The editors are grateful to many people for their assistance in the publication of this volume. The Robert Bosch Foundation Alumni Association and the authors have benefited from the financial support and encouragement of the Robert Bosch Foundation, its executive director Dr. Ulrich Bopp, and the Robert Bosch Foundation Board of Trustees. The authors submitted their chapters as papers to the Foundation from 1994 to 1996, and their contributions reflect their professional experiences as Bosch Fellows in the Federal Republic of Germany between 1993 and 1996. The Bosch Foundation's deputy director, Dr. Peter Theiner, and other staff members, particularly Dr. Günther Gerstberger and Jacqueline von Saldern, in addition to CDS International, Wolfgang Linz, and Elfriede Andros, deserve special thanks as well for their assistance. The authors also would like to express appreciation to the Robert Bosch Foundation Alumni Association officers during this period, particularly Presidents Roger Musgrave, Amy Houpt, and Eric Opp.

A board of outside experts, Patricia Davis, Ann Phillips, Carl Lankowski, A. Bradley Shingleton, and Jonathan Fleming, reviewed the chapters. We thank them for their time and efforts. Appreciation also is due to Debra Soled as copy editor and to Ann Scotti, who provided invaluable assistance in preparing the manuscript.

The views expressed in the volume are those of the authors and editors and do not represent the views of the institutions with which they are affiliated, the Robert Bosch Foundation, or the Robert Bosch Foundation Alumni Association.

G. A. M
G. D. O.
J. B. T.

Acronyms

AVE	Allgemeinverbindlicherklärung
BGB	Bundesgesetzbuch
CDU	Christlich Demokratische Union
CSCE	Conference on Security and Cooperation in Europe
CSU	Christlich Soziale Union
DDR	Deutsche Demokratische Republik
EU	European Union
FDP	Freie Demokratische Partei
FNP	Flachennutzungsplan
FRG	Federal Republic of Germany
GDR	German Democratic Republic
GL	Gemeinsame Landesplanungsabteilung für Berlin/Brandenburg
NATO	North Atlantic Treaty Organization
NLRA	National Labor Relations Act
OECD	Organization for Economic Cooperation and Development
OSCE	Organization for Security and Cooperation in Europe
PDS	Partei des Demokratischen Sozialismus
SED	Sozialistische Einheitspartei Deutschlands
SPD	Sozialdernokratische Partei Deutschlands

PART ONE

Germany in Transition:
Foreign and European Affairs

Introduction:
Foreign and European Affairs

GALE A. MATTOX

On November 9, 1989, the fall of the massive, concrete structure dividing East and West and German from German was met with jubilation accompanied by a fleeting period of surprising uncertainty. But after the brief shock of silence and apparent indecision for nineteen days, Chancellor Helmut Kohl announced his intention to pursue unification. His announcement was met with enthusiastic agreement on both sides of the former divide that unification was indeed the logical consequence of that eventful November night. The impressive national vote in the federal elections in December 1990 for the chancellor two months after unification reflected public support for the decision to unify. Unfortunately, the German unification process proved far more difficult than had been envisioned by the government or public. In the ten years since that fateful November evening, the enormity of the challenges posed by unification have emerged—from economic to political and from domestic to foreign policy issues.

The chapters for this book were written in the midst of one of the most challenging peaceful transitions in modern time. Except for the immediate postwar years, few societies have confronted the scope of transition necessary in Germany since those earth-shattering days of 1989. German policymakers on both sides of the former divide—but particularly in the east—have faced massive dislocations and restructuring. The challenges have been financial as well as psychological and the tasks have often been much more difficult than initially envisioned even by the most realistic policymakers. It is beyond the scope of this book to address all the myriad issues involved in unification; however, the chapter discussions afford insights into the complexity of the transition and its unique nature. The four sections of the book focus on themes ranging from foreign and European affairs, economic and business issues, and eastern Germany to minority rights issues, with a concluding section containing remarks given to the annual conferences of the Robert Bosch Alumni Association which focus on the role of Germany as an actor in the international community.

In the first section on foreign and European affairs, two of the authors examine the difficulties Germany has confronted in its relations with other states in the years since the spontaneous jubilation over the crumbling of the Berlin Wall and the collapse of the Communist system, while a third author illustrates with a series of environmental cases the challenge Germany confronts with its decision to subsume a portion of its sovereignty to membership in the European Union. The three chapters offer different approaches to the issue of Germany's identity since 1989, but also illustrate the challenge Germany will face in coming to terms with its identity in the future.

Unification has exposed deep misgivings by neighbors and allies grounded in long-standing historical and geopolitical realities, and prompted considerable soul-searching by the German public itself about its own national identity, both currently and in light of its history. Those musings and even strident debates, often behind closed doors but sometimes in public, have affected decisions about the direction of German foreign policy. Drawing on the fiftieth anniversary commemorations of the end of World War II, Crister Garrett considers the politics of public memory in an analysis of the German handling of its history. He concludes that the country will need to continue to discuss its history and aspects of national identity with justifiable nuance and reject the stereotypes imposed by many foreign, even neighboring states.

Damon Terrill addresses the new German question as it impacts the nexus of power and politics in Euro-Atlantic relations, strategy, and policy. He offers a framework through which to address the German question and understand the way in which very divergent assumptions about state behavior, particularly with respect to the issues of conflict and cooperation, make analysis difficult. He posits the necessity of understanding the changes both external to Germany in the international political system and within its domestic polity as expressed by interest coalitions. His analysis is directed toward understanding the challenges of Germany's relationships with other states, but has broader implications as well for defining its national identity.

In her chapter on the European Court of Justice, Molly Hall underscores the challenges of membership in the European Union on the basis of an analysis of four interesting environmental cases. From different perspectives, each of the cases represents an instance in which principles of state sovereignty are challenged by the broader dictates and viability of the concept of European unity. The implications of the German decision in 1957 to join the European Economic Community so as to regain and establish its legitimacy in the post–World War II era have been far-reaching. Hall uses concrete examples to illustrate the extent to which Germany has been willing to relinquish a degree of control and even sovereignty to the European Union. At the root of the issue is the question of the appropriate future direction for the nation-state in the march toward European integration. For German aspirations, it has meant a pursuit of national goals within the limits of multilateral organizations, not only the European Union but the North Atlantic Treaty Organization (NATO) and others.

The final section of the book contains remarks given before conferences of the Robert Bosch Foundation Alumni Association in which the speakers also addressed the difficulty of translating and adapting the realities of the German transition to everyday politics, primarily in the international arena. How does Germany balance its European and transatlantic relations? How should Germany react to the shift in the German-American relationship that inevitably has evolved since 1989? How should Europe, and Germany in particular, reconcile the need to develop its own foreign and security policy separate from the United States, without driving out U.S. forces and undermining the considerable stability on the continent as assured by the Atlantic Alliance over the past fifty years? Does history dictate continued modesty in German international aims or does Germany's increasing economic and political influence dictate a larger international role, even a seat on the UN Security Council?

From different perspectives, all three of the chapters in the first section and those contained in the fifth section point to the very complex decisions Germany will confront in the future. Common to all is the conclusion that the Germany of the next century will differ quite substantially from the Germany of the Cold War era. The Germany of the twenty-first century will have to come to terms with its new identity as a state incorporating East and West, and confront and deal with the residual tensions among its neighbors from the wars of the twentieth century. While it has made the decision to unify East and West Germans internally and to integrate with Europe, as it will do through the European Monetary Union, Germany has yet to come to terms with its appropriate role in the international community. In their speeches reproduced here, Paschke, Voigt, and Joffe all approach this issue, but a resolution remains unclear. While a seat on the UN Security Council would entail specific international commitments, the impact of this new role on German foreign policy and global involvement is an open question. The authors in this volume and the speeches reproduced here provide an excellent foundation for considering these issues, but a judgment on the impact of unification on Germany's international role will be a task for future Robert Bosch alumni and the next generation of policymakers.

1

From Locarno to Liberation?
Europe and the Politics of Public
Memory in Unified Germany

CRISTER S. GARRETT

With unification, the borders of Germany changed, but less so its geopolitical situation. It is still a country surrounded by officially friendly countries—the former German Democratic Republic (GDR), which stood in solidarity with Poland and Czechoslovakia, and the former Federal Republic of Germany's colleagues in the European Community. Away from the public podium, reality was different. Cold War clamps on German sovereignty allowed the appearance of international cooperation that belied the deep mistrust directed toward the birthplace of Nazism. When the Berlin Wall was brought down, the festivities among Germans were not replicated in Poland, Czechoslovakia, France, or Great Britain. Reactions outside Germany, by contrast, were nervous observances.

In 1995—five years after unification, and fifty years after Europe was liberated from Hitler—Germany had a unique opportunity to showcase what it stood for as a nation-state and as a member of the European community. The country's leaders seized the moment meant to commemorate the defeat of Nazism to send two political signals to neighboring countries and to key European allies: first, that Germany's political center is so thoroughly stable that any neo-Nazi impulses would be redressed immediately; and second, to help discourage neo-Nazi impulses, Germany would continue to pursue an uncompromising (*"erbarmungslos"*) engagement with its past.

Historical analogies can distort more than they clarify. The famous Locarno agreements in 1925, for example, stand in the German and European diplomatic lexicon as a codeword for the continent's great central power solidifying relations with west European powers while retaining visions of geostrategic revision in the East.

What possible relevance could Locarno have for a discussion of Germany's position in Europe today? It would seem a foregone conclusion that the diplomacy of Locarno has little relevance for contemporary Europe. Weimar Germany is not the evolving Germany of today. No revision is sought in the East. Relations with the West rest on a foundation of strong institutions and well-established working relations.

Yet stereotypes, doubt, and even mistrust remain unmistakable undercurrents between the main Locarno players. Moreover, Germany today is pursuing national interests more openly in the East than in the West. Unified Germany's *Europapolitik* is indeed not guided by the strategic calculations of Weimar Germany, but neither is the Germany with its capital in Berlin as reticent to consider, define, or pursue national interests as was the Germany with its capital in Bonn. The eastern and western components that together make up the country's strategy in and toward Europe became impossible to ignore as Germany pursued its politics of public memory in 1995 and afterwards.

The politics of public memory refers to the process whereby sectors of society compete to define what the public record of history should sound, read, and look like. The resulting consensus—the one that emerges for official purposes—becomes an integral part of pursuing national interests. German leaders insist that these are indivisible from those of Europe.

Germany indeed has been liberated from the ghost of Locarno. It has been freed from zero-sum choices with the demise of the Cold War and the survival of European institutions. Yet it has not been liberated from the geopolitical realities of Europe, and thus the legacy of Locarno remains a relevant issue. The distinction between the liberation from Locarno and its legacy is discussed in this chapter. For now, that difference ultimately lies in the nexus among public memory, domestic politics, and international relations, and underscores the uniquely daunting task Germany faces to become a seamless member of Europe.

Thomas Mann was wrong: The choice is not between a Germanized Europe and a Europeanized Germany. Neither will occur, but something in between might. This ambiguity allows Germany, on the one hand, to enjoy confidence among its neighbors but, on the other, to be the object of deep mistrust.

Enshrining Taboos, Gaining Legitimacy

German leaders, especially Chancellor Helmut Kohl, sought neither to distance themselves from the past nor to discuss relative degrees of guilt during the commemorations of the end of World War II. At every ceremony marking the liberation of a concentration camp, two historical lessons were emphasized: the daily and inescapable responsibility for the Holocaust (in Hebrew, *Shoah*) placed on Germans of all generations and the uniqueness of the butchery. Buchenwald, Ravensbrück, Dachau— what occurred at these concentration camps and others was unique and without precedent (*"einzigartig* and *beispiellos"*), as described by President Roman Herzog at Bergen-Belsen. History charged Germany's leaders with the principal task of passing on its lessons—along with responsibility for the past—to younger Germans. Herzog declared, "That is a fundamental mission for our generation."[1]

Germany's engagement (*"Auseinandersetzung"*) with its past is an agonizing and contradictory process. The issue is not about denying or concealing facts. *Verleugner*, those who deny that the Holocaust took place, do have supporters in Germany. They are intellectually as relevant as the Republikaner are politically; both are volatile phenomena but isolated in terms of representation in the political mainstream.[2] The political center, not the fringes, wins elections in Germany today.

The center in German society would mostly argue that the proper approach to history involves neither the concealment of the past nor its glorification, but soberness, reflection, and openness with the facts. This was the standard for historical debate set by then President Richard von Weiszäcker in 1985 during the fortieth commemoration of the events of 8 May 1945, the end of World War II. It is a standard that since has become accepted by the international community. German politicians repeatedly referred to it during the 1995 season of commemorations.[3]

The commemorations of the fiftieth anniversary of the end of World War II represented a peak of earnestness in the German preoccupation with self-examination. Throughout the country, churches, schools, museums, and various local groups convened conferences, organized exhibitions, and held commemorations. *Der Spiegel* commented in the spring of 1995: "The business of memory flourishes."[4] But why?

There are many reasons. The last allied occupation forces left in the fall of 1994, thereby putting the Germans truly to the test internationally as to whether they would continue to scrutinize—and how—their own history. Germans wanted to make sure they would pass the exam. In addition, witnesses are dying. How many survivors will remain in 2005 to tell about the Holocaust? German television devoted hundreds of hours in 1995 to interviews with witnesses—in prime time. Moreover, those who survived the war now have enough distance from those events to talk more freely; the 1968 generation is less interested in persecuting their elders and more willing to try to understand; and the youngest generation in Germany wants to learn what it was all about. In short, each generation has a motive to look at the past afresh or for the first time.

The generational politics of public memory and its *transparency* serve Germany's national interests in a variety of ways. The give-and-take among generations signals to the international community that Germany has an open and contentious civic debate (*"Streitkultur"*) in place regarding its history. That is a healthy sign for any democracy. The vigor of Germany's civic society, moreover, enhances its stature in international organizations, especially when that civic vitality is accompanied by healthy donations to those international organizations. Active participation in key international organizations and a vibrant civic society both serve to improve Germany's reputation as a trustworthy trading state and as a stable place to do business. The resulting international and domestic transparency make it clear that Germany houses no revisionist ambitions that could destabilize Europe and the global system.

Anglo-German Ties: No Romantic Illusions

In just one year Germany made great strides in its European politics of public memory. The fiftieth anniversary of D-Day in 1994 had left Chancellor Kohl sitting in the cold, as the United States, France, and Great Britain celebrated a key moment in the defeat of Nazi Germany. One year later, the chancellor was invited to London and Paris to commemorate the overthrow of Hitler. This was a clear step at reconciliation taken by two of Germany's key allies and a reflection of the trust it enjoys among Europe's most important powers.

Britain even sought in 1995 to address directly one of its most questionable acts carried out during World War II against Germany. The firebombing of Dresden has been an open wound in Anglo-German relations since the evening of 13 February 1945, when Allied bombers incinerated the city. Some 25,000 civilians died in the inferno.[5] All sides agree today that the action had little if any military purpose. Fifty years later, German officials and the country's press made it clear that remembering this "act of execution" (*"Hinrichtungsverfahren"*) would not lead to self-pity (*"Selbstmitleid"*)[6] or tit-for-tat justifications ("Aufrechnung"),[7] according to the *Frankfurter Rundschau*. Events in Dresden had already occurred in Coventry and Rotterdam at the hands of Germany. The *Süddeutsche Zeitung* reported at the center of the front page that the bombing could not be compared (*"aufgerechnet"*) with Nazi atrocities.[8] The *Frankfurter allgemeine Zeitung* carried the same message, in the same location.[9]

These three newspapers represent, respectively and roughly defined, the progressive, liberal, and conservative viewpoints in German politics and journalism. All three had twin missions in their reporting of the Dresden commemoration. That horrific episode revealed the Germans also to be war victims. However, noting this did not mean indulging in the kind of self-pitying historical memory that consumed Germany during the Weimar Republic. As a sovereign nation fifty years after the fact, Germany nevertheless had the right to observe that it, too, had been brutalized at the hands of a foreign power. This shows a widening liberation in mainstream Germany from constraints on discussing the past: One could not relativize historical responsibility (*Aufrechnung*), but one could acknowledge one's own suffering (*Anerkennung*). So British (and American) officials came to Dresden in 1995 to recognize the scope of what had happened to this city when the war was almost over.[10]

At home, the government of Prime Minister John Major used Britain's 1995 commemoration of victory in World War II to signal further rapprochement with Germany. While Kohl was noticeably excluded from the fiftieth anniversary ceremony for D-Day in 1994, he was included in London for the anniversary of VE-Day on 7 May 1995. The British deliberately kept the tone of this occasion subdued—reminiscent, even nostalgic, but not trumpeting the virtues of military zeal. The chancellor could be seen on German television being warmly greeted by Queen Elizabeth II and Prime Minister Major. Kohl's satisfaction with the proceedings was apparent.

Britain's handling of both the Dresden and London events reflected the government's desire to place World War II in the category of events never to be repeated, but in a way that emphasized reconciliation. The platitude that time heals all wounds can explain these efforts in part. Yet Britain also clearly realizes that Germany can be an important ally in several of its larger political goals, such as assuring that NATO continues to play the primary military role in European security issues and that the European Union (EU) does not become a regulatory leviathan. Reaching out to Kohl to show goodwill was a deft move by the Tory government to help support these objectives.[11]

As for Kohl, he could hardly argue with this reasoning. Like German leaders earlier in the century, Kohl sees Britain as a key supporter of Germany's European plans. At Locarno, this principally meant revision in the East. Today, it means a strong NATO, a streamlined EU, and a continuing active role for the United States in European affairs.

This is hardly to argue that the cause of World War II has been forgotten by either the government or the people of Britain. Major refused in 1995 to apologize for Dresden. The defeat of Nazism is for modern Britain a source of both great pride—the Battle of Britain has become an icon of national resiliency and will—and of lingering insecurity—the costs of victory forced Britain to step back from the front ranks of global power. The British attribute this loss of prestige almost exclusively to Germany. This has caused lingering mistrust and smoldering resentment.

The extent to which British thinking about Germany continues to be shaped by notions such as "national character" became evident in 1995 as one of the hoariest "Hun" clichés was dragged out and presented for all Britain to see. It has been argued repeatedly that romanticism provided much of the intellectual and emotional underpinnings for Hitler and his minions. This line of reasoning was confirmed fifty years after the Nazi capitulation in a German romanticism exhibition that opened in London and traveled to Munich. The British presentation of German romantic painters caused an uproar in Germany. Works in the exhibition, entitled "The Romantic Spirit in German Art," were arrayed in a chronological sequence oriented toward the conclusion that Caspar David Friedrich had led inevitably to the formation of the Hitler Youth.

German critics rejected this approach for its simplicity. When the exhibition moved to Munich, the paintings were reconfigured and the selection was expanded dramatically to underline the difficulty of defining romanticism. The paintings also were presented more haphazardly to emphasize the difficulty of presenting any chronological history of romanticism that tied it to Nazism. To be sure, art approved by the Nazis was portrayed in the Munich version of the exhibition, and no effort was made to conceal the Nazi usurpation of certain romantic themes—the exhibition was housed in Hitler's Haus der Deutschen Kunst. But that romanticism actually led to Nazism was a conclusion impossible to extract from the Munich version of the exhibition.[12]

The episode is a study in the shifting contours of Germany's engagement with its cultural history and sense of nationhood. There is clearly less predisposition in Germany to allow a discussion, either nationally or internationally, about the country's history that runs in roughly three stages: the precursors of Nazism, the height of Nazism, and the extent to which Nazism is or is not again on the rise. Germany is slowly matching its political sovereignty with a more confident intellectual independence. This is not a return to the historical revisionism of Weimar, however, nor is it an acceptance of the sort of historical simplicities evident in Bonn during the Cold War period. The muse of history is being put to more sophisticated uses today.

Franco-German Ties: A Question of Dialectical Deliberations

French elites and leading public figures in Germany joined in 1995 to celebrate the centennial of the birth of Ernst Jünger. The author of *In Stahlgewittern* (1920) and *Auf den Marmor-Klippen* (1939) is the last living German to have been awarded the prestigious order of merit by Kaiser Wilhelm II at the end of World War I. Jünger represents, as *Le Monde* noted, "a hundred years of Germanity."[13] The heads of the German government and state, Helmut Kohl and Roman Herzog, allowed themselves to be photographed next to Jünger at the birthday reception.[14] The ceremony was televised.

Although he was never a member of the National Socialist (Nazi) party, Jünger admired the energy of Hitlerian ambition. This association by affinity meant that Jünger was to be forgotten during most of West Germany's existence. After Kohl came to power, and French President François Mitterrand himself provided an intellectual benediction for the writer, it became politically feasible for him to be regarded as a national hero. Mitterrand had even received the German writer on such symbolic occasions as the 1984 commemoration of the battle of Verdun and the 1988 twenty-fifth anniversary of the signing of the Treaty of Elysée on Franco-German cooperation.[15]

This recognition by Germany's most important European ally made Jünger once again respectable (*salonfähig*). His appeal to Mitterrand and many of his compatriots lies in a writing style that possesses what Lucas Delattre, writing in *Le Monde*, calls "the rationality of Voltaire and the irrationality of Nietzsche."[16] Of course, this interpretation of Jünger confirms much French thinking that began with the reflections of Madame de Staël. It also reflects a French interpretation of German history similar to the British line revealed in the exhibition on romanticism: the German penchant for order and its admiration of strength.[17]

Order and strength were not the qualities in Jünger's writing that the German media focused on when covering the writer's hundredth birthday. That a conservative daily such as *Die Welt* reported on Jünger's birthday in its headlines should not have come as a complete surprise. The paper's editors regularly argue that Germany needs to develop a sense of national purpose and identity before it can fully understand its role in Europe and in the world. More surprisingly, the more circumspect *Die Zeit* also noted Jünger's appeal as a national symbol.[18] The complexity of Jünger's past was openly acknowledged by the progressive *Frankfurter Rundschau*: "There's no doubt that this hearty spirit can only be heralded or damned by those who skip over, repress, or set aside parts of his works."[19]

The debate about where to place Jünger in German literary history is similar to that which unfolded with German painting and the romantic paintings exhibition in Munich: There is no effort in Germany to conceal or distort connections and consequences. Yet Germans want to conduct the politics of public memory on their own terms, not according to a formula. Jünger provides an appealing symbol for this process because of his longevity and international respectability.

Mitterrand validated Germany's growing confidence in talking about its national history when he came to Berlin some two months after Jünger's birthday to participate in the 8 May 1995 commemoration ceremony—a visit that Mitterrand had proposed to Kohl. Mitterrand announced during his speech that this would be his last major international appearance before retiring from the presidency, and he wanted to use it "to pay my personal debt to Germany, the Germany of today, the Germany of always."[20] Mitterrand did not utter a word of criticism about Germany or its handling of the country's past.

Paris, London, and Bonn thus dignified the 1995 World War II commemorations with restraint and tact and were sincere in their efforts to signal reconciliation. This shows that they sought to move beyond the past to pursue more contemporary politics. Nevertheless, contemporary politics is pushing publics in western Europe to cling to that past. Western Europe's great powers are still occupied by national competition, regardless of what is happening in the EU. The French weekly *Le Nouvel observateur* put it succinctly: "The German question will not go away in France, be it about a common currency or something else, because it is ultimately a question about ourselves."[21] For both France and Great Britain, deliberations about national identity and purpose invariably involve a dialectical process connected with Germany.

Slights and Czechs

Unlike his British and French counterparts, the president of the Czech Republic, Václav Havel, was openly critical in 1995 of Bonn's handling of the historical record and bilateral relations over the past few years. Havel noted in an interview with a major German newspaper that, despite his apology in 1989 for the forced expulsion from Czechoslovakia in 1945 of Sudeten Germans (*Vertreibung*) and despite concrete efforts at addressing the Sudeten Germans issue, he saw little reciprocation from the Kohl government. Havel's comments were made two days before the 8 May ceremonies.[22] *Die Zeit* commented that Germany was conducting itself toward its eastern neighbor like a stiff giant (*starrer Riese*); it had done nothing since the 1992 Basic Treaty to support Havel's gestures, which had unleashed a firestorm of protest in his home country.[23] Why?

One could dismissively reply: "Because of 3.4 million Sudeten Germans." This response does provide much of the answer. Bonn leaves its Czech politics to the state government in Bavaria, the one that deals with the largest concentration of Sudeten Germans. Neither the Bavarian-based ruling party, the Christian Socialist Union (CSU), nor Chancellor Kohl wanted to earn the ire of this active voting constituency by openly discussing compensation for the victims of Nazism—a matter handled with Poland several years ago—without having something concrete to show regarding the property of Germans who formerly lived in the Czech Republic. Havel made it clear—as did the Czech Supreme Court—that no property is to be returned, nor is there to be compensation for lost property.

This represents a telling case of how public memory plays a defining role in domestic political culture and in the conduct of foreign policy. Are

Sudeten German pressure tactics so effective as to make the national government in Bonn reluctant to vigorously pursue reconciliation with its Czech neighbor? Or does this show instead some finely tuned calculation by the Kohl government that the Czech Republic needs Germany—and hopes for EU and NATO membership—more than Germany needs the Czech Republic—a sought-after market, but a medium-sized power at best? Regarding regional stability, moreover, Germany's eastern neighbor is clearly an important consideration, but not a determining factor. Bonn can, in short, allow Czech relations to slip a little without hurting German interests. Indeed, the ruling coalition's fortunes can even be improved by relations with the Czech Republic using domestic political calculations.

The point that the politics of public memory is inseparable from the politics of geostrategic power in the case of Germany, and in every other country, can be underlined by posing a pair of pointed questions. Would Kohl allow Franco-German relations to become as strained as Czech-German ties because of domestic politics? Would he permit German regional politics to lead to the delegation of Franco-German ties to a coalition partner? The answer to both questions is clearly no. Germany's *Europapolitik* begins with France. The Czech Republic does not enjoy this stature in Bonn.

Another comparison—this time with power politics farther east—further clarifies the connection between the politics of public memory and regional *Realpolitik*. We can contrast Germany's public memory calculus pertaining to the Czech Republic with that regarding Russia during the 1995 commemorations. Russia possesses vast economic potential and the ability to ignite Europe in conventional or nuclear flames. Russia's commemorations of 8 May were everything that the French and British ceremonies were not: bombastic, militaristic, loudly trumpeting the defeat of fascism. But Russia's public psychological needs differ from those of Britain and France. The latter countries are undergoing deep debates about national identity, to be sure, but they have not had an entire societal model and its historical justification swept away. Kohl understood the difference and thus the need as a German to go to Moscow and endure Russia's celebration of the martial spirit. *Die Welt* summed it up: "One can criticize Yeltsin, but one has to acknowledge his dilemma."[24]

Kohl certainly did not want to sanction Russian military nationalism in the form of the parade in Moscow trumpeting the glorious fighting past. The British, the French, and the Americans, however, had agreed de facto to do just that. Their agreement to attend the 8 May parade had been decisively influenced by the perception that such a spectacle would help to bolster the political fortunes of Yeltsin, and thus Russian stability. Germany is a sovereign country, but the sine qua non of its foreign policy is its European and transatlantic alliances. For Kohl to turn down the invitation to go to Moscow would have been an unmistakable snub of his closest allies.

Poland's Place at the Victory Table

Meanwhile back home, the chancellor wanted a decidedly lower-key affair to commemorate the end of World War II.[25] Originally, this meant Kohl's inviting a few German dignitaries to Berlin. Then French president François Mitterrand requested permission to give a speech during the ceremony. This grand gesture moved Kohl, and he could not refuse. Yet the French should not be the only foreign guests: but which others? In the end, Kohl restricted himself to participants at the July 1945 Potsdam conference, thereby ensuring that the affair would remain small.

Poland took umbrage. The country's foreign minister, Wladyslaw Bartoszewski, had proposed publicly—without consulting any of the key players in Germany or Poland—that Germany invite President Lech Walesa to speak at the 8 May ceremony in Berlin. This would be a symbol of reciprocation by Germany for the invitation extended by the Polish president to President Herzog in 1994 to speak at the fiftieth anniversary of the Warsaw uprising. Walesa had to fight domestically to sell his proposal for reconciliation, and was sharply attacked for it.

Kohl, however, did not budge, and no Polish official attended the 8 May ceremony in Berlin. Three political considerations probably shaped the chancellor's calculations. First, he did not want to put his French colleague in the difficult position of having Poland recognized as a victorious power and thus inviting comparison between the two countries' contributions toward the defeat of Nazism.[26] If Poland were invited based on resistance to Hitler, moreover, what about other European countries? This consideration can be dealt with fairly easily, however, by noting that Poland bore an inordinate amount of the Nazi onslaught and provided some of the most tenacious resistance to Hitler's rule. Such a recognition, however, would make Russia's participation in the 8 May ceremony all the more controversial. This, above all, Kohl wanted to avoid. His ally, Yeltsin, needed a boost back home, and the German chancellor wanted to provide it with recognition of the untainted glory bestowed upon Russia in defeating Nazism.

In the realm of *Realpolitik* and public memory or, perhaps more accurately, the *Realpolitik* of public memory, Kohl thus had to choose between (1) slighting a neighboring country and (2) causing an uncomfortable controversy for a key ally to the west and uproar in the government of a crucial partner to the east. Walesa was not invited to Germany.

Foreign Minister Bartoszewski was therefore asked to come to Bonn in April by the Bundestag and the Bundesrat invitation, in the words of

Bundestag President Rita Süßmuth, extended "from the German people to the Polish people." This point was further underscored by an invitation to Poland's foreign minister to address a joint session of the German parliament. The chancellor did not seek to quash the initiative. Kohl was thus trying to signal Poland—as he did with the Czech Republic by declaring German ties with this country a personal top priority—that it, too, was a key ally for Germany, a building block in German security as important in the East as France was in the West. Alas, "key ally" can mean different things at key moments in the geopolitical game.

Bartoszewski went to Bonn as part of the Polish government's overall effort to reduce the possibility of a "return to Yalta." Germany clearly had no interest in a neo-Yalta contract for Europe. Such a scenario would not serve its economic, political, or security interests. The agreements arrived at in the Yalta conference, after all, were imposed on Germany. Unification has meant that Germany no longer has to accept a diplomacy of *diktat*-from-above. Nor does Germany want to return to the politics of Locarno. German Foreign Minister Gustav Stresseman's attempt at a finely tuned East-West diplomacy at the time suffered from the same fundamental fault that doomed Bismarck's similar efforts: Too many factors influencing such a balance were beyond Germany's control. This observation by no means implies that Germany was not responsible for the choices made in August 1914 or January 1933. The point is, rather, that the twentieth century has taught Germany to pursue a diplomacy that will involve the fewest bilateral and regional trade-offs.

The two main forms of this resulting diplomacy are multilateralism and institutionalism. From Adenauer to Kohl, German leaders have thus sought to cement western and then unified Germany in the bedrock of European institutions. Its foreign policy could then avoid the fateful choice between the Locarno model—a seesaw diplomacy (*"Schaukelpolitik"*) of balancing east and west European interests—and the Yalta model—the potential for destabilization, military conflict, and the imposition of a security formula. Together, the end of World War II in Europe on 8 May 1945 and German unification on 3 October 1990 meant that a unified and sovereign Germany was largely liberated to choose a third foreign policy option.

Germany's handling of the 8 May ceremonies nevertheless left many Poles wondering unofficially to what extent Bonn would entertain notions of "spheres of influence." The potential damage to Polish-German relations from this suspicion should not be underestimated.[27] Chancellor Kohl, whose finest political skill is arguably an intuitive understanding of political timing, concluded that a trip to Poland was in order.

Kohl visited Poland for two days in July 1995, and the gesture was well received across the Oder River. Concrete steps were taken to improve communication between Warsaw and Bonn, including an agreement to install a direct telephone line between the two seats of government as well as a yearly meeting of their respective heads of government. Poland let its German neighbor know, however, that it would not forget the way the chancellor had handled the 8 May affair. The chancellor's office wanted Kohl to address a joint session of the Polish parliament during his visit. Warsaw left Bonn hanging for weeks before it finally acquiesced to the request.[28]

Conclusion

As is true of other modern nation-states, Germany's politics of public memory cannot be separated from geography, domestic politics, and international relations. How a country confronts the past is inseparable from how it will confront its future, which is itself inseparable from developments in the international system. The future of the international system likewise depends a good deal upon Germany. Simplistic scenarios cannot fully represent what is a complicated and shifting process.

The fiftieth anniversary commemorations of the end of World War II clearly revealed lingering mistrust and stereotypes among Germany's key allies and immediate neighbors. They underscored that, after the ceremonies were concluded, these sources of contention would remain for the foreseeable future for two reasons. One is unequivocally the record of the twentieth century: In both Poland and the Czech Republic, national identity is defined largely by suffering—suffering caused by Germany.[29] The other reason for continuing mistrust is Germany's vital statistics: a dominating country in the center of Europe that is largely defining the continent's economic and political debate. That kind of power breeds resentment and suspicion among the country's neighbors. At an assembly for Sudeten-German interests held in Nürnberg, Edmund Stoiber, the governor of Bavaria, alluded to the fact that Czech aspirations for EU membership were contingent on Prague's meeting Bonn's demands on the Sudeten issue.[30] Such statements confirm heightened national sensitivities in both Prague and Warsaw that, indeed, the road west runs through Germany. That geopolitical reality will assure that Locarno remains fresh in the minds of leaders in central and eastern Europe.[31]

The same is true regarding France and Britain. As Mitterrand stressed at the height of his reconciliation efforts (his unilateral request to speak at Germany's 8 May ceremony in Berlin), competition also will shape relations among the three European great powers. Competition among all industrial states for markets and political influence both in Europe and globally will only increase in the following decades. Varying degrees of success in the competition will inevitably be justified by analyses of differences in what underlies national performance. As the politics of public memory in France, Germany, and Great Britain in 1995 and subsequently in 1996 revealed, much of this analysis will turn on what makes up "national character." The problems that could arise as a result were suggested during the European soccer championship in 1996, when the British boulevard press compared Germany's national team to the Wehrmacht.[32]

No one should be surprised if that tone remains shrill. German press coverage of the bombing of Dresden, reactions to the exhibition on romanticism, and the celebration of Jünger's birthday all indicated a consensus in mainstream German opinion that the country has the right to discuss its history and aspects of national identity with nuance and the rejection of foreign stereotypes. That growing confidence, accompanied by Germany's substantial political and economic power, will lead to much ink being spilled on the question Whither Deutschland?

Perhaps this is what lay behind the éclat surrounding the publication of Daniel Goldhagen's *Hitler's Willing Executioners*.[33] The book contributes relatively little historical analysis, ignores important findings dealing directly with the subject, and simplifies history to the point of distortion. Yet the nature of the thesis—that Germany was a country whose fury was unleashed against another "tribe" because of Teutonia's deeper and darker psychosis—taps inevitably into, and reconfirms, a lingering assumption that the German juggernaut is ultimately powered by a combination of ruthless rationality and irrational impulses. Despite protestations to the contrary, Goldhagen has opened a fresh debate about national character by fueling the suspicion that such a thing exists.

An indispensable tool in the pursuit of German and European interests is thus a regular and permanent dialogue to combat such sweeping generalizations. The nature of global competition makes this tool of interstate relations just as indispensable in Germany's transatlantic relationship with the United States. There are basically two vehicles that can further the process of bilateral dialogue. Governments can fund exchanges and permanent forums, and private foundations and groups can encourage deeper understanding between countries. In an era of government cuts, this second source of funding will be more crucial than ever. For Germany, foundation spending in this area will provide high rates of return in terms of German interests, European interests, and transatlantic interests.

The 1995 commemorations emphasized how far Europe has come since 8 May 1945. It has been liberated from the tyrannies of Nazism, fascism, and communism, the three political plagues that visited Europe in this century. It also has been largely freed from the gross stereotyping practiced earlier in this century. These accomplishments can rightly be celebrated as universal victories for humanity. Yet humanity is only as strong as the communication that binds it. In this respect, one can speak not of victory but of ongoing struggle.

Notes

1. "Das ist eine ganz entscheidende Aufgabe unserer Generation." "Herzog: Die Erinnerung weitergeben," *Die Welt*, 28 April 1995. Interestingly enough, Herzog used *Aufgabe* (assignment or mission) and not *Pflicht* (duty). Perhaps he concluded that *Pflicht* would sound too heavy, too *verkrampft*, and that *Aufgabe* is more in tune with how every democracy must look at the role of history in contemporary politics.

2. There is no doubt that the problem of *Verleugnung* is real. Deborah Lipstadt has documented its existence and impact in her *Denying the Holocaust: The Growing Assault on Truth and Memory* (New York: Free Press, 1993). The neo-Nazi scene in Germany also is becoming more organized; it is not dying out. See "Rechtsextremismus in Deutschland: Wie gefährlich ist die Szene noch?" *Süddeutsche Zeitung* (hereafter, *SZ*), 13–14 January 1995.

3. Weizsäcker had drawn the definitive position for Germans in the politics of public memory, a position behind which, as Rita Süßmuth, president of the Bundestag, made clear, "kein Deutscher mehr zurückfallen [darf]." *Frankfurter allgemeine Zeitung* (hereafter, *FAZ*), 29 April 1995.

4. "Lust am Erinnern," *Der Spiegel*, 24 April 1995, 19.

5. Estimates had been for some time around 35,000. Latest figures are put at 10,000 less. See "Lähmendes Entsetzen," *Der Spiegel*, 6 February 1995, 44.

6. The term used by the noted German journalist Peter Sartorius in *SZ*, 10 February 1995.

7. *Frankfurter Rundschau*, 14 February 1995.

8. *SZ*, 14 February 1995. The word *aufrechnen* is hard to translate. It has an immediate emotional and intellectual meaning in German regarding the politics of public memory. Yet its meaning changes and is very hard to capture in English. The author asked several professional translators how they would tackle the issue, and they struggled, too.

9. *FAZ*, 14 February 1995.

10. The American ambassador to Germany, Charles Redman, and the chairman of the Joint Chiefs of Staff, John Shalikashvili, represented the United States. The duke of Kent represented Britain. No one from the government of Prime Minister John Major attended since there was no intention of offering a formal apology for the bombing. The bishop and lord mayor of Coventry concluded that the Allies had suppressed moral principles to carry out the bombing. For the political background to this story in Britain, see "Dresden's 35,000 Ghosts Haunt Anglo-German Friendship," *The Observer*, 8 January 1995.

11. See "Major Sees Kohl as Key Ally over Europe Strategy," *The Times*, 26 May 1995.

12. Like most points to be made, this one has its nuances. British curators had been lambasted in 1985, when they kept political connections out of their show, "German Art in the Twentieth Century." For the exhibition on romanticism, Ger-

man business assumed most of the costs. For a background story, see "Balanceakt zwischen Ideal und Wirklichkeit," *SZ*, 7 February 1995. For German reactions to the exhibition and the comments of its German curator, see "Entsetzliche Verdrehung: Christoph Vitali über eine umstrittene Romantik-Schau," *Der Spiegel*, 30 January 1995, 156–158.

13. Lucas Delattre, "Ernst Jünger, Cent ans de Germanité," *Le Monde*, 30 March 1995.

14. *Die Welt* published the picture on its front page (30 March 1995).

15. Mitterrand offered his views on Jünger for the centennial—in the *Frankfurter allgemeine Zeitung*. The former French president opined: "Few works are more subtle, few minds more active. A reflection of the inheritance from Goethe, Hölderlin, Nietzsche, but also of Stendhal, Jünger's ideas combine the richness of the Enlightenment with that of Romanticism, the discipline of the one with the abandon of the other." See *FAZ*, 29 March 1995.

16. Delattre, "Ernst Jünger, Cent ans de Germanité."

17. That France is keenly aware of its position in Europe and internationally vis-à-vis Germany was made plain with a cover for the popular French newsweekly *L'Express* (23 March 1995). A German flag filled the page along with a caption in capital letters that reads: "France Under the Weight of Germany." The story inside details the German model for success and how it differs from the business culture of France. Jerome Clement, head of the Franco-German television station Arte, summed it up: "The French never consult one another before a meeting, arrive late, or leave early. The Germans have preparatory meetings, stay until the entire agenda has been discussed, and always vote with one voice" ("Le secret de la puissance allemande," *L'Express*, 23 March 1995, 23).

18. While not forgetting to mention the sometimes politically incorrect nature of his writing—"Juenger's misogyny is more than tangential"—the journal nevertheless noted, "He has the stuff to be poet to the nation." Elke Schmitter, "Deutschland, Glückwunsch," *Die Zeit*, 24 March 1995, 65–66.

19. "Freilich, diesen rüstigen Greis kann verdammen oder bejubeln nur, wer Teile seines Werkes wegläßt, übergeht, verdrängt." *Frankfurter Rundschau*, 30 March 1995.

20. Mitterrand's speech was printed in almost its entirety in *FAZ*, 10 May 1995.

21. "Tout contre l'Allemagne," *Le Nouvel Observateur*, 17 January 1995, 50.

22. The interview with Václav Havel appeared in *Frankfurter Rundschau*, 6 May 1995.

23. Michael Thumann, "Starrer Riese," *Die Zeit*, 24 March 1995, 1.

24. "Jelzins Dilemma," *Die Welt*, 10 May 1995.

25. As *Der Spiegel* reported it, 27 March 1995, 18.

26. By any objective standard, Poland deserved to belong among the victors of World War II as defined by Potsdam if the French were included on this list. Any comparison of Poland's contribution with that of France to the defeat of Nazism makes this point abundantly clear. That it never had been recognized as such could be explained by the Allies allowing Stalin to pervert history and life in Eastern and Central Europe. The *Süddeutsche Zeitung* emphasized: "To commemorate without Poland would give Stalin a belated redemption" (Heiko Flottau, "Polen pocht auf seinen Beitrag zum Sieg," *SZ*, 30 March 1995).

27. The sentiment prevailing in Poland after the 8 May dispute was summed up in *FAZ*: "The Left and the Right in Poland agree on one thing: They feel misunderstood by the Germans and rejected by the international community" (*FAZ*, "Der bittere Nachgeschmack des Sieges," 29 March 1995).

28. See "Normaler, aber nicht normal," *SZ*, 6–7 July 1995.

29. Concerning Poland, see "Leiden an der Vergangenheit," *Die Zeit*, 7 July 1995.

30. Jan Kren, who received the Goethe Medal in 1996 (awarded by the Goethe Institute) for promoting German-Czech reconciliation, commented upon Stoiber's assertion: "That really shook me up." Kren is co-chair of the German-Czech Historical Commission, which seeks to arrive at a common narration of this century's history between the two countries. An interview with Kren about German-Czech relations appears in "Die Deutschen sollen nur kommen," *Der Spiegel*, 3 June 1996, 37–38.

31. Tensions between those of German origin still living in Poland and the local population are outlined in "Angst der Mehrheit vor dem Erfolg der Minderheit," *Die Welt*, 17 July 1996.

32. The tone of the British press did not go unnoticed outside Europe. See "England at Fever Pitch over German Match," *Washington Post*, 26 June 1996.

33. Daniel Goldhagen, *Hitler's Willing Executioners* (New York: Alfred A. Knopf, 1996).

2

Power and Politics:
The New German Question

DAMON A. TERRILL

The end of the Cold War has produced both consensus and a renewed division in thought about European and transatlantic relations. There is broad agreement that the Cold War's demise has profoundly altered the ways in which European states interact with one another and with the world around them. But there is less consensus, and often fundamental disagreement as to the types of international behavior that these changes may be expected to promote. As has been true for decades, Germany and the "German Question" serve as the starting points for analysis of Euro-Atlantic relations, strategy, and policy.

Since the peaceful revolution that toppled the communist regime in the German Democratic Republic (GDR), the German Question has emerged anew. Yet what that question is, and how best to begin answering it, has been no more concretely defined than many of the other issues with which post–Cold War politicians and strategists now contend. This lack of clarity can be traced to the divergent assumptions that form the basis for explaining state behavior and, above all, for explaining the dual phenomena of cooperation and conflict. Examining those assumptions yields a framework with which to address the "new German Question" that permits a better understanding and analysis of the now-united Germany.

Introduction

The end of the Cold War has rightly been hailed as an event of exceptional historical significance. Yet the long term significance . . . remains largely obscure. In part, the uncertainty is the consequence of the sheer pace, complexity, and pervasiveness of the transformations . . . (but it also) reflects a more fundamental uncertainty: is the process of change . . . yet another succession crisis in the long history of the rise and decline of states? Or . . . the transformation of the very patterns of international politics?[1]

After the fall of the Berlin Wall, generalized expressions of wonderment at the sweeping geopolitical changes brought about by the collapse of the Soviet alliance system (and later the Soviet Union itself) have become almost cliche. As the above passage suggests, it is no longer enough to marvel at the breathtaking spectacle of the Cold War's end, particularly when to do so carries with it the implied assumption that the "new world order" (and especially the new European order) will be more stable, more peaceful, and more prosperous than the old. Unfortunately, this is not always the case.

Structure, Agency, and the Nature of International Change

Since the nation-state's emergence in the seventeenth century as the principal actor in world affairs, the central question confronting those in the field of international relations has been why states do what they do. While theories of state behavior, especially those produced within the past century, have been both many and varied,[2] it is possible to separate them into two broad groups, characterized here as agential theories and structural theories.[3]

As used here, the term "agential" is at once broad and precise. Analytical frameworks explaining states' international behavior as primarily the result of the various characteristics of the state (the principal actor, or "agent," in international affairs) may be broadly termed "agential." Agential analytical frameworks might use as an explanation for state behavior one or a combination of both the characteristics of a specific state (i.e., the character or psychology of its leadership, its political or economic system, social structure, culture, and so on), or the "nature" of certain kinds of states as opposed to others (i.e., democracies versus dictatorships, communist countries versus capitalist countries, "revolutionary" versus "conservative" countries).[4] To be sure, there is a great deal of substance distinguishing the perspectives offered by scholars and others who look at very different components of states.[5] Yet, as much as these perspectives may differ from one another, they share an implicit (and often explicit) assumption that, all things considered, it is one or another set of characteristics of the state or its constitutive components that determines or most meaningfully influences its behavior.

"Structural" analytical frameworks, conversely, view state behavior as fundamentally the consequence of the structure of the international environment in which states must act. The defining characteristic of this structure is the absence of a central, suprastate authority with the ability to provide states with security from potential aggression by other states. Because the international system is in this sense anarchic, each state must provide its own security against would-be aggressors, and thus states need constantly to seek the maximization of their power relative to other states' security dilemmas.[6] Because of the demand, imposed by the international structure, that all states pursue the maximization of their power, state behavior will not vary fundamentally with differences in the characteristics of particular states.

In order to maximize their power relative to potential rivals, states often enter formal or informal alliances with other states faced with the same potential aggressor or aggressors. This can lead to a situation in which the political world (or significant parts of it) is divided into several "poles" of state groupings, which then interact as collectivities (though not, of course, ceasing to interact as states within the poles). These configurations of combined power are often described as "systems," distinguished by the number of poles within them: bipolar, multipolar, and, occasionally, unipolar systems in which one state possesses overwhelming power relative to all other states. Obviously, the concepts of structures and systems are central to structural analytical frameworks, but the two terms have specific meanings. Particular systems of distributed power are the result of states behaving in accordance with the demands of the structure of the international environment. It is the anarchic nature of this structure that all but compels states to pursue the maximization of their power relative to other states, regardless of their specific character or that of their peoples or leaders.

The use of either a structural or agential analytical framework often leads to disparate evidentiary choices and predictions, even when analyzing the same event or set of issues. This has been especially true of analyses of the implications of the end of the Cold War in terms of the patterns of state behavior it is expected to produce. The question is whether those changes constitute a fundamental transformation in the patterns of state behavior, or merely one more realignment of the configurations of power within an unchanged structure requiring power-maximizing behavior. Specifically, there has been broad disagreement as to whether the end of the East-West conflict will promote more peaceful and cooperative or more conflictual state behavior. In many (but not all) cases, the lines of this disagreement have been coextensive with the divisions between agential and structural analytical frameworks.

The principal aggressor in this century's two world wars and the object of both alliance and bitter conflict between the superpowers, Germany is viewed as critical to the future course of European relations. The larger question identified above can in many respects, metaphorically as well as

literally, be seen as the latest incarnation of the nearly two centuries–
old "German Question." As expected, how the new German Question is
conceptualized, and the preliminary answers given to it, reflect the
fundamental differences attending structural and agential analytical
frameworks, and will be central to the character of European and Euro-
Atlantic relations.

Europe and the New German Question

The German Question can still be said to preoccupy Europe in the 1990s,
even if in a vastly changed setting. The country has been formally unified, but its uncertain identity, its quest for true unity, its multifaceted
power, and its prominent role in world affairs continue to shape the often
ambivalent reactions of its many neighbors.[7]

For the reasons suggested above, most analysts view Germany's future
behavior as a pivotal variable in determining the character of European
and transatlantic relations in the post–Cold War era. The conviction that
active and enthusiastic German participation will be necessary if Europe's efforts toward monetary and political union are to succeed also enjoys broad consensus.[8] The new German Question thus can be simply
conceived of as asking whether Germany's behavior will promote cooperation and integration between itself and its European neighbors and
transatlantic allies, or encourage conflict. Put more concretely, the question becomes whether Germany will pursue a foreign and security policy
based on its singular national interests or on the interests of an integrated
Europe. Obviously, Germany acts and reacts in the context of the policies
pursued by its partners and potential rivals. As such, international perceptions of the Germans and their political behavior, as well as the course
taken by other states, assume at least equal salience.

For the purpose of this discussion, then, the new German Question
may be articulated as whether post–Cold War European politics will be
characterized by ever-deepening integration of sovereign nations into a
new Europe, or by the fractious politics of power in a renewed contest for
dominance.

Analysts using both structural and agential frameworks of analysis
have attempted to answer the new German Question. What follows is a
brief review of the essential features of both types of analyses. Special attention is drawn to how the chosen framework of analysis affects
the evidentiary and predictive choices made in the argument, and to
the analytical shortcomings of exclusively structuralist or agentialist
frameworks.

A New Germany and a New Europe

Agentialist approaches explain state behavior as primarily the consequence of the internal characteristics of states and their peoples. Elizabeth Pond's answer to the new German Question is distinctly agentialist.[9]

Pond contends that, since Germans "made the original conceptual leap to a post-national European identity four decades ago,"[10] the new united German state will continue to pursue policies that promote European integration and the transfer of strategic and foreign policymaking authority to European institutions. For Pond, the opinions and feelings of the people within the state of Germany will determine the state's behavior. That "all German policymakers and all major political parties" currently agree that "the German future can be secured only within a uniting Europe" suffices as a guide to the German state's future behavior.[11] Any renationalization of German international behavior is precluded, she argues, because "the German in the street remains resolutely non-nationalistic."[12]

Peter Katzenstein also is confident that the new German Question will be answered in favor of Europe and cooperation.[13] His analysis is consciously agentialist and he argues that a "focus on the character of international structures is unlikely to illuminate the likely future of Germany and Europe." Katzenstein contends that the "social and political attributes of these societies" will be most important in determining their behavior.[14] While stopping just short of the unqualified optimism that Pond expresses, Katzenstein is confident that the essentially egalitarian and democratic nature of Germany and other European polities will produce continued integration and cooperation.

As John Mearsheimer has observed, agentialist analyses of what is here being termed the new German Question are mostly optimistic.[15] Yet Conor Cruise O'Brien offers an analysis that is clearly agentialist and still offers a starkly different answer to the new German Question.[16] He characterizes the principal difference between the West Germany of the Cold War and the united Germany of the present and future (particularly after the end of Chancellor Helmut Kohl's administration) as "psychological."[17] After the transitional phase of Germany's internal unification has been completed, O'Brien insists, a "resurgence of German national pride" can be expected.[18] Partly as a result of the natural effects of the German identity no longer being split between two states, but also in reaction to other nations' suspicion and hostility toward Germany, this national pride will eventually impel Germany to "take the lead in the dismantling of the [European] federalist project."[19] Like most observers of the European integration process, O'Brien views the Franco-German partnership as critical to any hopes that the process will succeed in its goal of achieving political unity. He provides his own clear answer to the new German Question when he concludes, "Kohl's successor will sound more German, Mitterrand's more French—both less 'European.'"[20]

All three of the above analysts contend that the behavior of European states, and that of Germany in particular, can best be predicted and understood with reference to the internal characteristics of those states. While their specific answers to the new German Question differ, all agree that one must look primarily within the states to find an answer. Rejecting this agentialist view of state behavior, the analysts discussed below ask the new German Question and provide their answers with the international structure as a starting point.

Old Structures and the New Old Europe

Christopher Layne argues that the end of the Cold War is most importantly an end to systemic bipolarity and that the inevitable passing of the current "unipolar moment" (with the United States the lone truly great power) will attend the reemergence of multipolarity.[21] Germany will almost certainly be among the new great powers in a multipolar world in which the potential for conflict will increase markedly.

Whereas the global bipolar system of the Cold War served to solve the security dilemma for the European states (each superpower provided its European clients with security), the shift from bipolarity to multipolarity "means that the security dilemma and the relative gains problem will again dominate policymakers' concerns."[22] For Layne, whether or not a particular country's leaders or populace "want" their state to become a great power is all but irrelevant. Because the structure of the international environment is anarchic, states must provide their own security against "real or apparent threats," and thus must compete for power.[23] This fact alone "constrains eligible states to attain great power status."[24] Germany's already considerable power and the many potential threats to its security in the emerging multipolar system place it firmly among those states "eligible" to become great powers.

With the end of the Cold War's bipolarity, the "decisive variable" in that period's "Long Peace," the new multipolar system is bound to be more conflictual.[25] In Layne's view, Germany, as an eligible great power, will have to start behaving like one.

While differing somewhat from Layne in that he thinks the period of bipolarity has yet to draw fully to a close, Kenneth Waltz agrees that the end of the Cold War has left the structure of international politics essentially unchanged.[26] Because that structure remains "essentially anarchic," the international political realm continues to be an intensely competitive one.[27] Waltz also agrees that the competitive nature of the international environment all but compels potential great powers to pursue great power status, "whether reluctantly or not."[28]

Waltz views Germany, as well as Japan, as particularly well placed to become a great power, even more so than would be a hypothetical Franco-British combination.[29] Like Layne, Waltz sees the emergence of new great powers as all but inevitable, and the resulting multipolar system as inherently more conflictual.[30]

A structural analysis, then, anticipates dramatically increased German independence in its strategic behavior and at least a greater general tendency toward conflict over cooperation in European relations. These conclusions are drawn almost exclusively from the enduring structures of international politics and the shift from systemic bipolarity to multipolarity.

The Root of Divergence: Structure vs. Agency

Disagreement about the appropriate role afforded either structural or agential factors in explaining patterns of state behavior has hardly been limited to the current debate. Indeed, the debate between these two analytical traditions is ultimately about the "ontology" best suited to inquiry in international relations. That is, it is about the entities that constitute the substance of the social world and the relations among them.[31]

Structuralists maintain that the international environment's structure has independent ontological status (it comes into being as soon as autonomous political units arise, completely independent of any willed action by the units). The nature of this structure (decentralized, and without a single security mechanism both higher than and common to the units) both causes and constrains certain types of action on the part of the nation-states (units) within the structure. As discussed above, most important among these types of action is the competitive pursuit of power relative to other states. A structure which demands that all states increase their power relative to other states is bound to be conflictual. As Mearsheimer expresses it: "Conflict is common among states because the international system creates powerful incentives for aggression. The root cause of the problem is the anarchic nature of the international system."[32]

Agential frameworks of analysis tend to "explain international outcomes through elements and combinations of elements located at the national or sub-national level."[33] The units within the structure determine the relationships between the units and their behavior. For O'Brien, Pond, and Katzenstein, an answer to the new German Question could be found only by looking at the polities, peoples, and (in O'Brien's case) the psychologies of the Germans and their neighbors.

The difference, then, between these two types of analytical frameworks is essentially ontological. That is, the "concrete referents of [their] explanatory discourse" are different.[34] In the agential approach, the referents are the elements or combination of elements located at the national or subnational level. For Layne and Waltz, the referents are the unintended positioning and organization of units within a spontaneously emergent structure that predisposes those units to certain types of behavior, including conflict.

The empirical questions generated by the use of these two frameworks emanate from two fundamentally different assumptions about not only what is important in the world, but what the world *is*. In this sense, the two approaches speak past each other. The analysts first frame the question of Europe's future course as a question about either agency or structure, then proceed to amass evidence corresponding to their original assumptions about the nature of the question. Still, with Pond the possible exception, these writers all recognize some role for factors outside the ontology of their framework in affecting the most likely outcome.[35] What is needed, however, is an analytical framework that allows the examination of both structural and agential factors in light of rather than in spite of each other. In order to develop such a framework, the mutually exclusive assumptions undergirding each framework must be overcome. The work of Robert Gilpin has laid the foundation for doing just that.

Beyond Interaction: Systems and Interests

Robert Gilpin's use of concepts borrowed from sociological and microeconomic theory to characterize states and the international structure allows the conceptualization of a meaningful structure and sentient actors. While Gilpin, like most structuralists, considers the basic nature of the international environment anarchical (and thus characterized by states competing for power), his concept of power is operative only as a function of a set of rights and rules, employed in various "rule areas" in the service of state objectives that are nonunitary in nature.

Drawing from sociological theory, Gilpin concludes that the specific rights and rules governing international interaction at any particular time will have as their "primary foundation the power and interests of the dominant groups or states in the system."[36] The existence of these rules provides international interaction with a high degree of order, despite the system's lack of a central authority. It is possible, then, to study the structure of the international system in terms of the rules in place at a particular historical juncture. But because these rules, and the order they create, reflect the interests present in particular states, inquiry into the character of a particular system includes the study of those rule-making states.[37]

For Gilpin, states are nonunitary in nature,[38] and their objectives can and do change. He characterizes the state as a coalition of coalitions whose objectives and interests result from competition and bargaining among the several coalitions composing the larger society and political elite.[39]

As microeconomic theory suggests, because any one state is a conglomeration of often-competing interests, states will seek a "wide range of political, economic and ideological objectives."[40] The choices shaping an ultimate policy mix always involve trade-offs so that, as the coalitions that constitute a state change, so will the mix and character of that state's objectives. Still, the state's existence within a structure of rules characterized by the security dilemma necessitates that all states work to guarantee their own survival and protection. A more important element of the system in which states must act, though, is the common objective of states to exercise influence over other states and over the rules that govern interaction among states in pursuit of the interests possessed and articulated by its constitutive coalitions.

Gilpin's analytical framework overcomes the limitations of analytical frameworks grounded either in agential or structural assumptions. While individual analysts from both traditions may profess a recognition of the role factors not included in the ontologies their respective constructions may play, Gilpin's framework constitutes a fundamental reformulation of the ontological basis of what might otherwise appear as simply a variation on the structuralist theme. In short, the intellectual referents for Gilpin are both the structure and the agent. His system, concept of power, description of the international environment as ordered and ruled, and conceptualization of state objectives all must be considered with reference to both the interest coalitions within states and the minimum conditions of action presented to them by a structure in which the security dilemma is still operative. For Gilpin, the factors of "structure" and "agency" not only interact but constitute parts of a singular process of constant change.

Implications:
What Is New About the New Germany and the New Europe?

That the world has changed as a result of the collapse of communism, and that German unification has forever changed Europe and Germany, is clear. But analyzing what those changes mean, and what the future will likely hold, in the context of an analytical framework like the one presented above isolates the most important variables and produces concrete issues for further consideration.

First, a critical change has taken place in the systemic configuration of the political world in which Germany, Europe, and their partners must act. Political and economic power and influence are increasingly distributed among multiple states, rather than divided into competing spheres of influence dominated by two superpowers. U.S. global dominance in these respects seems preordained to be temporary. In the future, then, the states of Europe as well as the rest of the world will not be able to formulate their policies to revolve around the demands of either a dominant patron or an opposing bloc, nor will they be able to "import" their security from a friendly superpower. This growing diffusion of power among states, or groups of states, would be recognized by most structuralists as multipolarity. Germany will thus be faced with a world in which power is diffuse and in which its power is considerable relative to potential competitors.

At the same time that these changes have been occurring, the identity of Germany and the interest coalitions that will have to be accommodated within its polity have changed dramatically as well. Germany has been transformed from a rump state composed of two members of competing economic and security blocs into one. Where once there were two physical Germanies, one medium-sized and the other small, there is now the largest country west of the Urals. Its sovereignty, once highly circumscribed, is now as legitimate as that of its neighbors'. Its borders, once stable and secure, now constitute the demarcation between a wealthy European Union and developing, often unstable "new democracies." Simultaneously, Germany's economic interests in those border regions have multiplied both in number and in kind, its importance as an investor and source of aid to those countries by far greater than that of any others.[41] In short, Germany's relative power, especially its (equally salient) potential power, has increased substantially, while the reach of its economic and political interests has expanded.

Seen through the lens of an integrated structuralist-agentialist analysis, the following trends might be predicted. The simultaneous growth in both the substance and reach of important national interests, coupled with the decreased ability of patron powers to secure those interests, would be expected to encourage the development of significant political coalitions within the German polity on behalf of pursuing and protecting these new sets of interests. As such, increased demands would be made that the German state create the necessary "distribution of capabilities," or "power," as Waltz would put it, for doing so. In the absence of the creation of some new, supranational entity that might solve the security dilemma for Germany, and the rest of Europe, and considering the increasingly questionable ability of the erstwhile superpower patron (the United States) to provide Europe's security, one would expect a competition for power. Such competition would, at the same time, reinforce the demands placed on the state by the above-mentioned interest coalitions to obtain power. Both the facts of multipolarity and the increase in German power would, naturally, encourage other European states, and the interest coalitions within them, to increase their states' power relative to Germany's. The result would be a classic competition for power and influence among states, each pursuing control over emerging "rule areas" (as Gilpin characterizes them) and influence over the others. The potential for conflict among these states would be expected to rise markedly. The years since German unification and the collapse of the Soviet Union have provided ample opportunity to test some of these predictions.

Measured in sheer size, its influence over European and global economic policy, and potential military strength, Germany is without question the most powerful state in Europe. In the issues of critical importance to those countries, in particular the question of East European membership in the European Union (EU) and the North Atlantic Treaty Organization (NATO), Germany has taken a leading role. Corresponding interest coalitions, both in and outside the party system, have quickly formed around these issues. In many respects, then, Germany would seem destined to become a great power whether, as Lance might say, it wants to or not.

This increase in power has resulted in calls, both from the international community and from within the German polity, for Germany to begin assuming the responsibilities concomitant with its relative importance. This, in turn, has produced the need within Germany to consider what Germany, and the Germans, want as a country in relation to the rest of the world. Inevitably, but in contrast to the expectations expressed by Pond, such questioning has led to the reexamination of what Germany is, as a nation, and thus what its national interests are.[42] The issue of a permanent seat on the United Nations (UN) Security Council, its role in armed UN and NATO deployments, and EU peacekeeping measures in the former Yugoslavia have all raised the issue of Germany's new, and more complicated, national interests.[43]

The relative increase in Germany's power in general, and in its influence in important geographic and substantive issue areas, has not gone unnoticed, particularly by the states most directly in competition with Germany for that influence. Of special importance, because of the critical role played by the Franco-German partnership in driving European integration, has been France's often fearful reaction to its relative loss of influence in Europe in the face of growing German power. This fear has produced the rise of significant political coalitions within France that no longer see their interests represented in deeper integration with Germany, principally out of fear of being overshadowed.[44] This renewed concern about relative state power has considerably strained relations within the EU. Doubts are now often expressed as to whether the project of making the EU into an integrated and truly supranational, statelike body (the "United States of Europe") can succeed in what appears to be a climate of growing concern over national issues and national interests.[45]

So the patterns of state behavior, and the developments within Europe's various national political constituencies, seem to correspond in many important respects to those anticipated by the analytical framework. Bipolarity has yielded to (an emerging) multipolarity. Increases in relative state power have been uneven and have thus produced at least the beginnings of competition for power. National interests, and concern about the "nation" as such, have produced new interest coalitions acting to pressure states into concentrating more heavily on them.[46]

Yet a return to the potentially violent competition for power among Europe's states seems only a distant threat. Although the EU and NATO have experienced various difficulties, both remain essentially healthy. The Maastricht treaty, which created the union of the European communities, and its ratification tested the unity of the Union and the support of its peoples, but remains intact, and movement toward European Monetary Union is on track.[47] NATO (and the EU) were embarrassed in Bosnia, even raising calls for their replacement in security matters by some new organization. The transatlantic alliance, however, remains the only organization with the capacity and legitimacy to provide some degree of military security to its members against potential aggressors. The fact that EU and NATO membership remains the principal foreign and security policy goal of almost all the Central and East European states attests to those institutions' singular positions and enduring salience. Cooperation among Europe's states in a world with less clear lines of geopolitical demarcation has been decidedly more difficult, but continues. That this will remain so, however, ought not to be taken as given.

As the preceding discussion makes clear, the changes now taking place in Europe will provide increasing disincentives to cooperation and more opportunities for conflict. The analytical framework underlying this discussion suggests that the solutions to these issues will be critical in determining the future course of the relationship between Germany and Europe. First, unless the emerging security dilemma in Europe (that is, the fact that there is no body or state above the countries of Europe able to ensure their security) is solved, the incentives favoring competition for power, and the potential for conflict such competition brings with it, will only be strengthened. Solving that dilemma would entail either a substantial and permanent strengthening of NATO, and the U.S. position within it, or the successful creation of an effective and credible European security organ. At present, the political will to do either seems extremely limited in almost all of Europe's polities. The alternative is that each state must assume the responsibility for providing its own security in an increasingly insecure world; that means pursuing power.

The second critical variable will be the forms taken by the new, and reorganized old, interest coalitions within Europe's polities. Should Europe's collective institutions continue to fail to meet popular needs, both for material well-being and for security, pressure to seek national solutions within the individual countries will surely grow. Such a development would, of course, make the cooperation necessary for the creation of effective institutions even more difficult.

Third, the stability of Franco-German relations is of singular importance. Without the impetus provided by common Franco-German commitment and action, deeper European integration or broader expansion seems unlikely. France's near rejection of the Maastricht treaty, as well as a decisive shift toward politicians and parties in favor of reemphasizing France's particular national interests, reveals that the political coalitions in favor of continuing European integration are weak. As such, that polity's responses to the challenges posed by the post–Cold War world may be decisive in influencing the future course of both German and European politics.

Indeed, the electoral success of a Socialist-led coalition in France has opened once-latent cleavages in Franco-German relations. As the difficulty experienced by both countries in satisfying the respective national electorates demonstrated, the long-term stability of their relationship and its role as the driving force behind further European political, economic, and institutional integration is fragile.[48] Throughout the past four decades, the strength and sincerity of the Franco-German partnership has been the centerpiece of a "European" identity and mythos, promoted nowhere more actively than in Germany. Given the centrality of that partnership to real European integration, it is thus particularly unsettling, if not surprising, that fully 60 percent of Germans, and 77 percent among Germans thirty years old and younger, now view the Franco-German "friendship" as existing "only in the minds of politicians."[49]

Conclusion

The German Question, in its new form, remains as salient as ever to the future prosperity and security of Europe's peoples. The above analysis demonstrates that in order to determine whether and how Germany's behavior will encourage or discourage continuing European cooperation and stability, attention must be given to the changes both external to Germany (in the international political system) and within its domestic polity (its interest coalitions). Moreover, by employing such an analytical framework it is possible to identify the variables that will most directly affect that behavior. Despite the considerable degree to which Germany's (and the rest of Europe's) policies are constrained by the forces acting upon and around it, the choice to cooperate, or not, remains in the hands of decisionmakers and their constituents.

Notes

1. Michael T. Clark and Simon Serfaty, eds., *New Thinking and Old Realities: America, Europe and Russia* (Washington: Seven Locks Press, 1991), p. 193.

2. See Kenneth N. Waltz, *Man, the State and War: A Theoretical Analysis* (New York: Columbia University Press, 1959), for a comprehensive yet compact survey of the major innovations in international relations theory (even if it was not until recently known as such) from ancient thought to the mid-twentieth century.

3. Though they are characterized in a slightly different manner, Fareed Zakaria, in "Is Realism Finished?," presents a brief but informative overview of structuralist claims and the many agentialist challenges to it that have emerged (*The National Interest* [Winter 1992/93]: 21–32). Among the better-known agentialist theoretical schools are liberalism, neoliberalism, classical and Leninist Marxism (as pertains to the behavior of different state types), and idealism.

4. This general description corresponds, roughly but essentially, to Waltz's first and second "images" of world politics (Waltz, *Man, the State and War*, pp. 12–15).

5. Among some of those variables or characteristics not yet mentioned are institutions, ideologies and belief systems, economic systems or levels of development, political parties or movements, and particular histories and the "collective memories" of them.

6. Waltz, a structuralist, offers one of the clearest and (among structuralists) most broadly noted definitions of "power" in *Theory of International Politics* (New York: McGraw-Hill, 1979), pp. 183–193. For Waltz, power is the sum and consequence of the "distribution of capabilities" within a state that allow it to direct outcomes in ways that are favorable to it ("getting one's way"). Unless otherwise noted, the term "power" as used herein should be understood in this way.

7. Dirk Verheyen and Christian Soe, eds., "Introduction," in *The Germans and Their Neighbors* (Boulder: Westview Press, 1993), p. 6.

8. For a brief discussion of why Germany's participation in the European attempt at integration is so singularly critical, see Ann-Maria Leglonnec, "France, Germany, and the New Europe," in Verheyen and Soe, eds., *The Germans and Their Neighbors*, pp. 13–34, especially pp. 27–30.

9. Elizabeth Pond, "Germany in a New Europe," *Foreign Affairs* (Spring 1992): 114–130.

10. Ibid., p. 114.

11. Ibid., p. 118.

12. Ibid., p. 130.

13. Peter Katzenstein, "Taming of Power: German Unification, 1989–1990," in Meredith Woo-Cummings and Michael Loriax, eds., *Past as Prelude: History in the Making of a New World Order* (Boulder: Westview Press), pp. 59–81.

14. Ibid., p. 63.

15. See John Mearsheimer, "Back to the Future: Instability in Europe After the Cold War," *International Security* (Summer 1990): 5–56. Although his discussion takes a somewhat broader view in defining the differences in terms of general behavioral patterns of states, between the optimists and pessimists, his contention that (what are here characterized as) agentialist analyses produce optimistic predictions of post–Cold War stability remains generally accurate.

16. Conor Cruise O'Brien, "The Future of the West," *The National Interest* (Winter 1992/93): 3–10.

17. Ibid., p. 6.

18. Ibid., p. 5.

19. Ibid., p. 6.

20. Ibid., p. 10.

21. Christopher Layne, "The Unipolar Illusion: Why Great Powers Will Rise," *International Security* (Spring 1993): 5–51. See p. 7 for his specific clarification of what is meant by the phrase "unipolar moment." On pp. 40–41, he presents a classically structuralist argument in favor of viewing the Cold War as essentially a structurally determined bipolar conflict, and the end of that bipolarity as the most decisive (in terms of the future behavior of states) single variable.

22. Ibid., p. 42.

23. Ibid., p. 11.

24. Ibid.

25. Ibid., p. 41. The long peace (among Western states) characteristic of the Cold War was thus a "structural" peace resulting from the stability of the bipolar system and the temporary solution of the security dilemma in Europe. It was not a "liberal" peace based on the shared values or political systems of those countries.

26. Kenneth N. Waltz, "The Emerging Structure of International Politics," *International Security* (Fall 1993): 44–79.

27. Ibid., p. 59.

28. See ibid., pp. 64–68, for the reasons why this is so. Waltz's argument is slightly more nuanced than Layne's, but shares the same central contentions.

29. Ibid., p. 71.

30. Ibid., pp. 44, 66.

31. David Dessler, "What's at Stake in the Agent-Structure Debate," *International Organization* (Summer 1989): 441–473, offers an excellent discussion of the history of this debate in international relations theory. For his specific comments on the debate's roots in ontology, see p. 445.

32. Mearsheimer, "Back to the Future," p. 12.

33. Waltz, *Theory of International Politics*, p. 18.

34. Dessler, "What's at Stake in the Agent-Structure Debate," p. 445.

35. Most commonly, though, when such recognition is made, it is to argue that in any specific instance some agential factor "interacts" with some structural factor. The problem with these arguments is that they are most often made with little or no explanation of why the particular interaction took place in a particular case, why it was important in some cases but not in others, or whether such "interactions" can be expected to repeat themselves over time.

36. Robert Gilpin, *War and Change in World Politics* (New York: Cambridge University Press, 1987), p. 35.

37. Ibid., p. 30.

38. This is taken to mean that states do not constitute a singular, monolithic unit, but are in fact plural, composite units which contain within them many social components, some or all of which may have different interests at different times.

39. Ibid., p. 19.

40. Ibid., p. 22.

41. See Michael Dauderstädt, "A Comparison of the Assistance Strategies of the Western Donors," *Friedrich Ebert Stiftung, 1996*, especially p. 3.

42. One can hardly watch German television or listen to German radio without hearing such questions being hotly debated. For a few examples of the way in which these issues have manifested themselves, see Jürgen Leinemann, "Der Hunger nach Sinn," *Der Spiegel*, 23/1994, 6 June, 1994, pp. 40–58; Cordt Schnibber, "Das deutsche Wesen," *Der Spiegel*, 50/1993, 13 December, 1993, pp. 118–128.

43. Calls for increased military commitments by Germany also have led to the recognition that Germany's currently very modest military capabilities are no longer appropriate to its status as an emerging great power. See "Morgen die ganze Welt," *Der Spiegel*, 19 April, 1993, pp. 18–22; "Da müssen wir hin," *Der Spiegel*, 7 November, 1994, pp. 18–19.

44. See "Angst vorm Koloß: In Frankreich wächst der Argwohn gegen die vereinten Deutschen vor allem aus Sorge um Machtverlust," *Der Spiegel*, 32/1993, 9 August, 1993, pp. 22–25; "Das häßliche deutsche Haupt," *Der Spiegel*, 6/1992, 3 February, 1992, pp. 18–24. Regarding the particular concern that Germany's influence in Eastern Europe has grown too substantially, see "Nur nichts überstürzen," *Der Spiegel*, 14/1994, 4 April, 1994, pp. 32–33.

45. See, for example, "Rückzug auf die Nation?" *Der Spiegel*, 43/1993, 25 October, 1993, pp. 168–173; and "Die EG lebt gefährlich," *Der Spiegel*, 35/1993, 30 August, 1993, pp. 134–136.

46. This is true not only in Germany but in most of Europe's other larger countries. Political parties and nonparty movements demanding greater attention to national issues have enjoyed substantial (in some cases dramatic) gains all over Europe, including in France, Italy, Belgium, and Austria, not to mention in the states of Central and Eastern Europe.

47. For one example of the effects of the European Monetary Union process on the stability of once-solid political and interest coalitions within Germany, see Hans-Ulrich Jörges, "Der Euro-Krieg: Stoiber Contra Kohl und Waigel," *Die Welt*, 4 July 1997, p. 1.

48. This is true even in traditionally pro-integration and pro-EMU quarters. See, for example, Eric Bonse, "Mißklänge: Bonn und Paris steuern auf eine Eurokrise zu," *Handelsblatt*, 3 July 1997, p. 2.

49. The poll was conducted by Forsa and reported in various sources, including *Die Woche*, 27 June 1997, p. 5.

3

European Integration vs. State Sovereignty: The European Court of Justice and Harmonization of Germany's Environmental Law

MOLLY E. HALL

The Federal Republic of Germany has been described as one of the primary engines of the European Union's environmental program and a proponent of environmental legislation in many areas. Certainly the development of environmental laws applicable to the entire European Union (EU) has positive effects. Many environmental concerns recognize no boundaries: Air and water pollution travel any direction the winds, seas, or rivers may send them. In addition to the necessity of collaboration among neighboring states in addressing transfrontier issues of conservation and pollution, an EU-wide environmental policy is important because it provides initiative and concrete subsidies to countries that without the intervention of the EU, might otherwise lack the resources for environmental programs.[1] Finally, consistency of environmental laws, like the harmonization of European laws generally, reduces the difficulties that international investors might encounter as they expand their business from one member state to another.

Harmonization of European laws remains controversial for several reasons. First, as the EU develops a comprehensive program with jurisdiction over more areas of the law, the member states' jurisdiction as sovereign states is reduced. Second, states must coordinate their diverse political and economic agendas before legislation is enacted. Third, environmentally aggressive member states like Germany must conform their laws and existing EU legislation, often at the cost of stricter national standards.

Originally a trade entity, the precursor to the EU, the European Community (EC), aimed at enabling the free movement of goods, persons, and services across borders. Consequently, in its early years, the EC sought to achieve standardization in services, products, and methods of production in order to further the goals of free trade. More recently, as the EU, it has been willing to balance the goals of dismantling trade barriers with other objectives, including environmental ones. Recent decisions by the European Court of Justice (ECJ) involving German environmental legislation illustrate this delicate balance, as well as the competing desires of integration through the harmonization of European laws and preservation of sovereign authority.

This chapter examines ECJ decisions on four issues—Pentachlorophenol (PCP), crayfish, environmental impact assessment, and wild birds—relating to the Federal Republic of Germany's environmental laws and the extent to which Germany has been allowed to maintain environmental legislation deemed inconsistent with directives enacted by the EU or challenged for not enacting the EU directive.

In the German PCP case,[2] France and other member states challenged Germany's restrictions on the chemical Pentachlorophenol (PCP), which were stricter than the European directive on the same chemical. In the German crayfish case,[3] France and other member states alleged that Germany's ban on the import of freshwater crayfish was more restrictive than necessary for its stated purpose. In both cases, the ECJ addressed the permissibility of import bans that differed from existing EU directives. Although the challenge to the German trade measures was ostensibly motivated by trade interests, it was the inconsistency with European law that provided the legal basis for the ECJ to declare the German measures impermissible. In the German crayfish case, the ECJ's ruling required Germany to modify its law on the import of freshwater crayfish consistent with the EC directive. In the PCP case, Germany ultimately was allowed to retain the more stringent federal legislation banning the chemical PCP, despite its variance from the EU directive.

In the two other cases, the European Commission brought an action against Germany for failure to implement environmental directives. The issue in these cases was not a clash between environmental and trade interests, but the role of the EU in requiring member states to enact European rather than national or local law.

In the environmental impact assessment (EIA) case,[4] the EU alleged that Germany's failure to transpose the European EIA directive had caused the district of Darmstadt to assess improperly the application for a coal-powered station at Grobkrotzenburg. The ECJ decided not to assess penalties for German tardiness in implementing the European EIA directive because Germany had since transposed the directive and because Darmstadt's use of the German EIA procedures included adequate consideration of the environmental impact of the proposed extension for the power plant.

In the Wild Birds III case,[5] the European Commission brought an action against Germany for failure to modify properly its national law to conform to the European Council Directive 79/409/EEC on wild birds. The ECJ decided that the Germans had not properly enacted the wild birds directive because the German law for the protection of nature exempted agricultural and forestry interests from the law's requirements for protection of the endangered species of wild birds.[6]

In each of the four cases, the European Commission challenged the German federal legislation as inconsistent with the EU directives on the same topics. In the German crayfish and PCP cases, the European Commission's challenges were that German import bans were overly restrictive of intra-EU trade. In contrast, the EIA and wild birds cases illustrate Germany's tardiness or failure to transpose the relevant European directives and to balance the perception that Germany is consistently more environmentally correct than other EU members. Taken together, these four cases represent the ECJ's varying approach to harmonization and the range of deviation from EU directives that the ECJ will tolerate.

Development of a Harmonized
EU Environmental Policy

Critical to understanding these cases is the political context in which the ECJ makes decisions. The EU is a supranational, treaty-based organization consisting of four central institutions: the Commission, the Parliament, the Council of Ministers, and the Court of Justice.

Since 1957, member states have become integrated through the gradual harmonization of political structures and laws covering trade within the Community and through their growing willingness to develop a European agenda ranging from a common currency to measures for sustainable development and the environment. The Treaty of Rome established the European Economic Community in 1957 as "an extended customs union."[7] The harmonization of laws was seen as an important tool; one set of rules for several countries facilitated trade efficiency between the countries of this emerging common market. In addition, the European Commission saw harmonization as a way to promote its sphere of influence, thereby restricting member states' power to legislate in areas in which the Community had already taken action. The Treaty of Rome provided one of the early tools for achieving harmonization in Article 30, by forbidding undue restrictions on trade. The Treaty of Rome also empowered the ECJ to rule on the member states' compliance with

various treaty obligations, suggesting that EC law was superior to national law.[8]

The 1957 Treaty of Rome did not mention the word "environment"; the
first explicit legal basis for EC environmental policy came thirty years
later with the Single European Act (SEA) in 1986.[9] The SEA also was significant in that it changed the number of votes necessary for passing
most environmental laws from an absolute to a qualified majority,
thereby allowing greater harmonization of the EC's environmental law
and programs, including conservation and animal protection.[10] The EU
has enacted approximately 220 environmental directives, many since the
SEA changed the necessary number of votes in 1987.[11]

With this change in the voting requirements, the SEA also provided an
opportunity to opt out of specific Community directives for accepted objectives, including environmental objectives. Specifically, Article 100a(4)
gave member states the option of voting against a given directive to opt
out and following their own stricter national legislation. To qualify for an
exception under Article 100a(4), the EU treaty requires a member state to
receive confirmation from the Commission and ECJ that the derogation is
justified and not simply a disguised trade restriction.[12] Article 130t allows
member states to introduce new laws that are inconsistent with existing
EU law.

The willingness of member states to accommodate an increasingly
closer union was confirmed with the ratification of the Maastricht treaty
of 1992, which created the EU and extended explicit EU jurisdiction beyond purely economic matters. In terms of environmental matters, the
Maastricht treaty amended Article 2 of the SEA to include "sustainable
and noninflationary growth respecting the environment" as one of the
EU's tasks.[13] Maastricht's Article 3k required the development of "a policy in the sphere of the environment." Article 130r provided that "Community policy on the environment shall aim at a high level of protection
taking into account the diversity of situations in various regions of the
Community" and provided financial support to member states unable to
bear the costs of implementing environmental measures. Finally, Article
171 extended the ECJ's jurisdiction to enable it to impose fines upon
member states for failure to comply with Court judgments. Although the
ECJ has yet to require payment of sanctions, Article 171 may have increasing significance in achieving compliance with environmental directives.

The first articulation of the ECJ's approach to harmonization is seen in
the 1978 ECJ decision *Pubblico v. Ratti*, which holds that, once the EU has
acted, member states may not enact legislation that is more stringent
under the theory that inconsistencies in federal legislation may result in
restriction of intra-EU trade.[14]

Since the 1978 *Ratti* decision, opponents of harmonization have framed the discussion using the principle of subsidiarity. Subsidiarity can be defined as allowing the EU institutions to make as few decisions as possible, with the majority of decisions being made at the national or local level of government. They maintain that boundaries can be drawn between the respective responsibilities of the EU, the member states, and regional and local authorities, with preference given to the most local governmental level. They argue that the preservation of a degree of national sovereignty, or what Europeans call "federalism," should take precedence over continued harmonization of European laws.

Not surprisingly, the extent of Europeans' willingness to restrict their countries' national jurisdiction in order to accommodate the common will of fifteen member states is as varied as the members' legal and political structures. In addition to a more general desire to retain state sovereignty, many Europeans perceive the EU as an inefficient top-down bureaucracy in which taxes are high and democratic accountability is low. Moreover, Germany and several of the other northern member states contend that the EU's environmental programs are inadequate, and they are reluctant to modify existing national environmental laws in order to conform with EU directives.[15]

Much has changed since the EC's one-dimensional approach to unification of standards articulated in the 1978 ECJ *Ratti* decision, including the inclusion in the Maastricht treaty of the explicit opt-out clause in Article 100a(4) and a provision on the principle of subsidiarity.[16] Nevertheless, Europeans will continue to debate the question of the appropriate level of intervention that the EU should exercise in member states' national jurisdiction. This debate is reflected in the ECJ decisions in the PCP, the German crayfish, the EIA, and the wild birds cases where the ECJ seems to be groping for a balance among European integration, state sovereignty, and preservation of national environmental laws.

European Court of Justice Decisions

The European Court of Justice German Crayfish Decision

The German crayfish case involved the practical question of whether a German ban on the import of crayfish was an allowable restriction of trade between member states under the Maastricht treaty. The Commission brought the procedure against Germany before the Court pursuant to Article 169 of the treaty in March 1993, arguing that German legislation imposing a general ban on the import of all types of freshwater crayfish and issuing import licenses under special circumstances restricted trade. Issued pursuant to Sections 20 and 31 of its Federal Law for Nature

Protection (*Bundesnaturschutzgesetz*), the 1989 legislation set out to protect the native crayfish population classified as "protected" or "in danger
of extinction" from a crayfish epidemic that had originated in North
America. The purpose of the German system was twofold: first, to prevent the spread of the crayfish epidemic; and second, to prevent a threat
to the native wild crayfish population by the introduction of foreign crayfish (*Faunen Verfälschung*), which, because of the foreign crayfish's different eating habits, would result in a change of the natural ecosystem.

The German government conditioned the crayfish permits upon receiving information on the precise number and type of crayfish, their
land of origin, end use, and whether they had been disinfected. Valid for
only six months, the permits could be revoked by the government at any
time. The Germans maintained that the import legislation, while restrictive of trade, was not in conflict with Article 30 of the Maastricht treaty
because the legislation fell under the exceptions governing allowable restrictions provided for by Article 36 of the treaty.

The standard of nondiscrimination embodied in Article 30 prohibits
"quantitative restrictions on imports and all measures of equivalent effect"
among member states and is thus a cornerstone of the Common Market.
Under Article 30, all commercial rules that act as barriers to trade are dis-
allowed. Article 36 provides for exceptions to Article 30 when justified.[17]

The three criteria for exceptions are (1) whether the aim of the measure
falls within the scope of the exception and is recognized as a necessary
objective of the EU; (2) whether the measure has been applied on a
nondiscriminatory basis; and (3) whether the measure satisfies the principle of proportionality requiring that the measure be necessary to accomplish its purpose. The Court conceded that the German measures restricting imports were indeed taken with the aim of protecting the health
and life of native crayfish and were therefore justified under Article 36 of
the EU treaty.

The ECJ's second condition for application of an Article 36 exception is
that the measure be nondiscriminatory. For the EU to be an open market,
any charges or conditions a member state imposes on foreign imports
must not be more burdensome than those that the member state imposes
on its national goods. To the Commission's suggestion that the German
legislation restricting imports was discriminatory in its intent and was
disguised protectionism, the Germans retorted that the legislation did
not bring about a complete ban on imports but, rather, allowed many exceptions in the form of permits.

The Commission argued that the German legislation was discriminatory in its effect because the number of imports of crayfish to Germany
had fallen between 1989 and 1993. The Germans responded that, although importers might suffer, the damage was not so extensive as to

represent a threat to their financial existence. According to the ECJ, the German argument did not address evidence about other conservation measures taken within Germany to protect the crayfish.

It was the third condition for an Article 36 exception, that is, that the measure in question must be essential to its purpose and the least available restriction, which the ECJ found the Germans had not met. The ECJ found that the decision whether to issue import permits was left to the discretion of the German border officials. In addition, the Court found that there were less restrictive measures than import restrictions for protecting the native crayfish population from the epidemic caused by the introduction of foreign crayfish, such as the French random health checks on the border to control the epidemic.[18]

In response, the German government argued that a spot check of imports at the border would have been inadequate because border inspectors would have had to examine each individual crayfish and because the fungus was known not to appear for a week, by which time the diseased crayfish would have been approved and admitted into the country.

The ECJ noted that the German legislation was not proportional to its aim and that as of January 1, 1993, Germany was required to transpose and implement into German law Directive 91/67/EEC covering animal disease. By that date any discussion of Articles 30 and 36 and "proportionality" were moot. The Germans decided not to seek an exception through Article 100a(4), which would have allowed Germany to rely on its own law rather than implement the EU directive. By the time Germany was required to implement this directive, the disease threatening crayfish had been brought under control, and thus the European directive was sufficient. As illustrated by the ECJ's decision on the PCP case the following year, the ECJ might have interpreted the divergent German law with more tolerance (despite the existence of the directive) if not for the discriminatory effect of the German law.

The German PCP Case

In 1991, the European Council of Ministers adopted Directive 91/173/EEC, modifying restrictions on Pentachlorophenol (PCP) and other dangerous substances by a qualified majority.[19] Germany, Denmark, and the Netherlands voted against the directive because it relaxed the previous restriction on imports of the chemical.[20]

Germany notified the Commission that it wished to retain its own national PCP legislation.[21] Greece, Belgium, Italy, and France opposed Germany's request on the grounds that the stricter German measure would hinder trade within the EU.

The Commission decided that Germany's derogation was eligible for an exception under Article 100a(4), given that (1) it met the narrow interpretation of the exception to the uniform application of EU law; (2) the German ban on PCP was more stringent than the EU law; (3) the aim of the German ban was necessary and justified in that PCP was acknowledged as a dangerous chemical; (4) the terms of the European directive on PCP required reevaluation in three years; and (5) while the German ban did constitute a barrier to trade, the measure was proportional to a legitimate interest and not arbitrary or a disguised discrimination to EU trade.[22]

The French government appealed the Commission's decision on the grounds that Germany had not justified the proportionality of its trade restrictions. France argued that the Commission should explain why the stricter German measures were proportionate to the health risks posed by PCP, since this was the first application of the Article 100a(4) exception. The ECJ agreed, holding that Article 100a(4) allows variance from the EU's directives only with a well-reasoned basis for the derogation by the Commission.[23]

The Commission then issued a second decision to provide the necessary rationale for allowing the German derogation from the EU directive, describing the uses of PCP, the chemical's health risks, and Germany's evenhanded application of the law with respect to domestic and nondomestic production of the chemical. The Commission then concluded that there was little trade of the chemical PCP or its substitutes between Germany and other member states and that Germany had no special economic interest in the development, production of, or exportation of PCP substitutes.[24]

By initially annulling the Commission's approval of the German law and requiring the Commission to justify its reasons for the derogation, the ECJ was able to determine whether the German use of the opt-out provision of Article100a(4) presented trade obstacles. Finding that the German PCP law had no effect on EU trade, the ECJ could ultimately allow the German derogation from the EU directive to stand. Thus, the ECJ left open the door for a corrected Commission decision on Germany's derogation, as well as the future use of the Article 100a(4) exception by other states.

The German Environmental Impact Assessment Case

The Commission brought the EIA case pursuant to Article 169 in order to protect the integrity of the EU's recently adopted procedures for conducting environmental impact assessments. The ECJ assessed the significance of the district of Darmstadt's failure to use European procedures to evaluate the environmental impacts of a proposed extension to a power plant. The ECJ found that Germany, although late in transposing the European directive, had ultimately adopted its national law to the directive so that there was no possibility of future deviations from the directive, and that the Hessen procedures that had been applied in approving an extension of a power plant had not resulted in a significantly different assessment from that which would have taken place using the European EIA procedures.

No economic or trade interests were at stake in the case. The significance of this case for legal scholars is that the ECJ decided that the question of whether to award damages was a question of national rather than EU law. If the German EIA law awarded damages, then the Court would award damages. As the German law did not provide for damages, the Court found that damages could not be awarded. The significance of the case in the context of European integration is that it shows the Court's willingness to evaluate member states' implementation of the EU directives according to whether the state had correctly interpreted and transposed the spirit of the directive, rather than requiring a strict translation of each provision.

The Wild Birds III Case

Although this case was decided in 1987, it may have more significance for the future than for past patterns of ECJ decisions. The Commission's 1987 case concerning wild birds was one of a series of cases brought against Germany, Belgium, Italy, and the Netherlands for their failure to transpose Directive 79/409/EC on the protection of certain species of wild birds, their eggs, and their habitat. Although more than ten years have passed since the European Court of Justice ruled against Germany, Germany still has not implemented the wild birds directive. Therefore, the Commission is considering bringing an action against Germany pursuant to Article 171 of the EC Treaty for sanctions.[25] It is unclear, even to ECJ specialists, why the Commission should single out Germany for its failure to implement the directive, given that other countries failed to implement other directives over similarly long periods of time. Certainly Germany has the "pretension of being the greenest of the green" among the European member states and, unlike Greece or Portugal, cannot argue that it does not have the financial resources to implement the directive. Most likely, the Commission will bring an action against Germany and other similarly situated countries that have failed to implement the 1979 directive.[26]

In the eyes of the Commission and ultimately the ECJ, the 1979 directive on wild birds required member states to prioritize the protection of wild birds. Although the failure of Germany, as well as other countries, to transpose the directive had no impact on EU trade, the ECJ justified the enforced implementation of this early directive on the grounds that "effective bird protection is typically a trans-frontier environmental problem entailing common responsibilities of the member states."[27] Germany, Belgium, and Italy all argued that their existing laws complied with the goals of the directive on wild birds. Specifically, Germany asserted that Paragraph 22 of the Federal Law on the Protection of Nature (*Bundesnaturschutzgesetz*)[28] prohibits the hunting, capturing, wounding, or killing of animals of species given special protection. However, the same paragraph exempts conduct "in the course of the normal use of the land for agricultural, forestry or fishing purposes" from the prohibition regarding birds, thus allowing farmers, fishermen, or those engaged in forestry to continue business as usual.[29]

The ECJ agreed that Article 9 of the wild birds directive would allow a derogation for individual member states if those states can show that it was necessary to prevent "serious damage" and went on to find that the problem with Paragraph 22 was that it did not include any provision requiring farmers to take measures to protect birds, as long as their fishing, forestry, or farming activities were part of normal uses. Had the Germans succeeded in modifying the federal law so as to improve the protection of the bird species, the ECJ might have decided that the German federal law was not inconsistent with the directive.

Summary

The ECJ's jurisdiction extends over member states whose concept of the EU are both diverse and constantly evolving. As interpreter of EU law, the ECJ has had to feel its way in deciding when to promote European law and when to allow member states to maintain national law inconsistent with EU objectives. In each of the four cases, the European Court of Justice first needed to decide to what extent the environmental and conservation objectives of the German legislation were already covered by a legislative regime of the EU, and, if they were, whether the EU should require the Germans to harmonize their law with the EU legislation or allow the German measure to remain in place, thereby retaining sovereignty in the determination of their own level of conservation and environmental protection.

In the PCP case, the ECJ ultimately allowed the German legislation restricting imports to stand, even though it varied from the European directive squarely addressing the same chemical. The ECJ deemed the health goal behind the German ban on the chemical PCP worthwhile and the German ban proportional to the aim of protecting human health and the environment pursuant to the Article 36 exception. From a procedural perspective, the Court found that Germany had properly followed the opt-out provision provided in Article 100a(4) of the EU treaty. In addition, the ECJ was persuaded that Germany did little trading in the chemical and did not have an economic interest at stake.

In the German crayfish case, the ECJ found that the German measure was inconsistent with the recently enacted European directive on animal disease. And although the ECJ found that the aim of protecting the native crayfish was worthwhile, it found the ban on freshwater crayfish neither proportional to the aim nor consistent with the opt-out provision of Article 100a(4) of the EU treaty.

In both cases, the Commission and the ECJ put the burden on the member state attempting to implement varying legislation to show that the measure was necessary and proportional, and that no less restrictive alternative existed. In both cases, the ECJ was able to use Article 100a(4) as a vehicle to assess the necessity of legal harmonization and could avoid making an ultimate decision on whether the environmental interest at issue justified a restriction of EU trade. In the PCP case, the Court initially rejected the Commission's decision to allow the derogation on the procedural grounds of inadequate rationale. After the Commission issued its second decision with an articulated reasoning on why the German derogation was necessary, the ECJ concurred. In the German crayfish case, the ECJ commented on the impact of the trade restrictions as well as the aims of the ban, but it ultimately relied on the existence of a new directive on animal disease for the decision declaring the German law impermissible.

The EIA and wild birds cases show how the ECJ has handled Commission challenges based on a member state's failure to implement two European environmental directives. In the EIA case, the ECJ reprimanded Germany for failing to transpose the EIA directive for two years and considered whether this delay had substantively affected the district of Darmstadt's processing of the power plant's extension application. The Court's decision reflected a moderate approach. Since Germany had implemented the EIA directive by the time of the decision, and there was not much difference between the procedures applied by the district of Darmstadt and the European EIA procedures, the Court ultimately decided that Germany was not liable for damages.

In the wild birds case, on the other hand, the Court found that there were significant legal implications to applying the German Law for the Protection of Nature rather than the European wild birds directive. Although the EU directive provided for some narrow exceptions to prevent "serious damage" to agriculture, its exceptions were by no means as broad as those in the German federal law. The German failure to incorporate the European directive into the federal law illustrates a national version of the subsidiarity problem. Specifically, the federal government has yet to persuade the sixteen German states to transpose and help implement the European directive.

Although the delay associated with the legal implementation of complex and cost-intensive directives is understandable, it is doubtful that the Commission will continue to grant latitude to member states such as Germany that fail to transpose directives for years on end. Thus, it is not surprising that in 1997 the European Commission was considering using the newly available sanctions provided for in Article 171 of the Maastricht treaty to push Germany to transpose the wild birds directive. Most likely, the threat of becoming the first country subject to sanctions under Article 171 also will motivate Germany to amend its federal law to conform to the European directive. If, however, the Commission brings the action to the ECJ before the Germans can modify the law, the Court will be hard-pressed to find grounds not to impose sanctions. Imposition of sanctions would signal a willingness to use an even stronger tool to achieve European integration at the cost of state sovereignty.

Notes

1. The former head of the Legal Matters and Application of Community Law in Directorate General XI of the European Commission has written that if not for Community environmental rules, large parts of the European Union would have no environmental rules at all. Ludwig Krämer, *Focus on European Environmental Law* (London: Sweet & Maxwell, 1992), p. 53.

2. C–41/93, *France v. Commission*, 1994 ECR 1829.

3. C–131/93, *Commission v. Germany*, 1994 ECR at 3302.

4. In re the Grobkrotzenburg Power Station: *EC Commission v. Germany*, C–431/92, 1 CMLR 196 (11 August 1995).

5. C–412/85, *Commission v. Germany*, 1987 ECR 3503, 3506–7.

6. See the European Community Treaty (EC Treaty), Articles 155–163 (1992), for the responsibilities of the European Commission, Articles 193–198 (1992) on the responsibilities of the Court of Justice, Article 145 (1992) for the duties of the Council, and Articles 137–139 (1992) on the election procedures of the European Parliament. The European Court of Justice differs from other international courts in that it is a permanent standing court with compulsory jurisdiction and independent legal authority. The foundation of that legal authority is the willingness of the respective EU member states to limit their sovereign rights. Kurt Riechenberg, "The Merger of Trading Blocks and the Creation of the European Economic Area," *Tulane Journal of International and Comparative Law* 4 (1995) 63, 68.

7. Treaty Establishing the European Economic Community (EEC), 25 March 1957.

8. See EEC Treaty, Articles 169–172; see Tamara L. Joseph, "Preaching Heresy: Permitting Member States to Enforce Stricter Environmental Laws Than the European Community," *Yale International Law Journal* 20 (1995): 227, 234. The First

Community Environmental Action Programme of 1978 may be the first explicit nonlegal basis for an EU environmental policy. The First Action Programme provided a multi-annual review and framework for Community environmental initiatives, including legislative proposals. The Environmental Action Programmes of 1978, 1983, 1987, and 1993 describe harmonization of environmental policy programs as important in avoiding unilateral actions and achieving coordination of policies without hindering the environmental progress of the member states.

9. Krämer, *Focus on European Environmental Law,* p. 28.

10. The Maastricht treaty still requires an absolute majority for legislation involving border, fiscal, or matters involving local planning and land use, management of water resources, and choices of energy supply. See Maastricht treaty, Article 100A, 130s(2).

11. Krämer, *Focus on European Environmental Law,* p. 180.

12. According to Kurt Riechenberg, the ECJ has yet to answer specifically the question of whether a member state must actually vote against a directive in order to have standing to opt out. Author interview with Riechenberg, 15 April 1997.

13. The Maastricht treaty, Common Provisions' Article B, refers to "economic and social progress which is balanced and sustainable." Thus, while the Maastricht treaty does not refer to sustainable development explicitly, it does place environmental concerns on an equal footing with economic objectives.

Moreover, the treaty increased the role of the European Parliament, the only democratically elected institution of the EU. Before the treaty was signed at Maastricht, the European Parliament could only reflect its views on proposed legislation in a cooperative procedure or through consultation. Articles 189(b) and (c) of the treaty set out co-decision and cooperation procedures for the Parliament.

14. Case 148/78, 1978 ECR 1629, 1643.

15. Germany, the Netherlands, and Denmark have all favored more aggressive levels of environmental protection than the other member states. Krämer, *Focus on European Environmental Law,* pp. 37–39.

16. See Maastricht treaty, Article 3B. In addition, the treaty provides that "the Union shall respect the national identities of its member states." The treaty on the European Union (Maastricht), Article F(1) amending the Treaty Establishing the European Economic Community of 25 March, 1957, 298 UNTS 11.

Local authorities are typically better suited than a central authority to assess local needs and solve the problems. Harmonization requires agreement and ultimately implementation by member states with diverse legal and administrative systems. Moreover, transferring information back and forth from the center to the region can be inefficient.

See Cliona Kimber, "Comparison of Environmental Federalism," *Maryland Law Review* 54 (1995): 1658, 1672.

17. Exceptions included the grounds of public morale, order, security, protection of health and life of persons, animals, or plants, or the national cultural good of artistic or historical grounds.

18. None of the parties addressed the question of whether spot checks were adequate for controlling the second threat of introduction of foreign species (*Faunen Verfälschung*).

19. PCP is a chemical used for many purposes, including the treatment of leather, wool, paper, industrial textiles, and soil sterilization. It is toxic to humans and damaging to the aquatic environment.

20. Before the modification, states could ban imports of products where the concentration of PCP exceeded 0.01 percent; after the modification, states could only ban concentrations exceeding 0.10 percent of the product's content. The directive included a deadline of July 1992 for each member state to transpose or implement the directive.

21. German Federal Law Registry (*Bundesgesetzblatt*), 1989, p. 2235, adopting *Pentachlorophenolverbotverordnung* (regulation prohibiting PCP), entered into force 23 December 1989.

22. PCP, 1994 ECR 1845; see Joseph, "Preaching Heresy," p. 252.

23. PCP, 1994 ECR 1845.

24. This was substantiated by the fact that none of the member states challenged the Commission's decision within the two-month period (as provided by Article 173 of the treaty of the European Union); the Commission allowed the German legislation to stand.

See Commission Decision of 14 September 1994 Concerning the Prohibition of PCP Notified by the Federal Republic of Germany, 1994 *Journal of the European Communities* (L 316) 43, 44–48.

25. At the time the chapter was written, no judgment had yet been rendered on this issue.

26. Author interview with Riechenberg.

27. *Wild Birds I, Commission v. Belgium*, Case 247/85, 1987 ECR 3029 at 3059.

28. 20 December 1976 (*Bundesgesetzblatt* I, p. 3574).

29. Ibid.

PART TWO

Germany in Transition:
Economic and Business Issues

Introduction:
Economic and Business Issues

GEOFFREY D. OLIVER

In recent years, Germany, along with many other countries, has faced social and technological developments that have caused great changes in the domestic economy, which in turn has experienced changes that have caused considerable social disruption. In addition, technological advances and international trade agreements have led to a rapid growth of international trade, which has increased competition in many sectors of the economy. This competition has been intensified by the emergence of developing countries in Asia and Latin America, joined recently by east European countries. In an effort to reduce barriers to investment and trade and to promote efficiency, the European Union has adopted measures intended to open state-owned and -operated monopolies to international competition.

Both opportunities and challenges have been created. Many of the changes taking place promise increased economic productivity and thus economic growth and improved living standards. Many businesses and individuals now enjoy unprecedented opportunities. At the same time, many industries and businesses face greater competitive pressures to reduce costs and increase efficiency, leading to pressure on many individuals to accept reduced compensation and altered working conditions as well as causing a sense of loss of economic security.

While these developments have affected all industrialized countries in varying degrees, they have had an unusually strong impact in Germany because they have occurred simultaneously with the economic difficulties caused by the unification of East and West Germany. Unification has led to sizable and persistent budget deficits despite an increase in taxes and cuts in government spending; unification, together with underlying economic causes, has resulted in record levels of unemployment.

The result of these developments has been a growing debate on reform in Germany. The *"Standort"* (literally, location) debate revolves around the question of whether Germany is losing its competitive position as a center of investment and manufacture. The debate arises in particular from the relative importance of manufacturing to the German economy. To a much greater extent than in most other developed countries, manufacturing occupies a central position in the German economy. The success of the German economic model since the conclusion of World War II has depended on Germany's ability to attract domestic and foreign investment in manufacturing facilities and to export its finished products. Germany has concentrated on producing high-quality, high-performance products that generally sold at relatively high prices. Markets for such products were often less competitive than for lower-end products, allowing for higher profit margins. German companies enjoyed considerable success despite the relatively high costs of manufacturing in Germany.

The recent economic changes have created increasing challenges for Germany's manufacturing sector. On the one hand, German manufacturers of high-quality products face more competition as companies in other countries are increasingly able to match the quality and performance of even the best German products. On the other hand, relative costs of manufacture have risen in Germany over the past decade because of both increases in direct and indirect costs in Germany and the strength of the German mark.[1] As a result, German exports face increasing price competition in foreign markets. More troubling, the balance of investment flows has turned sharply negative as foreign investors and German companies alike choose to locate new facilities outside Germany.

In the late 1980s and early 1990s, business interests and commentators both within Germany and abroad began to question whether Germany remained a competitive location for investment and manufacture. As Michael Zumwinkle described in an article published in the previous volume in this series,[2] the debate has focused on direct and indirect labor costs, the level of taxation, the burden of regulation, and the role of research and development in Germany.

Calls for reform have intensified in recent years as investment in Germany has declined, unemployment has soared to the highest level in 60 years, and German manufacturers have increasingly opted to manufacture in other countries.[3] U.S. and other foreign commentators have been almost unanimous in concluding that Germany has suffered a serious decline in international competitiveness. Two separate studies of international competitiveness in 1997 ranked Germany from 14th to 25th among countries, behind not only the United States, the United Kingdom, the Netherlands, Japan, Singapore, and Hong Kong but, in one study, also emerging exporters such as Chile, Malaysia, South Korea, and Indonesia.[4] Foreign commentators assert that Germany cannot remain attractive as a center of manufacture competitively without undertaking significant reforms, including reducing both direct and indirect labor costs, increasing worker flexibility, easing government regulation, and reducing levels of government spending and taxation.[5]

From the U.S. perspective, the debate in Germany has been difficult to understand. Most parties have agreed that reforms are required, but U.S. observers have noted little concrete progress so far. Many observers have concluded that, while German employers have issued strident calls for reform,[6] their actions have often been limited.[7] For example, few German companies have gone so far as to adopt more open accounting standards or seek foreign stock exchange listings. Likewise, many believe that the government has acknowledged the need for reform, but has limited any specific reform to largely marginal measures. Few steps have been taken to reduce the regulatory burdens facing business.[8] However, U.S. observers generally have overlooked the considerable number of less visible changes taking place in Germany.

Likewise, U.S. observers have focused on the resistance of unions and workers to reform. In doing so, they have often failed to note that many unions and workers, while contesting the need for drastic reforms, have quietly accepted the need for more flexible hours and workplace practices and have departed from the principle of uniform nationwide industrial agreements in order to permit more flexible company-specific contracts where appropriate.[9]

John Leslie explains why economic reform in Germany has not followed the pattern expected by many U.S. and other foreign observers. He describes the history of consensus that has long characterized economic and industrial relations among business, labor, and the government in Germany. As he explains, the unique system of consensus has served all parties well in the past. He views the *Standort* debate as a departure from this German model of consensus. He argues that Germany's economic condition is not so grave as many proponents of reform claim. Rather, Leslie believes that the *Standort* debate should be perceived as an effort by proponents of reform to shift economic costs and burdens within German society. Despite the heated rhetoric of the *Standort* debate, Leslie believes that business, labor, and the government will be reluctant to abandon the German model. Instead, they ultimately will be most likely to seek a compromise. He concludes that reform is occurring and will continue, but within the framework of the German model rather than in the form anticipated by many outside observers.

Andrew Johnson and Lisa Creighton-Hendricks provide specific examples of some of the reforms currently under way in Germany. Spurred by the requirements of European Community (EC) legislation, the challenges and opportunities of global competition, and the lingering costs of unification, the German government has taken steps to privatize some leading publicly-held companies and open monopolies to competition. Utilities, telecommunications, air and rail transport, and health care are among the industries currently undergoing drastic restructuring in Germany.

Johnson describes the reform of the Deutsche Bahn (the German train company), referred to as *Bahnreform*. Although the west German Deutsche Bundesbahn had experienced consistent losses for years, the catalyst for reform was the unification of the Bundesbahn with the east German Deutsche Reichsbahn in 1990. As with privatization of the rail system in the United Kingdom, the crucial element of reform was the separation of the operating system (rail services) from the rail infrastructure to allow new providers to enter the market for rail services. The government's assumption of the substantial past debts of both the Bundesbahn and the Reichsbahn was a necessary component of the privatization, to permit the new operating companies to begin operations free of debt. The result has helped separate the private function of providing transportation services on a competitive, cost-effective basis from the public functions of maintaining basic infrastructure and ensuring the provision of transportation services in regions where it might not be profitable.

As Johnson points out, *Bahnreform* has not eliminated the substantial cost to the government of rail transport, nor has it resolved the issue of the proper extent of public support for rail transport. By separating private and public rail functions, however, *Bahnreform* has increased the efficiency of the provision of rail transport services, on the one hand, and permitted more open debate concerning the appropriate level of government support, on the other. Johnson concludes that, in the three years since *Bahnreform* was initiated, initial results have been positive with respect to the goals of improving financial performance and increasing market share, but it is too early to judge yet regarding the goal of increasing regionalization of local passenger rail transport.

Creighton-Hendricks compares the reform of telecommunications services in Germany and the United States, which started with considerably different systems. The United States has a tradition of private service providers. Although there are many large providers, each of the regional Bells retains a monopoly on local service within its region. Thus, the U.S. regulatory authorities are attempting to increase competition by permitting providers to expand operations to other market segments. As an incentive, the regulatory authorities are requiring each provider to open its segment to competition before permitting it to expand its own operations.

Telecommunications services in Germany, by contrast, are dominated by a single, state-owned provider. While reform has been promoted in Germany, much of the incentive came from EC initiatives. Legislation has already eliminated the state-owned provider's monopoly over certain telecommunications services and will introduce competition throughout the telecommunications market. At the same time, the telecommunications operations of the Deutsche Bundespost have been split off to a separate entity, Deutsche Telekom. Deutsche Telekom has been partially privatized through a share floatation on the German stock exchange, although the German government is scheduled to retain a majority shareholding at least until the year 2000. As Creighton-Hendricks points out, potential conflicts of interest are inherent in the German government's dual role as impartial regulator, responsible for ensuring that conditions permit new entrants to compete on equal terms with Deutsche Telekom, and majority owner of Deutsche Telekom. Despite the differences in the approaches to reform pursued by the regulatory authorities in the United States and Germany, Creighton-Hendricks believes that the ultimate goal of the reform efforts is the same.

Notes

1. The German mark increased in value against the U.S. dollar from 1.43 DM/$ in 1989 to 1.88 DM/$ in 1995, before falling again to 1.73 DM/$ in 1997. Federal-Reserve Statistical Release, Foreign Exchange Rates (Annual), 5 January, 1998.

2. Michael Zumwinkle, "Standort Deutschland: Can a Changing Germany Complete in the Changing World Market?" in B. Shingleton, M. Gibbon, and K. Mack, eds., *Dimensions of German Unification: Economic, Social and Legal Analyses* (Boulder: Westview Press, 1995).

3. German firms' overseas investment increased by 60 percent in 1995 alone to a record DM 80 billion. "Doom and Gloom in Germany," *The Economist*, 5 April, 1997: pp. 57–58. By 1999, Siemens AG expects that the majority of its employees will be located outside Germany, and Hoechst AG, which has cut the number of its employees in Germany from 80,000 to 45,000, now employs only 30 percent of its workforce in Germany. "Germany Inc. Flees Homeland for Cheap Labor, "*Washington Post*, 8 April, 1997, p. A10.

4. World Economic Forum, *Global Competitiveness Report 1997* (21 May 1997) (ranking Germany in 25th place); International Institute for Management Development, *World Competitiveness Yearbook* (19 May, 1997) (ranking Germany in 14th place, down from 5th place in 1992).

5. "Europe Hits a Brick Wall," *The Economist*, 5 April, 1997: p. 21; "Germany Inc. Flees Homeland for Cheap Labor."

The International Institute for Management Development reports: "Germany...continues to muddle through reforms that may take more time to implement than anticipated. The cost of doing business in Germany, the late restructuring of certain companies, the rigidity of labor laws and the effort to upgrade competitiveness in the Eastern part of Germany is taking its toll on the performance of the country as a whole" (*World Competitiveness Yearbook*, Executive Summary, p. 2).

The World Economic Forum concluded that Germany, together with a number of other European countries, "ranks especially poorly in government and in labour flexibility, but relatively better in infrastructure and technology" (*Global Competitiveness Report* 1996 30 May, 1996).

6. "Wirtschaftsverbände: Reformen jetzt zügig umsetzen, "Reuters, 22 April 1997.

7.For example, on 18 March 1997, after failed negotiations to merge Krupp-Hoesch and Thyssen in order to rationalize the German steel industry, the management of Krupp-Hoesch launched a hostile tender for the shares of Thyssen. Not only Thyssen management but also union representatives and representatives of the federal and state governments opposed the plan. Employees of both Krupp-Hoesch and Thyssen demonstrated outside the offices of the Deutsche Bank and Dresdner Bank, which had agreed to provide financing for the transaction, causing the banks to fear a consumer boycott. On 24 March 1997, Krupp-Hoesch withdrew its offer and, instead, agreed to a limited joint venture with Thyssen in steel production. *The Economist* summarized the development in a cartoon showing a tombstone bearing the caption, "Anglo-Saxon Capitalism in Germany, 18.3.97—24.3.97" ("Auf Wiedersehen, Shareholders," 29 March 1997: 68).

8. Even where the government has reduced the regulatory burden on business, it sometimes acts to minimize the effects of deregulation. In 1996, for example, the government enacted a provision allowing employers to reduce the amout of sick pay owed by employees to workers on medical leave from 100 percent to 80 percent of their regular pay during a portion of their absence. Many companies, including Daimler-Benz AG, were parties to collective bargaining agreements negotiated under the former law, and provided for sick pay of 100 percent of regular pay. When the new law became effective, the government opposed efforts by Daimler-Benz and other companies to alter the amount of sick pay owed under the collective bargaining agreements. See "Chaotische Kapitalisten," *Der Spiegel*, 16 December 1996

9. See, e.g., "Deshalb bin ich vor geprescht," *Der Spiegel*, 21 April, 1997.

4

The Politics of *Standort*: Germany's Debate About Competitiveness

JOHN LESLIE

The German economy is in the doldrums. The eastern part of the country continues to struggle with the problems of forty years of state socialism and, since 1993, West Germany has experienced stagnant growth and rising unemployment. Like past recessions, the present economic downturn in Germany requires adjustment and the movement of resources among occupations. As is appropriate to this endeavor, discussions have taken place at all levels of society about how to adjust the German economy not only to the present recession but also to related economic problems arising from German unification, European currency union, and changes in the world's economies.

In the media, less impassioned analyses of these processes have been pushed from public attention by a highly politicized discussion of Germany's economic competitiveness. Led by publicists, politicians, and leaders of Germany's business associations, this discussion has become known as the "*Standort* debate." Although some observers would include all discussion of Germany's economic future in the *Standort* debate, I use this term here to refer only to the highly focused "debate" on economic competitiveness taking place in the media.

The *Standort* debate, as it has been conducted in newspapers and on television, is not a true debate between opposing positions. Rather, it is a convenient instrument that has the effect of foreclosing discussion about adjustment in the German economy. A single argument is presented, repeated, reformulated, and presented again. This argument holds that Germany is no longer competitive in the international economy. The logic behind this assertion maintains that, in a "globalized" economy, firms are free to choose where they locate production and that, increasingly, they are choosing to invest outside Germany in order to avoid the high costs and rigidities of the German economy. As a result, capital and jobs are flowing out of the country. The solutions most often proposed for dealing with this situation are "deregulation" and increased "marketization" of the German economy. Occasionally, voices from the Left demand the creation of international institutions to restrain an uncontrolled global market. Interestingly, the underlying assumption of the *Standort* debate—that the German economy is no longer competitive—is questioned by neither side, even though Germany consistently runs a large and growing export surplus.

The motivations for maintaining this intense media "debate," despite the questionable nature of its principal assertion, are the subject of the present study. The argument presented here sees the causes of Germany's present economic problems in a combination of forces emanating from European amalgamation and changing international conditions and other factors. Predominantly, however, the cost of German unification has been the source of Germany's present lackluster economic performance and the current *Standort* debate. The *Standort* debate, however, does not seek the causes of Germany's economic problems; it merely asserts them. In doing so, it preempts the search for other causes and, therefore, other solutions to the problems of adjustment. By eliminating alternatives to the argument that globalization and declining competitiveness are the reasons for Germany's economic problems, a loose coalition of policymakers, political party actors, and employers hope to make deregulation the default answer to the problem of economic adjustment—a solution that conveniently fits their interests. Budget-cutters acquire a seemingly neutral economic rationale with which to absolve themselves of responsibility for trimming popular public expenditures, particularly welfare payments. Political advocates assume an electorally legitimating mantle as the champions of "change" and "renewal." Employers seek to shift a greater percentage of the gross domestic product from employees to the owners of capital.

Analysis of this argument proceeds in four parts. The first section reviews the institutions and functioning of West Germany's postwar social market economy (SME), or, as it is sometimes called, the "German model." It demonstrates the striking incongruities between the argumentation of the *Standort* debate and the SME's historical solution to the twin problems of economic competitiveness and political stability. The second section analyzes, in light of economic data, claims made by those who insist that "globalization" has undermined Germany's international competitiveness and is the source of such economic problems as unemployment. It reveals striking discrepancies between such claims and the economic evidence. The third section offers an explanation for the continuance of the *Standort* debate despite such discrepancies. It contends that the *Standort* debate is motivated by the fiscal, electoral, and economic interests of a loose coalition of state actors, electoral politicians, and employers. The final section considers four recent examples of economic conflict to determine whether and how economic adjustment is occurring. These cases suggest that changes are taking place in Germany, but not according to the simple model of deregulation that some adherents of the *Standort* debate claim is inevitable. Rather, these examples reveal that adjustment is proceeding according to West Germany's postwar pattern of negotiation and consensus among management, labor, banks, and the state.[1]

The German Model

Until unification and the present recession, most observers agreed that the German social market economy provided a unique combination of economic competitiveness and political stability. Capital tolerated intervention by state and social institutions to create a more equitable distribution of national income. In return, state and social actors provided the economic infrastructure and ever-rising skill levels among the labor force necessary for German firms to compete in high-quality, high value-added sectors of international markets. The result was both rising profits and rising wages.

Recent claims that high labor costs have crippled German competitiveness stand in striking contrast to the assumptions underlying this model. To test the validity of such claims it is first necessary to understand the organization and functioning of the German model.

Germany's social market economy rests on a competitive market system. Both the protection of private property rights and the maintenance of competitive market conditions are anchored in law. However, in contradiction to the Anglo-Saxon conception of the "natural market,"[2] markets here are considered political constructs, intended to serve the welfare and goals of the general public. Consequently—as in all industrial democracies—some sectors of social life, such as education, health care, and social insurance, are managed by the state outside the market system; other sectors operate in the marketplace, but are regulated because of a belief that unrestrained competition will produce undesirable results.

Further, as is the case with labor and capital markets, regulation takes place through private and quasi-public institutions, such as banks, unions, and producer organizations, as well as state intervention. Since the end of World War II—and as the result of bitter experience—institutions such as unions and employer organizations generally have operated according to a spirit of compromise and mutual accommodation rather than the irreconcilable rancor that characterized their relations in Wilhelmine and Weimar Germany. Through intervention, social regulation, and a generous welfare state, government and social institutions have achieved a mutually acceptable and considerably equitable distribution of wealth in competitive markets. State intervention and history also have affected the structure of the economy by considerably segmenting markets and thereby limiting possibilities for mass production and price competition.[3]

The German economic system differentiates itself from both more interventionist systems, such as those found in France and Japan, and more laissez-faire economies, such as those of the United Kingdom and the United States. The division of authority between the federal and state *Länder* governments, the independence of agencies such as the Reserve Bank (*Bundesbank*) and the Federal Cartel Office (*Bundeskartellamt*), and the legal autonomy of social institutions in shaping important economic activities limit the ability of the state to pursue political goals in the economy. At the same time, the central government maintains the ability to charter social organizations to regulate or intervene in the economy. It does this by codifying (1) the consolatory status of certain organizations in the preparation of legislation and contracts; (2) the authority of these organizations over their membership; and (3) the legal nature of their agreements with other organizations. (For example, some wage contracts between employer organizations and unions become legally binding even with respect to employers and employees who are not members of the respective employer organizations or unions.) In this way, the state can affect outcomes in economic arenas such as industrial relations while avoiding excessive direct involvement in the economy.

The results of interdependence between state authority and social institutions are visible in both the organization of firms and the role of organizations in the German economy. Firms are treated not merely as assets to be traded by shareholders like other forms of private property but as integral components of the social order subject to the influence of many interests. Rather than intervening directly in firm decision making as the proxy of societal interests, however, the state has created mechanisms to foster negotiation directly among social actors themselves. For example, legislation grants employees representation on company supervisory boards and thus a voice in major corporate decisions. Further, legislation restricting managers' ability to hire and fire employees has the effect of transforming labor from a variable to a fixed cost, thereby reinforcing incentives to cooperate and negotiate in the workplace. Unable to shed employees easily, managers acquire a strong interest in training and retraining their workers to shift activities inside the firm to meet changing market conditions, while employees acquire a long-term interest in the economic health of the firm.[4]

Moreover, in most cases, independent shareholders do not exercise ultimate control over firms. Rather, such control usually is exercised by banks, which, in addition to lending to companies, may own a significant portion of their customers' equity and control the proxy votes of other shareholder-depositors.[5] Share ownership and proxy rights give banks both the incentive and the means with which to oversee the performance of management. The presence of labor and bank-lenders on supervisory boards encourages management to pursue the common interests of shareholders, creditors, and employees, and thus the long-run performance of the firm, rather than short-run equity value.

Perhaps more organized than any other Western industrial democracy, German society is enmeshed in a dense network of nonprofit corporations and associations encompassing everything from sports and leisure-time activities to critical functions of industrial policy and the welfare state.[6] These nonprofit corporations and associations are entrusted with the performance of certain functions and the production of certain collective goods. To help these organizations take effective collective action, the state often makes membership legally or practically obligatory.

In regulating economic outcomes, the state has delegated the most important role to business associations—the constituent members of the Federal Association of German Industry (*Bundesverband der Deutschen Industrie*, BDI), the Federal Association of Employers' Organizations (*Bundesvereinigung der Arbeitgeberverbände*, BDA), and the German Chambers of Commerce (*Deutsche Industrie- und Handelstag*, DIHT)—as well as the 15 centralized industrial unions of the German Federation of Unions (*Deutsche Gewerkschaftsbund*, DGB). By setting high technical standards and promoting specialization in product markets, the sectoral producer organizations under the BDI refocus firm competition away from price and toward quality. They facilitate this goal by organizing R&D activities and technology transfer. In labor markets, employers' associations and unions in certain sectors or industries avoid downward wage competition by negotiating high standards for the quality of work. To ensure a sufficient supply of workers with the necessary skills for high-quality production, these organizations have created an extensive apprenticeship system based on long-term cooperation among competing firms, the government, and unions. The German system's legitimacy has always rested on the resulting rising standard of living and relative equality in income distribution.[7]

The economic foundation of the German system has been the international competitiveness of its firms, especially small and medium-sized companies. Because of their relatively small size, these firms rely on long-term cooperation within economic organizations to maintain an infrastructure of R&D, product innovation, export marketing services, financing, wage determination, rationalization, and training. Coordinating these essential activities requires firms to expose a great deal of proprietary information to outside scrutiny. The desire of managers to protect proprietary information could inhibit cooperation, especially if the government is involved. When banks and producer associations assume the role of coordinator, these sensitive activities are removed from the arena of competitive politics, thereby alleviating businesses' concerns that politicians might be unable to place business interests before the demands of electoral politics.[8]

Similar arrangements modify the behavior of employer and union representatives in industrial relations. Integration in management decisionmaking educates employee representatives in the practical economic realities of the firm. More symmetrical access to information and the experience of cooperating in management decisions reinforces labor's trust in the good faith of managers and gives both sides the confidence to engage in agreements that place long-term mutual interests ahead of immediate payoffs. Aggregation of such information at the sectoral level by producer associations and unions also makes it more likely that cooperative solutions in industrial relations can be brought into line with macroeconomic objectives; wage restraint in the face of stagflation during the 1970s is the primary example.[9] Here the "semi-sovereign" role of the state is especially important. Legally embedded "wage autonomy" *Tarifautonomie* removes industrial relations from the electoral realm, forcing management and labor to deal directly with each other. Yet the state provides such resources as obligatory membership in employers' organizations and the codification of "blanket" contracts, which ensure each "social partner" that the other will be able to enforce the terms of negotiated bargains among its members. Finally, the legally defined role of labor representatives in plant-level decisionmaking and a certain tolerance among union leaders provide a mechanism through which local management and labor representatives can interpret sector-level contracts to conform more closely to their needs.[10] Thus, institutional arrangements help overcome problems of confidence and trust among competing firms and among different groups of workers, as well as between capital and labor, to make possible mutually advantageous, long-term agreements. At the same time, they provide considerable flexibility to assimilate overarching sectoral and societal goals to diverse local needs.

In the postwar era, producers in Germany have remained competitive in the international economy although the German system has resulted in hourly labor costs that are among the highest in the world. In effect, by raising wage rates, the system has forced firms to seek productivity gains elsewhere to compensate. Indeed, German workers have attained high levels of skill and training and are among the most efficient worldwide. Adherents of the *Standort* debate assert that this system is no longer sustainable. The next section assesses the evidence for these claims.

"Globalization" and Unemployment: Rhetoric and Evidence

Discussions about competitiveness in the German media rest on a seductively simple logic. This logic holds that globalization, or the increasing propensity for economic activities to take place across national borders, has had two consequences. First, it has brought producers in Germany into direct competition with high-skill producers in lower-wage countries, primarily in Asia and Eastern Europe. Second, capital and technology have become completely fungible, effectively allowing owners and managers to choose freely among potential production sites those offering the most advantageous cost and wage levels. Given these incentives and constraints, domestic firms increasingly are choosing to move production out of Germany while foreign firms have chosen not to enter. Germans are being squeezed by low-wage competitors while declining investment means Germany is falling behind Japan and the United States in competition to produce high-technology goods. The result is rising structural unemployment. The simplicity of this logic gives it great power in public discourse.

The evidence on which such arguments rest also seems straightforward. By international comparison, nominal wages and payroll costs in Germany are quite high. Some of Germany's most important exporters have made highly publicized decisions to open production facilities outside Germany, including BMW, which opened a production facility in Spartanburg, South Carolina, and Daimler-Benz, which built its first production facility outside Germany in Tuscaloosa, Alabama. In April 1997, while statistics showed the U.S. unemployment rate to be 5 percent, the German rate had reached a postwar high of 11.3 percent.[11] These developments seem to point clearly to both the causes and consequences of developments in the German economy.

Upon closer analysis, however, economic assumptions underlying the *Standort* debate begin to unravel. If one considers unit labor cost of production, rather than nominal wages and payroll costs, for example, German labor costs fall in the midst of the range of labor costs of other leading industrial economies.[12] Further, productivity in Germany's automobile, turbine, machine tool, and nonindustrial chemical industries remains among the highest of the industrial countries, as do its exports of such products—to both high- and low-wage countries.[13] In fact, Germany's consistent position as the world's largest or second-largest exporter, its constant trade surplus, and the long-term revaluation of the deutsche mark all confirm the extreme international competitiveness of producers in Germany.

Patterns of investment also fail to support the globalization arguments. First, in terms of both total investment and total private domestic investment, Germany ranks second worldwide behind Japan, but ahead of all other industrial democracies, including the United States.[14] More important, significant evidence contradicts the assumption that capital flows know no borders and that companies are unconstrained in their selection of investment locations. The vast majority of productive investment, R&D, and high value-added activities by all transnational corporations (TNCs), including those in Germany, takes place within their home country.[15] When TNCs invest abroad, investment, like trade, takes place largely in other advanced industrial countries. Furthermore, a significant portion of TNCs' foreign investment occurs in their geographic region of origin: most North American firms invest largely within the North American free trade area, many Asian firms concentrate foremost on Asia, and many European firms invest primarily within the EU. Rather than seeking out low-wage/low-cost environments, TNCs often invest abroad to improve their ability to respond to local market conditions and to circumvent trade restrictions.[16] In doing so, they increase both the volume of highest value-added activities and total economic activity in their home country.

Finally, unemployment statistics also fail to indicate that the German economy is falling behind in comparison with the economies of other countries. The *Standort* argument frequently contrasts inflexible labor markets and high unemployment in Germany with the flexibility of the deregulated U.S. economy. However, if the two economies are compared using standardized OECD (Organization for Economic Cooperation and Development) data over a period longer than the past three years, as is done in Table 4.1, the differences are far less dramatic. Two factors tend to inflate German unemployment figures in comparison with those of other industrial democracies. First, German definitions of unemployment are much broader than those in other countries. (The standardized calculations of the OECD adjust for this discrepancy.) Second, the figures for Germany in Table 4.1 after 1992 include the unemployed in eastern Germany, where the rate of unemployment is nearly twice as high as in the West. Since proponents of the *Standort* debate claim that it is the rigidities of the West German social market economy that threaten German competitiveness, it seems disingenuous to include data from an economy still in the process of transforming itself from a centrally planned economy in a comparison of advanced industrial economies. To the extent that all-

Table 4.1 Comparative Unemployment Figures

	1984	1985	1986	1987	1988	1989	1990	1991	1992	1993	1994	1995	1996 (est.)
FRG[1]	7.1	7.1	6.4	6.2	6.2	5.6	4.8	4.2	4.6	7.9	8.4	8.2	10.3
OECD (nat.)	(7.9)	(8.0)	(7.7)	(7.6)	(7.6)	(6.9)	(6.2)	(6.7)	(7.7)	(8.9)	(9.6)	(9.4)	
USA	7.4	7.1	6.9	6.1	5.4	5.2	5.6	6.8	7.5	6.9	6.0	5.5	5.4
OECD (nat.)	(7.5)	(7.2)	(7.0)	(6.2)	(5.5)	(5.3)	(5.6)	(6.8)	(7.5)	(6.9)	(6.1)	(5.6)	
France	9.7	10.2	10.4	10.5	10.0	9.4	8.9	9.4	10.3	11.7	12.3	11.6	12.4
OECD (nat.)	(9.7)	(10.2)	(10.4)	(10.5)	(10.0)	(9.3)	(8.9)	(9.4)	(10.4)	(11.7)	(12.3)	(11.7)	
U.K.	11.7	11.2	11.2	10.3	8.6	7.2	6.9	8.8	10.1	10.4	9.6	8.7	7.6
OECD (nat.)	(10.7)	(11.0)	(11.0)	(9.8)	(7.8)	(6.0)	(5.8)	(8.2)	(9.9)	(10.2)	(9.2)	(8.2)	
Japan[2]	2.7	2.6	2.8	2.9	2.5	2.3	2.1	2.1	2.2	2.5	2.9	3.2	3.3

SOURCE: *OECD Economic Outlook 1996* (January 1997), Annex Table 21.

NOTE: Upper figures in each cell represent OECD standardized measurement of unemployment for the country/year. Lower figures are the nationally reported figure for unemployment.

[1] Until 1992, figure represents unemployment measured in West Germany only. After 1992, figure represents unemployment for all of Germany.

[2] Japanese employment statistics do not vary from OECD figures, therefore only one number is given.

German unemployment figures are used as evidence of the lagging competitiveness of the West German economic system, the inclusion of eastern unemployment data contributes to an overstatement of the differences between West Germany and other industrial democracies.

More important, the spectacular difference between the United States
and Germany reflects a marked economic upturn in the United States
and a downturn in Germany after 1992. A longer horizon of comparison,
together with West Germany's superior performance vis-à-vis the rest of
Western Europe (including the flexible and deregulated labor markets of
the United Kingdom, if one separates East and West German data),
paints a much different picture of the development of German employment. Long-term increases in the unemployment rate are not the product
of the peculiar structural weakness of a rigid West German economy but,
rather, have occurred in all industrial economies since the 1970s. Furthermore, Germany seems to have done an above-average job of managing
this problem. The real source of the current difference between the U.S.
and German economic performance appears to be cyclical; although Germany was able to postpone the effects of the recession in most developed
countries at the beginning of the 1990s with a temporary boost from unification, it suffered an economic downturn as the U.S. and U.K.
economies were recovering. Unemployment is a serious dilemma for
Germans, and similar levels of unemployment may even represent a
greater problem for the German economy than for others.[17] However, unemployment cannot be used as an indicator of the "structural" weakness
of German economic performance vis-à-vis other industrial economies.

Interests and the *Standort* Debate

If evidence of the competitive decline of Germany's economy is less than
compelling, why do proponents of globalization and the *Standort* debate
continue to insist with such vehemence that resisting deregulation, wage
decline, and the triumph of global economics over national politics is not
only futile but dangerous? Further, why do their appeals find public acceptance? One possible answer is that the *Standort* debate is not so much
an explanation of economic developments as an instrument with which to
shape them. Pursuant to this view, the *Standort* debate is a set of arguments
promoted by a loose coalition of actors with parallel fiscal, electoral, and
economic motivations of shifting the enormous costs of unification.

First, the members of Bonn's governing coalition, driven by the necessity of financing the DM 150 billion–a–year cost of unification, have embraced the *Standort* debate as an instrument of fiscal consolidation. The
government already has exhausted many sources of funds trying to
cover this cost. Ongoing tensions within the coalition over the rising tax

burden associated with unification—particularly the "solidarity surcharge" (*Solidaritätszuschlag*)—indicate that the government has reached its own limits for raising revenue through taxation. Having staked its electoral future on the popularity of a "no new taxes" stand, the coalition's junior partner, the Free Democratic Party (FDP), extracted a commitment from its partners, the CDU/CSU, to begin phasing out the "solidarity surcharge" by July 1997. The FDP has made clear its unwillingness to raise even indirect taxes to cover the expense of unification.[18]

The German government's ability to finance unification through debt also seems to have reached its limits, effectively exhausting a second source of funding. A growing budget deficit, a rise in interest rates, and an increase in the value of the mark relative to other European currencies after unification contributed significantly to the demise of the European Monetary System/Exchange Rate Mechanism and stagnant growth in Germany and the rest of Europe. Further, the German government's inability to maintain public-sector debt below the 3 percent threshold specified by the Maastricht treaty has raised doubts about the future of the European Monetary Union. Despite its own demands for strict compliance with both the Maastricht convergence criteria and the 1999 start date, the German government itself will likely have to request either a loosening of the strict fiscal requirements or a postponement of monetary union.

With its access to new tax revenues and further borrowing effectively closed, the German government has sought to reduce government spending in other areas, especially social welfare programs, to finance unification. The government's fiscal shortfall was exacerbated by the extension of West German pension, unemployment, and health-care systems to include the East German population following unification. The treaty on economic, social, and monetary union between East and West Germany has had two effects which, in combination, produced a massive transfer of resources from western contributors to eastern recipients through welfare accounts. First, it translated East German debts, accounts, and wages into deutsche marks at a highly inflated exchange rate. Second, it integrated East Germans into West German social security systems. As inefficient enterprises became unprofitable and closed, large numbers of East Germans claimed unemployment benefits. Similarly, retired East Germans, including a far higher percentage of formerly employed women, were now entitled to pensions at or near the West German rate from the now all-German pension system, although they had never paid into the system. Developments in the quasi-public medical insurance system follow a similar pattern. These benefits are all financed by contributions paid equally by employers and employees. Although they had paid little or nothing toward these systems, easterners received benefits from systems funded largely by employers and employees in the west. As a result, these claims for benefits resulted in substantial transfers from western to eastern Germany.

With the slowdown of economic growth since 1993, a widening gap between revenues and expenditures in social security accounts became not only a fiscal but a political problem. Although rising payroll costs (*Lohnnebenkosten/Lohnzusatzkosten*) for pensions, health care, and unemployment insurance are not popular among employees, they may expect someday to be recipients of them. Rising payroll costs are opposed even more vigorously by employers, for whom they represent an additional cost of labor. Confronted with growing discontent over payroll costs, the Kohl government has attempted to turn fiscal necessity into a virtuous national struggle to save the "German *Standort*" against the external threat of global competition. As further increases in taxes and borrowing became politically more difficult, the government had to persuade the public to accept the equally unpalatable idea of cutting benefits. The result was the present *Standort* debate. In public statements explaining the government's position, Chancellor Kohl has sought to convince Germans that they have "lived above their means"[19] and that they can no longer afford high wages, long vacations, and a generous welfare state. The chancellor has argued that, to face the demands of international competition, "personified" by aggressive "Asian tiger states," the nation must sacrifice. This means "leaner" business, a "leaner" state, and, above all, "leaner" welfare benefits.

Financially strapped *Länder* governments of all political parties, including those led by the SPD (Social Democratic Party), share the fiscal concerns of the Bonn coalition and have offered qualified support for a campaign that promises to help them avoid political responsibility for budget cuts. Western *Länder* governments face increasing budgetary pressures caused, in part, by transfers to the eastern states. In the German federal system, many administrative functions and their fiscal burdens are borne by the states. To ensure rough parity in administering programs, the largest sources of revenue (value-added taxes, income taxes, and corporate taxes) are pooled by the federal and state governments and distributed back to the states according to a formula of rough per-capita equality.[20] Thus, until economic output and revenues in the new states of the east reach levels comparable to those in the west, there will be a net flow of fiscal resources from western to eastern *Länder*. Budgetary pressures caused by unification and recession have led state leaders, even within the SPD—many of whose most important constituencies are employed by or dependent on social programs—to embrace *Standort* rhetoric as a justification for painful cuts in administrative and overhead costs.

The timing and selectivity of SPD governments' contributions to the *Standort* debate reveal their fiscal motivation. Numerous statements in early 1996 from representatives of SPD-led *Länder* governments, such as those in Lower Saxony and Rheinland-Palatinate, corresponded closely with their support for Bonn's demand that public-sector employees forgo wage increases in the 1996 round of contract negotiations. However, as coalition negotiations on lowering the "solidarity surcharge" threatened to further decrease revenues available to the states, *Länder* governments proved unwilling to make their own sacrifice for the good of the German *Standort*.[21]

Important differences separate the interests of the coalition parties in the *Standort* debate. While the CDU/CSU Union parties regard the *Standort* debate more as a useful tool for consolidating the federal budget than as an appeal for winning votes, the Free Democrats have gained a new lease on electoral life as the champion of tax reduction and small government. Having difficulty projecting a political profile independent of its coalition partners, the party faced electoral extinction as it failed to surpass the 5 percent threshold for parliamentary representation in twelve of thirteen state elections between 1993 and 1995.[22] Since 1995, its new leadership has recast the FDP as a reform party dedicated to economic renewal through deregulation and emancipation of individual initiative.[23] Borrowing from the programs of economic liberals in the United States and the United Kingdom, the new leadership has criticized "entitlement democracy,"[24] proposed a moratorium on new public debt,[25] and considered a pledge to permit "no new taxes."[26] After better-than-expected results in three state elections in March 1996, the FDP reasserted an independent image and firmly tied its electoral fortunes to the appeal of its position in the *Standort* debate.

Furthermore, to the extent that the government campaign halts the growth of or actually reduces payroll costs, employers generally support it. Some business leaders even advocate the far more controversial step of shifting a larger portion of such costs, historically divided equally between employees and employers, onto employees. However, there are too many potential divisions among employers—large versus small firms, manufacturing versus service industries, export versus protected sectors, rising versus declining industries, and so on—to generalize about the role of employers in the *Standort* debate.[27] While the debate finds some of its most vociferous proponents among the leaders of business organizations such as the DIHT, the BDI, and Gesamtmetall, an "alliance" between the state and employers on the issue of payroll costs rests on potentially conflicting calculations of interests. To cover ever-widening fiscal shortfalls, the state must maximize revenues while limiting expenditures. Representatives of business, however, would like to see cuts in benefits translate into a reduction in their contributions. Further, to the extent that efforts to redistribute costs to employees and welfare recipients threaten to provoke conflict with unions or undermine the autonomy of contractual negotiations (*Tarifautonomie*), many employers will be hesitant to support such redistribution efforts.

While fiscal, electoral, and economic interests have driven the *Standort* debate in the German media, they explain neither why this interpretation of the economic situation in Germany has met little organized opposition nor how change is actually taking place. The answer to both questions might lie in the complex nature of the adjustments currently occurring in the German economy. Markets and economies around the world are changing, perhaps more rapidly and fundamentally than neoclassical economic theories can explain.[28] Furthermore, in contemporary Germany, where the nature and course of economic change are compounded by German unification and European integration, two forces reinforce the view of economic developments proposed in the *Standort* debate. First, the underlying logic of the debate is loosely grounded in neoclassical economics. Therefore, its proponents lay claim to a widely accepted theoretical economic framework. Second, the *Standort* debate provides a clear perspective as to who should make important economic decisions.

Proponents of deregulation in Germany generally assume that firms are abstract entities, the embodiment of the neoclassical production function, and not complex human organizations. Further, they assume that firms are driven only by the motives of maximizing efficiency and profit and that deviations from such behavior originate not within firms but with external, "market-distorting" regulations. Consequently, it is argued, all such distortions should be removed and economic decision-making authority should be concentrated in the hands of managers and owners. This helps explain the popularity of this perspective among those who stand to exercise such power or profit from this type of economic organization.

Although the adherents of deregulation offer the most forcefully articulated perspective on economic change in Germany at present, their views do not necessarily correspond to the way most Germans view economic issues. Forty-five years of successful economic performance and favorable experience with cooperative institutions have created vested interests and deeply ingrained beliefs regarding cooperation and social solidarity. While such perspectives remain prevalent in German society, advocates of reform within the traditional German model suffer from two weaknesses in the *Standort* debate. First, they cannot formulate a preferred vision of social organization in conveniently transmittable soundbites such as globalization and deregulation. Second, during a recession, when the need for reform is obvious, it is a greater rhetorical challenge to make the case for promoting certain changes while resisting others than it is to advocate the fundamental transformation of the economy.

At present, adherents of reform are attempting to use the *Standort* debate to delineate starkly opposing camps regarding the process of economic change in Germany. On one hand, they place themselves as the proponents of deregulation and marketization, who have recognized the necessary direction of change in an increasingly global economy. On the other, all those who disagree with them are labeled "traditionalists," accused of intransigently clinging to the past, the institutions of the social market economy, and their narrow self-interest. This schema permits no room for those who would maintain and adapt the role of existing institutions to changing economic conditions, although this position probably describes the majority of German society.

Because of the extent of organization in the German economy and the preponderance of norms of cooperation embedded in such organizations, however, the *Standort* debate is unlikely to produce a sweeping reorganization of the German economy. Yet, as demonstrated in the next section, this does not mean that change and adjustment have ended in Germany.

The Course of Change in the German Economy

Recessions and recoveries raise the problem of structural change in an economy. Investors and laborers are confronted with the prospect of moving from one occupation to another, often at considerable cost. The present situation in Germany is no different. Rather than opening a societal "debate" in the conventional sense about how this adjustment should take place, however, the *Standort* debate appears much more an attempt to foreclose discussion of these questions and impose the views of one coalition of interests about how the costs and benefits of adjustment should be distributed. Rhetorically, the *Standort* debate proposes that Germany's current economic difficulties are the result of the organization of its economy and that the solution is to liberate the market by sweeping aside the institutional constraints of the social market economy. The question that is raised only implicitly—and which the *Standort* debate attempts to preempt—is whether adjustment to the dislocations arising from unification, and elsewhere, can take place within the carefully constructed mechanisms of consultation and negotiation institutionalized in the "German model."

Four examples of economic conflict between spring 1996 and summer 1997 demonstrate that economic adjustment is occurring in Germany.

These examples indicate that economic adjustment is not resulting in the systematic reorganization that adherents of the *Standort* debate claim is unavoidable; rather, adjustment generally takes the form of negotiated compromises broadly consistent with Germany's traditional economic model.

The first example is the attempt of managers in the metal industries to shift unilaterally a portion of the cost of sick pay regulations (*Lohnfortzahlung im Krankheitsfall*) to employees at the end of 1996.[29] At the behest of employer associations, the government included in its 1996 "savings package" a provision permitting employers to reduce payment of sick workers from 100 percent to 80 percent of normal wages for at least part of their absence. Because existing contracts were written under the old regulations, some employers, led by Germany's largest firm, Daimler-Benz, announced their intention unilaterally to abrogate existing labor agreements and to impose the new regulation in subsequent negotiations with employees. The maneuver was viewed by many Germans as so heavy-handed that it provoked not only the resistance of the unions but also public demonstrations and sharp criticisms from government representatives, including Chancellor Kohl and President Roman Herzog.[30] After backing down in the face of pressure, employer organizations in the metal industries, as well as those in other sectors, have been unwilling to risk a similar reaction by raising the issue in subsequent contract negotiations.

This episode presents two insights into attempts to reorganize the German economic model. First, employers severely overestimated their influence with respect to public and political opinion when they attempted unilaterally to impose costs on employees. In spite of apparent public acceptance of many aspects of employers' arguments in the *Standort* debate, neither the public nor political leaders were willing to allow such a sudden departure from postwar norms concerning "social partnership" and "solidarity." Second, the government's attempt to extend its influence in contract negotiations seems to have backfired, leading to a strengthening of wage autonomy and resistance to state influence in industrial relations. In passing the sick pay legislation, the government signaled its consent to a redistribution of costs in industrial relations toward employees. As a result of employers' overzealous leap to embrace this signal, however, unions have been able to resist management demands regarding sick pay, not on the basis of material self-interest but as the defenders of wage autonomy and social peace against partisan political interference in the economy.

The second example concerns ongoing tensions within the Bonn coalition over fiscal policy. In preparation for the budget debate in 1996, the leader of the CDU/CSU parliamentary group, Wolfgang Schäuble, warned members of his party not to focus purely on savings and consolidation, but to emphasize the growth and jobs that would be created by cutting pension, unemployment, and health-care budgets.[31] By spring 1997, however, with the deadline for inclusion in the first round of European Monetary Union approaching and the prospect that Germany's budget deficit would exceed the Maastricht criteria, considerations of growth and jobs largely were replaced by intracoalition discussions of a narrow, intractable issue: how to reconcile the government's commitment to a European currency that is as stable as the deutsche mark with its desire to avoid raising taxes to consolidate the budget.

Those concerned primarily with ensuring that a single European currency will be as strong as the mark are more willing to raise taxes to ensure that Germany's budget deficit complies with the Maastricht convergence criteria. Facing continued public skepticism toward a single European currency, hard-liners within the Bonn coalition, especially the CSU under Finance Minister Theo Waigel, have led a public campaign for strict compliance with the convergence standards established in the Maastricht treaty. Strict compliance would, as a practical matter, exclude several countries (notably Italy, Greece, Spain, and Portugal) from participation in the first round of monetary union. Unfortunately, in 1997 Germany's own projected deficit threatened to put it outside the Maastricht threshold as well, leaving the Bonn government—should it not find a new source of revenues or means of reducing expenditures—to choose between two unpleasant options: postponing the introduction of the new currency or acquiescing in a flexible interpretation of the convergence criteria. The latter option would likely diminish both Germany's authority to demand fiscal restraint by other European governments and the credibility of the new European currency in Germany. Consequently, many members of the Union parties have advocated increasing petroleum and value-added taxes to control the deficit.[32]

On the other side of the issue stands the FDP, which has reversed its declining fortunes by advocating tax reduction as its central policy. By doing so, however, the FDP has left itself, and thus the coalition, no room for maneuver in efforts to consolidate the budget. Having cut expenditures where it could, sold government shares in Deutsche Telekom, and even attempted to revalue the Bundesbank's gold reserves, the government is left with two options to reduce the budget deficit: cut welfare programs, which would probably require (and would probably not receive) consent from the SPD-dominated upper house of the parliament (the Bundesrat), or raise taxes. The example of employers' efforts to shift the costs of sick pay demonstrated that employers lack government and public support to make significant alterations to the German economic model unilaterally. The example of the 1997 budget debates confirms that much of the government is unwilling to sacrifice other social, political, or economic objectives in order to implement sweeping economic reforms.

If these first two examples indicate that the proponents of reform behind the *Standort* debate lack the cohesion to alter radically the nature of
the German economic model, this does not mean that adjustment itself
has ceased. Rather, the final two examples—the attempt by Krupp A.G.
to buy out fellow steel manufacturer Thyssen A.G. and the labor contract
in the chemical industry negotiated in mid-1997—indicate that social and
economic adjustment is occurring, but according to a very different logic
from the one advocated by the proponents of the *Standort* debate.

The third example involves Krupp A.G.'s hostile bid for Thyssen A.G.
in March 1997. Sensing an opportunity to sanitize their own company's
troubled balance sheet through further rationalization in the Rhein-Ruhr
steel industry, managers at Krupp approached Thyssen with offers of a
merger. Thyssen's management, which had shortly before conducted a
reorganization and returned the company to profitability, failed to see the
advantages of union with the beleaguered Krupp and rebuffed the over-
tures. In secret consultations with Germany's two largest banks,
Deutsche Bank and Dresdner Bank, Krupp managers devised a strategy
for a hostile takeover of Thyssen. Announcement of Krupp's bid for
Thyssen caused surprise and shock among German managers and
bankers. Thyssen's management denounced the Krupp managers' "Wild
West manners" and vowed to fight.[33] In contrast to the United States,
where they are primarily the prerogative of managers and shareholders,
mergers and acquisitions in Germany often involve negotiations among
management, labor representatives, banks, and state authorities. Krupp's
attempt to circumvent such consultations precipitated dramatic resistance from workers and the government. Expecting that Krupp's move
signaled the next round of plant closures in the Rhein-Ruhr steel industry, plant-level employee representatives *(Betriebsräte)* and officials of the
metalworkers union (IG Metall) in the state of North-Rhein-Westphalia
called on employees in both firms to take to the streets to protect their
jobs. Within hours of Krupp's announcement to Thyssen shareholders,
the governor and finance and economics ministers of North-Rhein-Westphalia summoned the top executives of both firms to Düsseldorf for consultations.

State and labor leaders objected less to the proposed rationalization
than to the unilateral strategy Krupp and the banks had employed to
carry it out. Rather than blocking the merger outright, state authorities
brokered a compromise union of the two firms' steel divisions. In addition, IG Metall's top functionary for North-Rhine-Westphalia joined
management of the two firms in the negotiations on the condition that
worker layoffs from the merger would not be tied directly to plant closures *(betriebsbedingte Kündigungen)*. This stipulation assured workers
that they would not bear the entire cost of rationalization. Resistance was

less a reaction against rationalization than against attempts to implement it entirely according to a single set of shareholder interests. The Krupp-Thyssen case demonstrates that German firms have continued to adjust to changing economic conditions, and that they have done so according to the postwar German pattern of negotiation among various interests.

A fourth example, the mid-1997 contract in the chemical industry, demonstrates that the mechanisms of the social market economy themselves are adjusting to the changed economic environment according to a similar pattern. In June 1997, the chemical workers' representatives *IG Chemie-Papier-Keramik* and employers organization (*Bundesarbeitgeberverband Chemie*—BAVC) concluded a tariff agreement governing wages and benefits in the chemicals industry. Following the typical German pattern, the contract not only covers all employers in the BAVC and their employees but also sets the standard for other employers in the industry. For the first time in the postwar history of German industrial relations, however, this contract includes an opening clause that allows plant-level negotiators to adjust not only hours and overtime compensation to local conditions but also wages.[34] Because the new contract opens the possibility for wage cuts of up to 10 percent "to secure employment and to improve competitiveness," some observers, particularly in the American press,[35] have concluded that the arrangement signals not only labor's full retreat in the face of the "globalizing" chemical industry but also the end of sector-wide blanket contracts (*Flächenverträge*).

In fact, despite the headlines, the arrangement appears to be a balanced and innovative approach to dealing with changing market conditions in the chemical industry. While the contract permits deviation from sectoral wage norms in individual plants and firms, wage cuts require the consent of plant-level employee representatives (*Betriebsräte*) and are permitted only for the specific purpose of preventing job losses and maintaining the firm's competitiveness. Further, downward deviations from the specifications of the sectoral contract are limited to a 12-month period. This "wage corridor" was created not to squeeze labor but to keep a group of about two dozen firms in Germany's depressed rubber and chemical fiber industries within the sectoral bargaining mechanism. The alternative to the present agreement was the creation of contracts for individual branches within the chemical industry—a solution both employers' organizations and unions feared would precipitate the eventual collapse of centralized negotiations.[36] Observers proclaiming a defeat for labor overlook the precedent of similar arrangements providing for plant-level flexibility in work hours and overtime compensation (although not in wages) in other industries.[37] They also neglect the fact that employers and labor unions apparently continue to see advantages in the maintenance of centralized bargaining when its results can be flexibly interpreted by credible representatives on both sides at the plant level. It is not an accident that innovation involving the blanket wage contract—a mechanism fundamental to the social market economy— evolved in an industry where no serious labor conflict has occurred in the past 25 years.[38]

Conclusion

Since the media discussions of Germany's economic future dominated by the *Standort* debate during 1993, there has been a noticeable disparity between economic developments and the explanations offered for them on television and in newspapers. Despite claims that Germany's economic system, based on high wages, high skills, and high-quality production, cannot survive in a globalized economy, there is little evidence that capital and jobs are fleeing the country for havens of cheap labor. Nor does it seem that entrenched interests have blocked the process of economic adjustment, thereby intensifying current economic difficulties. Rather than conforming to the purely competitive economic logic of a global market, economic adjustment in Germany is proceeding according to a different, more political pattern.

Power and influence are distributed differently in Germany from elsewhere. As employers' failed attempts to redistribute unilaterally the economic burdens associated with sick pay demonstrate, German managers, unlike their American counterparts, are unlikely to dominate the politics of economic adjustment. Further, the Bonn government has shown that it lacks the unity of purpose to formulate policies radically to reorient the German economy, let alone impose such a program. Where change has taken place in the German economy, it has occurred not as a response to economic necessity or the imposition of will by certain political or economic interests, but as a settlement negotiated by managers, banks, labor representatives, and the state. This pattern of negotiated settlement represents a continuation of the postwar German model.

In Germany, as in other industrial democracies, not only are international issues increasingly relevant to domestic politics, but social forces are more deeply involved in the policymaking process. Highly publicized debates about globalization and competitiveness in Germany and elsewhere demonstrate the recognition by politicians and other policymakers that prevailing on certain policy issues depends on winning public support or, at least, ensuring the absence of active resistance. As Suzanne Berger has pointed out, the new politics of globalization raise a common set of potentially explosive questions with which policymakers in every country must attempt to deal.[39] Can the social and even cultural peculiarities of different national systems survive as ever more economic processes transcend national borders? Are changes occurring in connection with increased internationalization the result of impersonal technological and market forces or the voluntary choices of individuals and groups in society? Finally, whose interest does change serve and when, where, and how should issues of such societal importance be resolved?

Debates about globalization and economic competitiveness have suggested different answers to these questions in different countries. In Germany, the outline of possible answers is discernible in the responses to the *Standort* debate. While it is too early to say whether the German model will survive and adapt to the post–Cold War economic environment, recent experience indicates that any demise will result from political choices guided by concrete interests rather than from the need to deregulate forced by the global market. The institutions of the German social market economy will be abandoned only if and when their constituencies see their interests served better elsewhere and they withdraw their political and financial support. While advocates of the *Standort* debate portray this process as a forgone conclusion, they do so because this serves their interests.

The survival of the social market economy depends on its ability to adapt to changing conditions, confront new challenges, and reconcile a broader spectrum of interests. The evidence presented here indicates that, so far, the social market economy has proved sufficiently resilient to adapt to changing economic conditions while retaining popular support throughout most segments of German society.

Notes

1. The following draws heavily on the works of Peter Katzenstein and Wolfgang Streeck, particularly Peter J. Katzenstein, *Policy and Politics in West Germany: The Growth of a Semi-Sovereign State* (Philadelphia: Temple University Press, 1987), and Katzenstein, ed., *Industry and Politics in West Germany: Toward the Third Republic* (Ithaca: Cornell University Press, 1989); as well as Wolfgang Streeck, "On the Institutional Conditions of Diversified Quality Production," in Egon Matzner and Wolfgang Streeck, eds., *Beyond Keynesianism* (Worcester, UK: Edward Elgar, 1991), pp. 21–61, and "Der deutsche Kapitalismus: Gibt es ihn? Kann er Überleben?" (translation from Colin Crouch and Wolfgang Streeck, eds., *Modern Capitalism or Modern Capitalismus?* [London: Francis Pinter, 1995]). For a similar treatment of the same subject from the popular press, see Michel Albert, *Kapitalismus contra Kapitalismus* (Frankfurt: Campus Verlag, 1991).

2. For a classic reconsideration of the myth of the "natural market," see Karl Polanyi, *The Great Transformation* (Boston: Beacon Press, 1944).

3. Streeck, "Der deutsche Kapitalismus," pp. 36–37. The absence of prefabricated or "tract" housing in the market for freestanding housing offers one important example of such segmentation.

4. For discussion of various types of "flexibility" in labor relations, see Wolfgang Streeck, "The Uncertainties of Management in the Management of Uncertainty," *International Journal of Political Economy* 17, no. 3 (Fall 1987): 57–87.

5. For the classic discussion of the relationship between German banks and their industrial customers, see Andrew Schonfield, *Modern Capitalism: The Changing Balance of Public and Private Power* (London: Oxford Press, 1965), particularly chaps. 11 and 2.

6. For a treatment of Germany's nonprofit sector, see Wolfgang Seibel, *Funktioneller Diletantismus* (Baden-Baden: Nomos Verlag Gesellschaft, 1992).

7. Streeck, "Der deutsche Kapitalismus," pp. 40–41.

8. On the capacity of the institutions of the German economy to create "trust" relationships between actors, see David Soskice, "The Institutional Infrastructure for International Competitiveness: A Comparative Analysis of the UK and Germany," in Anthony B. Atkinson and Renato Brunetta, eds., *Economics for the New Europe* (London: Macmillan, 1991), pp. 45–66.

9. For discussion of "corporatist" bargaining during the 1970s, see the contributions in John H. Goldthorpe, ed., *Order and Conflict in Contemporary Capitalism* (New York: Oxford University Press, 1984).

10. For discussion of relations between centralized unions and local works' councils on the "interpretation" of sectoral contracts at the plant level, see Kathleen Thelen, *Union of Parts* (Ithaca: Cornell University Press, 1991).

11. *Süddeutsche Zeitung (SZ)*, 7–8 June 1997, p. 6.

12. See Deutsches Institut für Wirtschaftsforschung (DIW), "Hat Westdeutschland ein Standortproblem?" *Wochenbericht* 38/95 (21 September 1995): 653–661.

13. Ibid., pp. 655–656.

14. Ibid., pp. 655–656.

15. See Laura D'Andrea Tyson, "They Are Not Us: Why American Ownership Still Matters," *American Prospect*, no. 4 (Winter 1991); and U.S. Congress, Office of Technology Assessment, "Multinationals and the National Interest: Playing by Different Rules," OTA-ITE–569 (Washington, D.C.: U.S. Government Printing Office, September 1993); and idem, "Multinationals and the U.S. Technology Base," OTA-ITE–612 (Washington, D.C.: U.S. Government Printing Office, September 1994).

16. See Tyson, "They Are Not Us," pp. 41–42.

17. Streeck makes this argument in "Der deutsche Kapitalismus," but, ultimately, he, like Albert in *Kapitalismus contra Kapitalismus*, sees the dilemma confronting the German model as being distributional and political rather than one of international competitiveness. Although both authors come to a pessimistic conclusion about the future of German or Rhein capitalism—and not without good reason—their arguments do not directly contradict the one presented here. Rather, their works and this essay are separated by the chosen tone of their authors.

18. See the platform of the FDP party congress in Wiesbaden in *SZ*, 26 May 1997.

19. Helmut Kohl in *Der Spiegel*, no. 36 (6 September 1993), p. 30.

20. For a detailed analysis of German federalism, see Heinz Laufer, *Das föderative System der Bundesrepublik Deutschland*, 6. *Auflage* (Munich: Bayerische Landeszentrale für Politische Bildungsarbeit).

21. In spring 1996, a government plan to lower the "solidarity surcharge" and cover the loss in revenue to the federal government by reapportioning VAT revenues from the states back to the federal government met with stiff opposition from not only SPD-led state governments but also the Union states. This restructuring of revenues was critical to the "savings package" the government was attempting to sell as an employment program.

22. Jürgen Falter and Jürgen Winkler, "Die FDP vor dem Aus?" *Aus Politik und Zeitgeschichte*, no. 6 (2 February 1996): 57–59.

23. "Es liegt an den Steuer" (interview with Hermann-Otto Solms), *Der Spiegel*, no. 2 (8 January 1996): 57–59.

24. "Seele verlieren," *Der Spiegel*, no. 6 (5 February 1996): 34–36.

25. Guido Westerwelle in *SZ*, 17–19 May 1997, p. 6:1.

26. *SZ*, 26 May 1997, p. 1.

27. For a discussion of the divisions within and between Germany's industry associations, see "Chaotischen Kapitalisten," *Der Spiegel*, no. 51 (16 December 1996): 22–24.

28. For the classical discussions that view present economic changes as representing transformations deeper than the "regulatory" transition envisioned by liberals and neo-Marxists, see Michael Piore and Charles Sabel, *The Second Industrial Divide: Possibilities for Prosperity* (New York: Basic Books, 1984), and Horst Kern and Michael Schumann, *Das Ende der Arbeitsteilung? Rationalisierung in der industriellen Produktion* (Munich: Beck, 1984).

29. Sick pay was first won by the metal union in a bitter sixteen-week strike in 1956–1957. Indirectly, the strike forced the Bundestag to legislate sick pay regulations. See Michael Schneider, *Kleine Geschichte der Gewerkschaften* (Bonn: J.H.W. Dietz Nachf. GmbH, 1989), pp. 286–287.

30. See comments by Kohl and Herzog in "Chaotische Kapitalisten," pp. 22–24.

31. See Schäuble's comments in *SZ*, 19 April, 1996, p. 2.

32. *SZ*, 17–19 May 1997, p. 1.

33. *SZ*, 19 March 1997, p. 1.

34. *SZ*, 5 June 1997, p. 1.

35. See, for example, "German Union's Consent to Wage Cuts Signals New Erosion of Labor's Power," *Wall Street Journal*, 5 June, 1997, p. A10. In the German press, "Tarifpolitik: 'Rutsche nach unten,'" *Der Spiegel*, no. 24 (9 June 1997): 93–94; Arne Daniels, "Geordneter Rückzug," *Die Zeit*, 13 June 1997, p. 26.

36. *Frankfurter allgemeine Zeitung (FAZ)*, 6 June 1997, p. 15.

37. See Thelen, *Union of Parts*.

38. *Der Spiegel*, 9 June 1997, p. 93.

39. Suzanne Berger, "Introduction," in Suzanne Berger and Ronald Dore, eds., *National Diversity and Global Capitalism* (Ithaca: Cornell University Press, 1996), pp. 1–25.

5

Economic Reform: Restructuring the German Railway System

ANDREW P. JOHNSON

By January 1994, the German railways were in dire need of reform. They were horribly out of shape, both fiscally and physically, and their popularity as a mode of transportation was in serious decline. The *Bahnreform* (railway reform) adopted in December 1993 resulted from nearly five years of planning, deliberation, and political wrangling. Indeed, this was far from the first attempt made at reforming the German railways.[1] Even so, the *Bahnreform* began in 1994 with political fanfare and great enthusiasm. With fresh resolve, the reformers set out to break the railways free of what seemed a perpetual cycle of declining market shares and increasing deficits. Although the *Bahnreform* is expected to take nine or ten years to complete, it has now reached a point where an interim evaluation appears useful.

The first two sections of this report are historical. The first section briefly addresses the situation leading up to 1994 and the urgent need for some form of *Bahnreform*. The historical summary is then followed by a description of the political, legal, and organizational steps that brought the *Bahnreform* to fruition. Thereafter, the report focuses on the structure and results of the *Bahnreform*: the privatization model adopted for the *Bahnreform* is outlined and explained, and the changing but ever-present role of the German government is considered. Finally, the *Bahnreform's* progress is assessed in terms of both its financial results and its broader goals. Overall, the picture is encouraging.

The Situation Before the *Bahnreform*

The problems, costs, and fears that led to the *Bahnreform* were substantial. The postwar history of the German railways had been characterized by sharply decreasing market shares and increasing deficits. In West Germany, the Deutsche Bundesbahn's market share of passenger traffic in 1950 was 36 percent. By 1993, that percentage had fallen to 6.3 percent. With respect to freight traffic, the Bundesbahn enjoyed a market share of 62 percent in 1950. Its market share in 1993 was less than 23 percent.[2] These sharp declines in market share occurred during a period that saw a tenfold increase in passenger-kilometers traveled and a fivefold increase in ton-kilometers transported. To a large extent, these trends were international and not particular to Germany. The relative decline in the role of railways is inversely related to the phenomenal growth in the importance of automobiles and trucks as passenger and freight carriers in modern industrial societies. But the declining market shares of the railways in Germany are particularly noteworthy when one considers both the natural advantages of railways and the quantity of resources devoted to the German railways in that time period.

Rail transportation enjoys natural advantages over road transportation in Germany, including energy efficiency, environmental friendliness, safety, reliability, and near-immunity to poor weather conditions. The availability of rail transportation makes individual travel affordable and comfortable without a large initial investment in an automobile. And the presence of rail-transport hubs in city centers is both an advantage for the railways and an important factor in the quality of life in and preservation of urban centers. These advantages explain the political support that the railways have long enjoyed in Germany. They also suggest that the railways might benefit from a certain competitive advantage over other modes of transportation in certain markets. Nevertheless, even when combined with the particular disadvantages to the consumer of road transportation (i.e., high initial investment and maintenance costs, high fuel prices/taxes, tolls, delays resulting from congestion, parking concerns), these advantages seem to have been incapable of halting the inexorable trend away from the rails and onto the roads.

Regrettable as they may have been, declining market shares alone would never have brought about the *Bahnreform* as it exists today. The true catalyst for reform was the fact that, with declining market shares, this once-profitable state enterprise had been incurring ever-larger losses (paid from the public budget) for more than twenty years. In the early 1990s, this trend reached alarming proportions. In 1970, the Deutsche Bundesbahn received subsidies of DM 3.5 billion, realized losses of DM 1.3 billion, and had a cumulated debt of DM 14 billion. In 1990, despite subsidies of DM 13.3 billion, the Bundesbahn lost DM 4.9 billion, bringing its total debt to DM 47 billion. Germany's transportation minister, Günther Krause, forecast that the Bundesbahn's debts would exceed DM

80 billion by 1996. "The financial collapse of the Bundesbahn as a government agency was calculable and foreseeable."[3]

German unification in 1990 also played a decisive role in bringing about the *Bahnreform*. With unification, the assets of the Deutsche Reichsbahn, the railway of the GDR, were assumed by the federal government. Clearly, the railways would be critical in managing the ever-increasing transportation needs of a unified Germany. The highways were already overcrowded, and Germany's position at the center of an increasingly open and integrated Europe promised to increase the volume of traffic.

But just as clearly, after unification, the German railways were not up to the task. After decades of government direction within the planned economy of the GDR, the Reichsbahn was ill prepared to operate in a commercially viable manner in the newly reunified Germany. Within a year of the unification, passenger and freight traffic on the Deutsche Reichsbahn fell to half of what it had been in 1990. Declining revenues and rising expenses resulted in losses of DM 2.9 billion and new debts of DM 2.2 billion in 1991. Major investments were needed in infrastructure and equipment, and the enterprise was significantly overstaffed.

Taken together, the Deutsche Bundesbahn and the Deutsche Reichsbahn had by 1993 amassed debts totaling DM 66.2 billion. If no action were taken, Germany's transportation minister calculated, those debts would rise during the period from 1994 to 2003 to DM 382 billion. In the same period, the government could expect to pay subsidies totaling DM 257 billion.[4] Without reform, annual losses of the combined railways were expected to rise to DM 49.2 billion by 2003.[5] The absorption of the Reichsbahn was by no means a singular enterprise resulting from unification. But the costs that ensued from its incorporation into the federal government supplied increased urgency to the reform proposals already under consideration in the West.

Finally, the *Bahnreform* was motivated in part by developments at the European Communities level. On July 29, 1991, the EC Council adopted Council Directive 91/440/EEC, which was intended to "facilitate the adaption of the Community railways to the needs of the Single Market and to increase their efficiency."[6] Prior to the *Bahnreform*, the legal and economic structure of the German railways was inconsistent with the requirements of this directive. The *Bahnreform* created the legal framework necessary for Germany to comply with the directive.

Steps Toward Reform

The German government took the first concrete steps toward reform in early 1989 with the appointment of the Federal Railway Governmental

Commission. This commission included representatives of industry, science, politics, and railway employees, and was given the mandate to study the situation of the German railways, placing particular emphasis on their fundamental structure and potential for future competitiveness. Chaired by Günther Sassmannshausen, the former chairman of the board of Preussag AG, the commission was empowered to act independently and to maintain neutrality with respect to the views of interest groups.

The Deutsche Bundesbahn also received new leadership on January 1, 1991. Heinz Dürr, the former chairman of the board at AEG and a member of the board of Daimler-Benz AG, was named chairman of the management board of the Deutsche Bundesbahn. He was expected to bring new direction to the Bundesbahn by beginning to move it toward commercial viability even before the Federal Railway Governmental Commission had submitted its report. His role as head manager of the German railways was extended to the Deutsche Reichsbahn in September 1991.

In June 1991, the commission submitted an interim report outlining the results of its two-year inquiry, in which it proposed "revolutionary" reforms that went far beyond anything suggested in previous attempts at reforming the railways. In its report, the commission emphasized the looming financial catastrophe and suggested that only comprehensive reform could be effective: "Without a fundamental rehabilitation plan, there is no hope of stabilizing the railways."[7] The proposals presented by the commission in its interim report, and set forth in greater detail in its final report on December 19, 1991, were to form the basic scheme under which the *Bahnreform* was realized in 1994. The most important proposals included the following:

- The Deutsche Bundesbahn and the Deutsche Reichsbahn should be amalgamated to form a government-owned joint-stock company, the Deutsche Eisenbahn AG (DEAG).
- The DEAG should be managed as a commercial enterprise and report on its successes in accordance with German commercial law.
- The DEAG should be divided into the following divisions: track infrastructure, freight traffic, and passenger traffic.
- The DEAG's freight traffic and passenger traffic divisions should compete with each other and with third parties for use of the track. They would pay the track division fees for the use of its facilities.
- If fees for the use of track and operating costs cannot be covered in the field of passenger traffic (and, in particular, short-distance passenger traffic), the deficits arising from these services—which the DEAG offers in the public interest—must be covered by the

federal government, the federal states, special-purpose associations, and companies involved in passenger transportation.

- The DEAG's freight traffic and passenger traffic divisions would bear the commercial responsibility for investment in rolling stock, stations, and freight centers.
- The DEAG's infrastructure division would bear the commercial responsibility for maintaining and extending track.
- The DEAG would procure material and equipment according to exclusively commercial considerations and no longer primarily to serve the national interest.
- The federal government would assume responsibility for the financial obligations and debts incurred by the Deutsche Bundesbahn and Deutsche Reichsbahn.
- The federal government would take over the Deutsche Bundesbahn's obligations arising from the former civil service status of its employees. It also would assume the burden of the Deutsche Reichsbahn's surplus personnel and the obligation to pay pensions to retired employees.[8]

These proposals established the structural framework for *Bahnreform*. The next step was for the government to hammer out a package of specific reform measures that would receive the necessary political support in both houses of the German parliament, the Bundestag (the lower house) and the Bundesrat (the upper house, which acts essentially as a representative body of the state governments at the federal level).

In February 1992, Günther Krause was instructed by the Cabinet to develop a plan to reform the railways based on the commission's report. The essential features of the plan were as follows: setting fair conditions for the railways to compete on the open market; making the railways competitive; protecting the legitimate interests of the staff of the Deutsche Bundesbahn and the Deutsche Reichsbahn; solving the debt problem; and ensuring that the railway could provide services in the public interest.[9]

In April 1992, Krause submitted his ministry's proposals for discussion by the Cabinet and other affected ministries. He put forward a number of alternative draft proposals, each with slightly different organizational or ownership structures. In the discussions that followed, a proposal that envisioned the privatization of the railways under the ownership of a holding company that could later be broken down into its constituent parts gained favor. As suggested by the Federal Railway Governmental Commission, the plan proposed first to amalgamate the Deutsche Bundesbahn and the Deutsche Reichsbahn, and then to transform the whole into a joint-stock company, the DEAG. In the short term, this joint-stock company would remain in the exclusive ownership of the federal government but would have the legal status and commercial objectives of a private corporation. Within the framework of the DEAG as holding company, the infrastructure, passenger traffic, and freight traffic divisions were to be separated financially and organizationally.[10] Each division would form its own joint-stock company (*Aktiengesellschaft*) and, after a period of not more than five years, the umbrella of the holding company would be dissolved.

In the summer of 1992, Krause submitted the necessary bills to the Cabinet. The principle of railway reform was supported by every political party represented in the Bundestag, and the need for rapid action was widely accepted. The government set the goal of completing the legislative process and implementing the *Bahnreform* within a year.[11]

In the end, two issues dominated the political debate and were principally responsible for delaying the *Bahnreform* until the beginning of 1994. The first arose within the Cabinet of Ministers. Krause's proposals, like the Federal Railway Governmental Commission report, assumed that the existing debts and liabilities of the Deutsche Bundesbahn and the Deutsche Reichsbahn would not pass to the newly formed, private corporation but would remain with, and be financed exclusively by, the federal government. Theodor Waigel, the finance minister, believed that these liabilities would continue to accumulate after privatization of the railways and was concerned about the effects of those liabilities on the general budget. Waigel demanded that the "funds required to implement plans to privatize the railways must come from the transport sector," and he called on Krause to come up with proposals to that effect.[12] A road toll and an increase in the gasoline tax were considered solutions. But Krause objected to the linking of such measures to the *Bahnreform*.

The second major issue involved the burdens that *Bahnreform* would place on the states. One of the main tenets of the proposed *Bahnreform* was the regionalization of local public transportation. It was unclear, however, whether the federal or state governments would bear the costs of this beneficial but perpetually loss-generating service. Waigel saw the *Bahnreform* as an opportunity to eliminate this burden, estimated at about DM 14 billion per year, from the federal budget. Under Krause's proposed "Federal Consolidation Program," the federal government would "cease payment of government subsidies for deficits arising from short-distance passenger traffic by rail and payments stipulated under the Local Transport Financing Act at the end of 1994."[13]

Of course, the states objected to the Federal Consolidation Program as a passing of responsibility without any corresponding financial support. The states warned of potential "catastrophic developments" in local public transportation, particularly in the major cities, if the Finance Ministry's plans were adopted.[14] The states' opposition to this one point of the *Bahnreform* plan posed a legitimate threat to the entire process because any decision to privatize the Deutsche Bundesbahn and the Deutsche Reichsbahn involved a change in the text of Article 87 of the German Basic Law, or constitution (*Grundgesetz*), which required approval by two-thirds of the representatives in both the Bundestag and the Bundesrat.[15] Although the states were, in principle, solidly in favor of *Bahnreform*, the proposed legislation would not obtain the support of a two-thirds majority in the Bundesrat without a satisfactory resolution of this financing issue.

The Cabinet missed its initial goal of approving a plan for *Bahnreform* by November 1992. Following the personal intervention of Chancellor Helmut Kohl in late January 1993, the states were reassured that the finances would be worked out as part of a general restructuring of revenues and expenses between the states and the federal government. Further progress was made in the middle of February, when the parliamentary group of the CDU/CSU (Christlich Demokratische Union/Christlich Soziale Union) voted to support Krause's plan and he reached an agreement with Waigel on financing the *Bahnreform*.[16] On February 17, 1993, the Cabinet gave its final approval to Krause's package of legislation enacting the *Bahnreform*.[17]

The government's proposed *Bahnreform* legislation was introduced in the Bundestag on March 26, 1993, and in the Bundesrat on May 7, 1993. Difficult negotiations stretched over many months. The states held fast to their original demand for additional funding and, in some cases, added special requests to their list of conditions.[18] At a summit meeting at the Chancellery on November 30, 1993, federal and state government representatives reached a compromise whereby the text of the bill on *Bahnreform* would be amended to take into account certain state demands. Those amendments were as follows:

- The regionalization of local passenger rail transport would be postponed from 1995 to 1996.
- An amendment to the constitution would stipulate that the states had a right to funds from federal tax revenue for spending on local passenger rail transport. The regionalization act would stipulate that these funds were to be provided out of revenue from petroleum taxes.
- The compensation paid to the states by the federal government in 1996 would be increased from DM 8.2 to 8.7 billion. From 1997 onward, the states would receive DM 12 billion per year. This

sum would be raised over subsequent years at the same rate at which revenues from value-added taxes increase.

- The federal government would ensure sufficient funds to cover old obligations of the Deutsche Reichsbahn. The federal government also would provide DM 100 million in 1996 and 1997 for renovations to the Berlin *S-Bahn* urban railway system, which had been split in two as a result of the building of the Berlin Wall.[19]

This compromise cleared the way for quick approval of the *Bahnreform* by both the Bundestag and the Bundesrat. Two days later, on December 2, 1993, bills to amend the Basic Law and privatize the railways passed in the Bundestag with 558 out of 575 votes cast. Two weeks later, the Bundesrat followed suit with 61 out of 66 votes cast in favor of the *Bahnreform*.

Five years of study, planning, debate, and negotiation culminated in the adoption of a comprehensive legal and structural reform for the German railways. The enactment of reform legislation was only the framework and not the culmination of the *Bahnreform*, however. As Heinz Dürr stated: "The railway reform will not be completed as soon as a Deutsche Bahn AG has been established and the financial questions have been resolved. These decisions are merely the beginning of the real rehabilitation and modernization of the railways. The internal railway reform will actually be the more difficult part."[20]

Legal and Structural Reforms

The *Bahnreform* program will be implemented in several steps continuing into the next decade. In a preliminary reorganization before the adoption of the reform legislation, railway activities of a commercial or entrepreneurial nature were separated from tasks that were and would remain a special responsibility of the state. As a result of this reorganization, the Deutsche Bundesbahn, the Deutsche Reichsbahn, and the railway system in what was formerly West Berlin were merged to form the Federal Railway Property (*Sondervermögen Bundeseisenbahnen*). The Federal Railway Property continued to be an agency of the federal government; its activities included owning and managing the infrastructure of the railways, the provision of transportation services, and the operation of related businesses, such as travel agencies, resulting therefrom. Remaining state responsibilities included supervisory and regulatory tasks as well as the administration of and provision for the employees and the existing debts of the railways.

The *Bahnreform* proper began with the legislation referred to above in December 1993. The Deutsche Bahn AG was created on January 1, 1994, as a private corporation under the 100 percent ownership of the federal government, and the Federal Railway Property was transferred to the Deutsche Bahn AG. The *Bahnreform* required the Deutsche Bahn AG to establish at least four internal divisions reflecting its business segments: long-distance passenger traffic, local passenger traffic, freight traffic, and infrastructure. Separately, the state responsibilities remaining with the federal government also were divided between two agencies. The Federal Railway Office (*Eisenbahn Bundesamt*) took over the government's supervisory, regulatory, and planning functions with respect to the railways. In addition, a newly formed Federal Railway Property (*Bundeseisenbahnvermögen*) office assumed responsibility for the old debts and civil service personnel of the railways and any real estate previously owned by the Deutsche Bundesbahn or the Deutsche Reichsbahn but unrelated to the current business of the Deutsche Bahn AG.

Enactment of the reform legislation and the implementing steps described above established the foundation for the realization of the full program of reforms proposed by the Federal Railway Governmental Commission in 1991. Germany's railways are now operated by the Deutsche Bahn AG, a private company subject to commercial law and commercial accounting requirements. The Deutsche Bahn AG has divided itself into nine, not four, separate business units—each with the object of maximizing its individual revenues and profits. It is free of the enormous debts amassed by the Deutsche Bundesbahn and the Deutsche Reichsbahn before 1994. It is free to reorganize its structure or alter its operations in accordance with purely commercial demands.

Bahnreform is not yet complete; the remaining steps will increase the separation and commercial independence of the businesses forming the present Deutsche Bahn AG. In the third step, scheduled to take place by 1999, the Deutsche Bahn AG will be transformed into a holding company and its subordinate parts will be given independent corporate status. The fourth step envisions the dissolution of the Deutsche Bahn AG or the merger of the Deutsche Bahn AG into one of its parts. These final steps are intended to enable the individual business divisions to operate independently and even to compete with one another for the goods and services of other divisions.

Nevertheless, the links between the Deutsche Bahn AG and the government, and the funding and subsidies that flow to the Deutsche Bahn AG from the government, will remain substantial. In theory, the Deutsche Bahn AG will be free to act according to exclusively commercial considerations and no longer primarily to serve the national interest. Whether this can ever be completely true in practice, however, remains to be seen.[21] The Deutsche Bahn and the regulatory authorities will, of necessity, have to work closely together. Future government regulation and subsidies are not failures of the privatization or the *Bahnreform*, but rather essential components of the *Bahnreform* itself.

Regulation of the Deutsche Bahn AG (and ultimately its separate business divisions), as mentioned above, is the province of the Federal Railway Office, an administrative agency subordinate to the Ministry of Transportation. The Federal Railway Office's responsibilities include, among other things, issuing operating permits or licenses to infrastructure and transport units of the Deutsche Bahn AG and other railway operators, regulating access to the railway infrastructure where problems arise, deciding on the closure of particular sections of track or other railway infrastructure, developing and approving plans with respect to the track infrastructure, and supervising the technical aspects of railway vehicles and facilities.[22] In addition, the Federal Railway Office has the responsibility of reviewing applications made by the Deutsche Bahn AG for state financing of investments in the rail network. Applications are considered in light of the technical and economic standards set forth annually in the federal budget estimates. These standards determine whether a particular investment qualifies for funding out of that year's transportation budget.

The Federal Railway Office may approve either outright grants or interest-free loans to the Deutsche Bahn AG. In either case, funding comes from the annual budget of the federal Transportation Ministry. This raises a very important point in the larger scheme of *Bahnreform*. One of the most frequently cited explanations for the failure of the railways to compete successfully with other forms of transportation in the past is the fact that, unlike other forms of transport, railways had to finance infrastructure entirely out of their own budgets.[23] In order to make the railways more competitive, future investments in railway infrastructure are to be financed, in whole or in part, by the federal government.

Another responsibility of the Federal Railway Office is maintaining the distinction between commercial investments financed with government-provided interest-free loans, to be repaid from commercial operations, and noncommercial investments funded entirely by the government. Initially, the Deutsche Bahn AG approaches the Federal Railway Office with proposals for infrastructure investments that it believes will be commercially viable. In order to promote investment in the railways, the Federal Railway Office will finance those investments that it approves through interest-free loans.[24] The state, acting through the Federal Railway Office, may desire certain additional investments, however, even though they may not be in the commercial interest of the Deutsche Bahn AG. In such cases, the government may fund infrastructure investments through subsidies that the Deutsche Bahn AG is not required to repay. This system gives rise to at least two concerns. First, such a dual system involving loans that have to be repaid and subsidies that do not runs the risk of manipulation or abuse. Second, even after the *Bahnreform* is fully implemented, a significant amount of public investment in the railway infrastructure will continue to be directed by political rather than market influences, which may be appropriate but, depending on how it is implemented in practice, risks continuing a portion of the excesses and inefficiencies of the railways before reform. Thus, the Federal Railway Office has an important role to play as the intermediary between the Deutsche Bahn AG and the financial resources of the federal government.

The sister agency of the Federal Railway Office is the Federal Railway Property, an agency with a substantially different but equally important role. The Federal Railway Property is essentially the repository for the old debts and other obligations assumed by the government in order to give the railways a fresh start in 1994. In particular, the Federal Railway Property has the following functions:

- administration and management of real estate not essential to railway operations;
- cooperation with the Federal Debt Administration in managing and servicing the old debt of the former Special Federal Funds, Deutsche Bundesbahn and Deutsche Reichsbahn;
- management of the civil service personnel allocated to Deutsche Bahn AG;
- responsibility for the pensions of civil servant staff; and
- maintenance and continued operation of staff welfare schemes.[25]

These functions come at a high price to the federal government but are essential to the success of the *Bahnreform*. The freeing of the Deutsche Bahn AG from the debts of its predecessors, valued at DM 66 billion on December 31, 1993, is only the most obvious example. The creation of the Federal Railway Property as a repository for the civil service employees of the Deutsche Bundesbahn and Deutsche Reichsbahn solved a difficult problem. At the end of 1993, more than 100,000 civil servants were employed by the Deutsche Bundesbahn and the Deutsche Reichsbahn. Under the German Basic Law, these civil servants benefitted from employment guarantees and other benefits inconsistent with the privatization of the railways. The law required that these civil servants remain government employees, but their services would largely continue to be required by the privatized railways. The creation of the Federal Railway Property made it possible for these civil servants to retain their civil servant status, with the Deutsche Bahn AG contracting for their services at market rates. Differences in the amounts paid by the Deutsche Bahn AG for these services and the cost to the Federal Railway Property of the civil servants' salaries, benefits, and pensions are subsidized by the federal Ministry of Transportation. This arrangement will likely continue until the last civil servants working for the Deutsche Bahn AG retire.[26]

The costs to the federal government of funding the Federal Railway Property are, in a sense, the price of *Bahnreform*. Over the next twenty to fifty years, these costs are likely to decline and ultimately disappear. At the same time, the Deutsche Bahn AG may eventually generate significant revenue for its public shareholder. But the immensity of the short-term costs of the *Bahnreform* to the federal government is striking. Projections of the budgets for the federal Ministry of Transportation suggest average total transport costs of close to DM 50 billion per year through 1999. Of that amount, approximately DM 30 billion each year, or 60 percent of the total budget, will be expended on the railways. The projections suggest that of this DM 30 billion, approximately 20 billion will be required to support the functions of the Federal Railway Property. In other words, through at least 1999, about 40 percent of Germany's federal transportation budget will go toward subsidizing debts and expenses associated with the pre-*Bahnreform* railways. If these projections are correct, that amount will approach the amount spent in the same years on public investment in all forms of transportation infrastructure, including the railways.[27]

The preceding discussion makes clear that the legal and structural changes introduced by the *Bahnreform* were not an instant fix for the financial crisis described at the beginning of this chapter. Legal and structural changes have brought about a separation between public and private responsibilities. But public responsibilities and, in particular, public expenditures are still substantial. It should be remembered, however, that these costs mostly originated before the *Bahnreform*. The act of privatizing the railways and establishing the Federal Railway Property did not place additional or increasing burdens on the federal government—it merely consolidated existing liabilities. If anything has changed, it is that now the full measure of the inefficiency and debt of the old Deutsche Bundesbahn and Deutsche Reichsbahn can easily be seen. German taxpayers may surely regret the price tag revealed by the *Bahnreform*, but they also should be relieved to have faced the problem, knowing that, if the *Bahnreform* succeeds, they will have prevented future deficits.

Bahnreform: An Interim Evaluation

The success of the *Bahnreform* to date can be evaluated only in light of its original goals. Although rarely stated explicitly, the most important goal of the *Bahnreform* was ending the financial hemorrhaging of the Deutsche Bundesbahn and the Deutsche Reichsbahn. An important second goal was to obtain increased market share or, more generally, attracting more traffic to the railways. In doing so, the *Bahnreform* would "ensure mobility while protecting the environment." The *Bahnreform* was intended to allow the railways to compete on an equal basis with other modes of transportation as well as free the railways from "political directives and handicaps." Responsibility for "local passenger rail transport" was to pass to the states. The *Bahnreform* was also intended to provide a "legal basis" for allocating civil servants employed by the Deutsche Bundesbahn and the Deutsche Reichsbahn to the privatized railway.[28] Finally, and not least in terms of importance, the *Bahnreform* would bring Germany into compliance with European Communities Council Directive 91/440/EEC on the development of the community's railways as explained below.

Determining at this point whether the *Bahnreform* has succeeded is harder with respect to some goals than others. The first goal, "placing the railways on a sound financial footing and reducing the burden placed on the federal budget by the railways,"[29] seems to have been realized. Direct comparison of financial data from before and after the *Bahnreform* is made difficult by the structural changes that *Bahnreform* brought with it. The positive financial results of the Deutsche Bahn AG in each of its first two years might be an indication that a turnaround has been achieved. While it is possible that changes in accounting methods have simply hidden continued annual losses generated by the Deutsche Bundesbahn and Deutsche Reichsbahn, the government's estimates that future railway-related expenses (other than investment expenses) have leveled off provide an additional indication of a turnaround. The *Bahnreform* appears to have ended the pre-reform cycle of growing government expenses and increasing indebtedness. The Deutsche Bahn AG has been given what looks like a sound financial footing and seems to be holding its own.

The first indications with regard to the second goal, increasing market share, have been positive, although not dramatically so. In both 1994 and 1995, the Deutsche Bahn AG was able to achieve increases in the number of passenger-kilometers traveled in both long-distance passenger transport and local passenger transport. In long-distance passenger transport, those increases were 2.3 percent in 1994 and 3.6 percent in 1995. In local passenger transport the increases were even more substantial: 10.4 percent for 1994 and 5.8 percent for 1995.[30] These results were achieved, at least in 1994, during a period of stagnant growth in the number of motor vehicles registered and sinking real incomes.[31] Similar results were obtained in goods traffic and parcel services in 1994, where ton-kilometers increased by 9.4 percent and 5.3 percent, respectively, even though revenues decreased for the year. The year 1995 was less friendly to the goods traffic and parcel services divisions of the Deutsche Bahn AG, which lost three-fourths of the business it previously conducted for the Deutsche

Post.[32] Freight traffic tended to be lower in most branches. However, positive results were seen in the areas of international freight traffic and combined traffic (meaning traffic in containers that can be carried either by rail or by truck) in the direction of Eastern Europe.[33]

The Deutsche Bahn AG was creative in seeking new customers in 1994 and 1995 through special offers. These offers in some cases resulted in more passengers even where they did not succeed in increasing revenue. One such special offer was the *Schöne Wochenende-Ticket*, which allowed groups to travel together on weekends at a reduced rate. Eighteen million of these tickets were sold in 1995 and, as a result, approximately nine million additional passengers were enticed to take the train.[34] Clearly, for many years to come, there will be substantial room for the railways to increase their market shares in passenger and freight transportation. Even at this point, it seems safe to conclude that the *Bahnreform* has had and should continue to have success in that direction.

The question of whether the railways are, as a result of the *Bahnreform*, able to compete on an equal basis with other forms of transportation is, as previously mentioned, not something that can be answered here. The *Bahnreform* has certainly improved the position of the railways in this competition. The government has taken upon itself the costs of the mistakes and lack of competitiveness by the railways in previous decades. It is committed as well to an aggressive program of investment to benefit the railways.[35] Just as there are natural advantages to rail transportation, there also are natural disadvantages. Rail transportation excels at carrying heavy goods over long distances, but it suffers when compared to truck transportation in flexibility and responsiveness to special requests from customers. Achieving an equal basis for competition between modes of transportation is likely an impossibility because of these differences. Without a doubt, though, the *Bahnreform* has improved the competitive position of the railways.

There is little to be said about the success or failure of the regionalization of local passenger rail transport at this point because that process began only recently. Clearly, the federal states demanded much in exchange for their votes for the *Bahnreform* in 1993. They will continue to have the benefit of significant federal funding for local rail transportation. The real potential of regionalization lies not in the source of funding but, instead, in the locus of responsibility for this important service. State and regional governments will in the future determine what services are provided and what company provides those services. This implies that the provider may not necessarily be the Deutsche Bahn AG, although it will no doubt continue to be a major participant in this area. But regional transportation is likely to be one of the first areas where the access to the rail infrastructure for third parties that came with the *Bahn-*

reform becomes a legitimate invitation to compete with the Deutsche Bahn AG.

This opening of the railway infrastructure to third parties was just one of the requirements of Council Directive 91/440/EEC. Other requirements included ensuring the management independence of railway companies, improving the financial structure of railway companies, and separating the operation of railway infrastructure from railway transport. The proposals of the Federal Railway Governmental Commission and the package for *Bahnreform* put forward by the transportation minister in 1992 took into account these European regulations. The result is that the letter of the law in Germany, as with many other EC members, satisfies the requirements of European law. The Deutsche Bahn AG has advertised its program, allowing other railway companies access to its rail network as the first in Europe to offer equal access in accordance with Council Directive 91/440/EEC.[36] Unfortunately, there are still many artificial barriers to cross-border competition among European railways.

In 1994, the first year after the *Bahnreform*, the Deutsche Bahn AG earned profits from operations totaling DM 180 million; in 1995, that figure rose to DM 280 million. These are small beginnings for such a large company, but are encouraging nonetheless. Small, positive results may mean more at this point for company morale and public perception than they do for the business prospects of the Deutsche Bahn AG in coming years. The Deutsche Bahn is now in the process of the "internal reforms" that will decide issues such as market share and return on investment in the future. The *Bahnreform* of 1994 established new ground rules for that process. It was a remarkable decision by a government to face up to past mistakes and debts in the hope of preparing for a better future.

Notes

1. "Sixteen initiatives to reform the Bundesbahn were recorded in the period from 1949 to 1990 alone" (Werner Gerdes, *The Railway Reform* [Deutsche Bahn AG, 1994], p. 8).

2. *Bundesministerium für Verkehr, Verkehr in Zahlen 1994.* Isolating the period from 1970 to 1990, the decrease in market share for passenger traffic was from 8.4 percent to 6.2 percent and the decrease in market share in freight traffic was from 39.9 percent to 24.7 percent.

3. *The Railway Reform*, p. 8.

4. DIRI Dresdner International Research Institute GmbH, *Deutsche Bahn AG, Ein privatwirtschaftlich strukturiertes Unternehmen des Bundes am Kapitalmarkt* (1995), p. 3.

5. Deutsche Bahn AG, *Presentation on German Railway Reform* (1994).

6. Council Directive 91/440/EEC on the Development of the Community's Railways, *1991 Journal of the European Communities* (L237) 25.

7. *Federal Railway Governmental Commission Interim Report of June 21, 1991*, as quoted in *The Railway Reform*, p. 19.

8. *The Railway Reform*, pp. 30–33.

9. Ibid., p. 38.

10. Ibid., pp. 42–46.

11. Statements made by Heinz Dürr in late 1992 emphasizing the urgency of the situation and the need for the politicians to act quickly with regard to *Bahnreform* suggested that each additional month of delay would cost German taxpayers an additional DM 800 million. Ibid., pp. 54–55.

12. Ibid., p. 56 (quoting *Die Welt*, 12 November 1992).

13. Ibid., p. 60 (quoting *Deutsche Verkehrs-Zeitung*, 28 January 1993).

14. Ibid., p. 61.

15. Before the *Bahnreform*, Article 87, Paragraph I, of the *Grundgesetz* stated: "The Federal Railways are managed under federal administration with its own administrative authorities" (translation by Deutsche Bahn AG).

16. *The Railway Reform*, pp. 62–65.

17. Ibid., p. 67.

18. The state of Saxony, for example, said in November 1993 that its vote in the Bundesrat would depend on whether the city of Chemnitz was promised access to the International Rail Network. Ibid., p. 87.

19. Ibid., p. 92.

20. Ibid., p. 65.

21. A case in point is the February 1996 decision of the Deutsche Bahn AG, despite numerous critics within the company and much initial hesitation, to acquire a 12.5 percent interest in the operating company for the Transrapid magnetic levitating train to be built between Hamburg and Berlin. Critics of the Transrapid within the Deutsche Bahn AG and its predecessor companies had long supported the alternative construction of a high-speed rail link between the two cities. Whether the Transrapid will be a commercial success for the Deutsche Bahn AG and its other private participants remains to be seen. But the Transrapid clearly has a greater chance of succeeding with the active support and coordinative efforts of the railways behind it. It would not be surprising, therefore, if the federal government, as the sole shareholder of and principal source of funds for capital investments by the Deutsche Bahn AG, pressured the Deutsche Bahn AG to participate. Critics may cite this as interference with the commercial autonomy of the private Deutsche Bahn AG. Alternatively, it may be seen as a function of transportation planning, which is still very much a government responsibility.

22. Horst Stuchly, "Das Eisenbahn-Bundesamt. Organisation und Aufgaben," *Eisenbahningenieur* 45 (1994): 614–616.

23. This argument, of course, neglects to account for fuel and registration taxes that amount to an indirect charge on the users of roads and, in fact, bring far more revenue into the federal coffers each year than is spent on investments in road and highway infrastructure. Whether the *Bahnreform* has established what may rightly be called an "equal" footing for the railways is an interesting question—one that merits more research and more complex analysis than are offered here. For present purposes, it suffices to say that the goal behind this argument

was to improve the competitive position of the railways and that that goal has to some extent been reached in the *Bahnreform*.

24. Specific cases where federal funding is available under law include: the construction, expansion, or replacement of track infrastructure generally; investment in or modernization of the infrastructure previously belonging to the Deutsche Reichsbahn in order to bring it up to the standard of the Deutsche Bundesbahn; measures for the improvement of traffic conditions within communities; and measures to improve the safety and efficiency of railway crossings. Stuchly, "Das Eisenbahn-Bundesamt," p. 619.

25. Federal Republic of Germany, Federal Railways Fund, *Information Memorandum* (February 1995).

26. At the end of 1994, 108,561 civil servants were employed by the Deutsche Bahn AG. Deutsche Bahn AG, *Company Report 1994*, p. 25.

27. Figures were provided by the Bundesministerium für Verkehr, Budget and Financial Planning Department, and reflect projections current as of 26 October, 1995.

28. *The Railway Reform*, p. 95.

29. Ibid.

30. The figure for local passenger transport for 1994 must be considered in light of the fact that the *S-Bahn* in West Berlin was added to the Deutsche Bahn AG. *Company Report 1994*, p. 14.

31. Dresdner International Research Institute, p. 8.

32. This was a onetime loss for the Deutsche Bahn AG but a significant event with respect to the competition between rail service and road service. Namely, the Post, as part of its own privatization and rationalization process, developed a new freight and parcel concept in 1995 that was to be a move toward improved efficiency and customer service. That concept, unfortunately for the Deutsche Bahn AG, took freight off the rails and put it onto the roads.

33. "Bahn hat sich auch im zweiten Jahr als Aktiengesellschaft gut behauptet," *Süddeutsche Zeitung*, 29 February 1996, p. 23.

34. "Bahn beteiligt sich am Transrapid," *Stuttgarter Nachrichten*, 29 February 1996, p. 11.

35. Budget projections of the federal Ministry of Transportation plan on investment expenditures for the railways of DM 7.7 billion in 1998 and each of the next three years. The investment in federal highways, by comparison, will be about DM 10 billion annually for the same period. It may appear, at first glance, that the railways continue to be at a disadvantage in this situation. But that is not the case when one considers that approximately 37 percent of the Transportation Ministry's investment resources will be spent on railways that have not significantly increased their market shares from the 1993 figures of 23 percent for freight traffic and only 6.3 percent for passenger traffic.

36. Deutshe Bahn AG, "Die Deutsche Bahn öffnet den Fahrwegen für Dritt zum Trassenpreissystem" (1996).

6

Liberalization of Telecommunications Markets

LISA CREIGHTON-HENDRICKS

Currently, Germany and the United States are taking steps to liberalize and introduce more competition to their respective telecommunications markets. In the United States, the Federal Communications Commission (FCC) and the state commissions are in the process of implementing the Telecommunications Act of 1996 (1996 Act). In Germany, the federal government has enacted a new telecommunications law, the *Telekommunikation Gesetz* (TKG). In both countries, these legislative developments are intended to create the regulatory framework that will make a fully liberalized market possible. For both, this entails establishing a framework that will introduce competition to markets where monopoly providers have control of essential bottleneck facilities. In Germany, competition is being introduced for the first time in all segments of the market. In the United States, competition already exists in some segments. However, regulators and competitors are facing similar issues in trying to level the playing field in what has traditionally been a monopoly environment.

While both Germany and the United States are liberalizing their domestic markets, the global market is bracing for similar changes. In February 1997, 69 countries signed the Basic Telecommunications Service agreement negotiated through the World Trade Organization (WTO). In the WTO agreement, both Germany and the United States reaffirmed their commitment to liberalized telecommunications markets. Their success or failure in implementing their planned reforms will affect the many nations that, under the WTO agreement, must now begin work on opening up their markets and may determine whether the goals of the WTO agreement are realized.

This chapter briefly chronicles the historical development of the U.S. and German markets (focusing on voice services) and discusses the current status of the markets and implementation of liberalizing legislation.

United States

Historical Developments

In contrast to most other countries where telecommunications services have been provided by state-run entities, private-owned firms in the United States traditionally provided almost all telecommunications services. However, as in most other countries, the provision of such services was monopolized by one provider. With few exceptions, before 1982, American Telephone & Telegraph (AT&T) effectively held a monopoly on the provision of telephone services. The development and maintenance of AT&T's monopoly, however, was subject to the oversight of both the FCC and the state utility commissions.

The FCC was established under the Communications Act of 1934 to regulate interstate and foreign telecommunications. Interstate jurisdiction includes telecommunications that cross state boundaries, or what is commonly known as long distance. Interstate jurisdiction also reaches to activities that affect long-distance service, such as access to local networks through which long-distance calls are delivered. The FCC is composed of five commissioners, appointed by the president with the advice and consent of Congress. The president designates one commissioner as chairman.[1] The commissioners serve for five years, and only a majority may be from the same political party.[2]

Each state has a regulatory body, typically called the Public Utility Commission or Public Service Commission, which regulates intrastate telecommunications. Intrastate jurisdiction includes telecommunications that do not cross state lines and is commonly known as local services. In three-fourths of the states, the commissioners are appointed by the governor, subject to the approval of the state senate. The other one-fourth of the states elect their state commission directly.[3]

Both the states and the FCC played important roles in the attempts to penetrate AT&T's monopoly. Historically, the states have generally been the protectorates of the monopoly, arguing that it was necessary to ensure service to all residents at a reasonable cost.[4] While the FCC shared this goal, supported by the courts, it traditionally has believed that the monopoly should be well defined and limited. Before 1982, the FCC made several attempts to act on this concern. However, it was the Department of Justice (DoJ), with ultimate authority with respect to antitrust matters, which proved AT&T's final nemesis. In the 1970s, the DoJ sued AT&T, alleging that the company engaged in predatory pricing and continued to misuse its dominant position in violation of the antitrust laws. This led to a pivotal point in the introduction of competition in the United States—the Modified Final Judgment (the Judgment).[5]

In 1982, the United States District Court for the District of Columbia entered the Judgment under which AT&T and the DoJ agreed to divide AT&T's monopoly into two segments—a long-distance market and local markets. The DoJ and AT&T agreed that monopolies would remain in the local markets, but that the companies which provided local service to the monopoly would be divested from AT&T.

The divestiture of the local companies resulted in the formation of seven regional companies, frequently referred to as Regional Bell Operating Companies (Regional Bells). Under the Judgment, the Regional Bells were excluded from offering long-distance services. Further, AT&T was excluded from the local service area, leaving it to concentrate on the long-distance market. Under the Judgment, competition was successfully encouraged in the long-distance markets. In the ten years that followed divestiture, new competitors targeted AT&T's most profitable customers; AT&T lost 36 percent of its market share, and its long-distance prices fell 48 percent. In spite of this, AT&T's earnings and revenues continued to increase. Much of AT&T's continued success was due to the growth in the long-distance market that resulted from the introduction of competition—from 1984 to 1989, long-distance traffic grew more than 84 percent.[6] But the local service markets remained dominated by the Regional Bells, each controlling more than 95 percent of local telephone revenue in their regions.

In the 1980s, wireless providers entered the local markets as a supplement to the wire-based services, allowing extended mobile coverage. In the 1980s, the FCC, through a lottery system, assigned two cellular licenses per metropolitan area, one reserved for the local telephone company and the other for a competitor. Personal Communications Services, the latest addition to the wireless market, compete against existing wireless carriers and offer clearer communications and more secure lines. However, wireless remains a supplement to wire-based local service provided by the Regional Bells, although someday it may develop into an alternative.

The Markets in 1996

Thus, the U.S. telecommunications markets evolved into highly decentralized markets composed of multiple providers, service offerings, and regulators. However, until the 1996 Act, barriers remained between the markets, particularly the local and long-distance markets. The bases for such barriers largely vanished, however—modern technology was moving toward a convergence of markets, with cable providers able to provide telecommunications service and Internet users able to make long-distance calls without using long-distance networks. While the judicially created barriers continued to separate services, these barriers were increasingly seen as artificial and pressure to remove them was building.

The 1996 Act

On 8 February 1996, President Bill Clinton signed into law the 1996 Act, which marked the first comprehensive overhaul of telecommunications legislation since 1934. The signing of the new act indicated the liberalization of the U.S. telecommunications markets by removing existing barriers between competing industries and allowing the marketplace to function more freely.

The 1996 Act removes barriers in three major telecommunications markets: the long-distance market, the local market, and the video market. The 1996 Act recognizes that access to the existing local networks is fundamental to the development of competition in the local arena, as such networks are extremely costly to reproduce and provide the only landline access to customers.

Acting on this recognition, the 1996 Act requires all telecommunications providers to provide connection to their networks.[7] The existing local service providers are required to (1) negotiate in good faith concerning their obligation to offer nondiscriminatory connection to their networks at any technically feasible point; (2) offer unbundled access to their services; (3) offer resale of capacity on their networks at wholesale rates; (4) notify other carriers of changes in transmission and routing requirements; and (5) offer nondiscriminatory physical collocation of equipment for connecting providers.[8]

To ensure that competition has the opportunity to develop, the 1996 Act also directs the FCC to remove all barriers to local service competition,[9] and gives the FCC the power to refrain from applying any provision of the 1996 Act, if doing so would promote competitive market conditions and is in the public interest.[10] Further, in order to create a level competitive playing field, the FCC and the states were given the task of restructuring the complicated subsidies provided to local service providers to ensure universal access to telecommunications service.

The 1996 Act has several provisions applicable solely to the Regional Bells. These provisions set forth conditions for the Regional Bells to enter the long-distance market.[11] Most important, the Regional Bells must meet specified requirements facilitating the opening of the local market area.[12] They cannot offer long-distance services to their customers until they receive approval from the FCC.[13] The FCC has 90 days after receipt of a request for approval from a Regional Bell to issue a decision.[14] Within that 90-day period, the FCC must consult with the DoJ regarding the competitive effects of such an approval.[15] While the FCC must give substantial weight to the DoJ's opinion, it must make the final decision.[16] To date, the FCC has not granted any Regional Bell authority to offer long-distance services in their region.

In the past several years, the FCC produced detailed and voluminous regulations to implement the 1996 Act. Through these regulations, the FCC has established detailed guidelines intended to level the playing field within the local arena. However, the Regional Bells are not giving up their local monopolies without a fight, despite the incentive of being permitted to enter the long-distance market. Indeed, some Regional Bells and state commissions are challenging very important aspects of the FCC rules and have succeeded in postponing their effectiveness. While some hopeful competitors have negotiated or otherwise obtained interconnection agreements under which they can access portions of the Regional Bells' local network to compete head-on with them, they are finding that monopoly power provides the Regional Bells with many ways to frustrate competitors' access to their networks.[17] Further, the Regional Bells appear uniquely able to influence state legislators, ensuring that competition develops in a manner most beneficial to them.[18] Experience is quickly proving that despite a decade-long history of introducing competition into a monopoly arena, the United States still faces tremendous challenges.

Germany

Historical Developments

Under the post–World War II German Basic Law, or constitution (*Grundgesetz*), responsibility for the provision of telecommunications services rested solely with the federal government. As a result, as in many other European countries, the German government both regulated and supplied telecommunications.[19] Further, because a government monopoly was mandated by the Basic Law, legislative attempts to restrict it were not viable. For many years there were no serious attempts to lift the monopoly, as there was little public support for the introduction of competition. But during the 1980s, in several countries, particularly the United States, there was a growing awareness of the potential of a global telecommunications market and the need to push for regulatory reform to open up lucrative markets around the world. As the European market was almost entirely protected by state-owned and-operated monopolies, efforts were launched to get the European Community (EC), as well its member states, to open some segments of their telecommunications markets.[20]

The Commission of the European Communities served as the catalyst for Germany's move away from a federal-owned and-operated telecommunications service. In 1987, the Commission published the EC Green Paper on Telecommunications (referred to below as the 1987 Green Paper),[21] which aimed to liberalize telecommunications equipment and service markets throughout the EC member states.

The goal of the 1987 Green Paper was to encourage market developments that would provide Europe with a variety of low-cost, high-quality telecommunications services. The 1987 Green Paper recommended creating Europe-wide network integrity, opening common markets for services outside basic network or voice services (i.e., value added), providing standardization, promoting clear separation between regulator and operator duties, and creating transparent financial environments. Although the Commission's policy allowed voice services and infrastructure to remain protected monopolies, the Commission indicated that this was an interim policy and would be revised at a later date.

The Commission used its powers pursuant to Article 90 of the Treaty of Rome (which established the EC) to issue directives to the member states, requiring them to adopt measures to achieve reforms mandated by the Commission. The Commission's reliance on Article 90 in this manner was challenged on several occasions. On each occasion, the European Court of Justice ruled in favor of the Commission, holding that the directives were lawful and that exclusive rights regarding telecommunications service given to public entities could be abolished.[22] As a result of these decisions, the Commission assumed a dominant role in establishing telecommunications policy for the EC, now ELL.

The 1987 Green Paper and the Commission's subsequent measures forced Germany to consider reform. The result was legislation commonly referred to as *Postreform I*, passed in mid-1989 (officially titled The Telecommunications Installations Act of 1989).[23] Under *Postreform I*, the responsibility for regulating telecommunications was separated from the responsibility for supplying the service. In separating responsibilities, *Postreform I* created a separate public entity responsible for telecommunications operations called Deutsche Bundespost Telekom (DBT).[24] *Postreform I* also gave greater entrepreneurial independence to DBT and stipulated that it would operate under "business management principles." *Postreform I* facilitated the transfer to DBT of the federal government's authority to operate the federal telecommunications networks.[25] However, consistent with the 1987 Green Paper, *Postreform I* provided that DBT would maintain a monopoly over basic voice telephone networks and telephone services.

Under *Postreform I*, the Ministry of Federal Telecommunications and Post[26] retained regulatory responsibility over telecommunications. This regulatory responsibility included ensuring that DBT did not cross-subsidize its competitive services from its earnings on monopoly services, approving DBT's tariffs,[27] and ensuring that DBT continued to work toward providing service to all who requested it.[28] The minister in charge of this ministry is appointed by the chancellor and serves at his pleasure.

Several subsequent amendments to the Telecommunications Installations Act also provided for the liberalization of the markets for customer-premises equipment and data services. Introducing competition into mobile communications in December 1989, the ministry granted a license to Mannesman Mobilfunk to operate a national digital mobile network in competition with DBT (which included voice services). In February 1993, the ministry awarded a third digital mobile license to a consortium called E-Plus (which also included voice services).

During this time, the European Commission issued additional mandates and guidelines. One of the Commission's most important directives identified the principles and guidelines for open and effective access to, and use of, public networks, requiring transparent objective criteria, equality of access, harmonized technical features, and cost-oriented tariffs.[29] Other measures concerned the development of common markets for telecommunications services and equipment,[30] coordination of the introduction of European Integrated Digital Networks (ISDN),[31] Digital European Cordless Telecommunications,[32] and guidelines on the application of the EU's competition rules in the telecommunications sector.[33]

In June 1991, the ministry introduced the Telecommunications Ordinances (*Telekommunikationsverordnungen*, or TKV),[34] which governed DBT's relationship with its customers and competitors and which implemented some of the European Commission requirements. The TKV prohibited DBT from leveraging its control over infrastructure and voice services to gain unfair competitive advantages in competitive services. Thus, DBT was prohibited from providing components of infrastructure or voice service to itself on conditions more favorable than it provides to others who compete in markets such as data transmission and mobile communications.[35] DBT also was required to meet other requirements such as allowing connection to networks for nonvoice services, service quality, and information publication.[36]

In 1993, the German government and the European Commission each announced important decisions that would have a strong impact on the German market: (1) in June, the German government publicly announced its intention to privatize DBT; and (2) in July, the Commission announced that EC member states would be required to open their voice service markets to competition by January 1, 1998.[37] These decisions required further reform of telecommunications services in Germany. The result was the Law Concerning the Reorganization of Post and Telecommunications of 14 September 1994 (Reorganization Act), also known as *Postreform II*.

Under the Reorganization Act, DBT was transformed into a stock corporation, Deutsche Telekom AG, effective 1 January 1995.[38] Initially, 100 percent of the stock ownership remained with the government, subject to initial plans to begin privatization in late 1995 or early 1996. This transformation to a stock corporation was accompanied by an amendment to the constitution stating that it was no longer the duty of the state to provide telecommunications services.[39] The Reorganization Act also created a new agency, the Bundesanstalt, to hold Deutsche Telekom's stock as trustee for the federal government and to fulfill obligations as a holding company. Such obligations included managing relationships between Deutsche Telekom and its employees, who remained civil servants after the transformation to a stock corporation.

In transforming Deutsche Telekom into a stock corporation, the Reorganization Act established the internal structure of Deutsche Telekom as an ordinary private company with a management and supervisory board. Certain supervisory and regulatory responsibilities remain with the ministry such as approval of tariffs filed by Deutsche Telekom for monopoly services, as well as the conditions under which Deutsche Telekom makes its networks available to others.[40] The Reorganization Act also grants the ministry the ability to modify the scope and context of Deutsche Telekom's exclusive right to provide telephone network and switched voice services.[41]

The Reorganization Act gave Deutsche Telekom the "exclusive" right to provide infrastructure and voice services through 1997.[42] The Act introduced exceptions to Deutsche Telekom's monopoly on infrastructure services. These exceptions allowed (1) state and municipal authorities to construct facilities for their own internal needs;[43] (2) transportation organizations to provide similar facilities for their own needs;[44] and (3) owners of buildings within a 25-kilometer radius to construct networks for their own use.[45] In addition, electric companies were authorized to construct their own networks as long as such networks did not adversely affect Deutsche Telekom. The construction of corporate networks, private lines, and voice resale also was approved.

In 1994, the European Commission adopted a regulation that, in addition to voice services, eventually led to the liberalization of telecommunications infrastructures in January 1998.[46] Subsequently, the Commission announced that the exclusive right for the provision of network infrastructure for service other than voice services would be lifted in 1996.[47] In announcing the liberalization of the last remaining monopoly services, the Commission set out general guidelines and principles that member states should follow in structuring the regulations to achieve these goals. These broad guidelines include principles governing connection to networks, cost accounting, tariffs, and publication of, and access to, information.[48]

Contemporary Market

Unlike the situation in the United States, the German telecommunications market is not highly decentralized, nor is it characterized by multiple firms, markets, and regulators. In many, if not most, circumstances, the impetus for, as well as the broad guidelines for the content of, the ministry's policies originate not within Germany but at the European Commission. Within Germany the ministry plays an important role in determining how to implement Commission directives and establishes telecommunications policies. The main focus of the ministry's regulation is Deutsche Telekom, as the former monopoly provider continues to dominate the core infrastructure and voice markets. While there has been some opening of the infrastructure market, competition remains at an early phase. The stage has been set, however, for a period of rapid growth.

The cellular/mobile market is the most competitive market segment within Germany. As mentioned earlier, Mannesman was awarded a digital cellular license in 1989 and entered the market in 1992. Initially, Mannesman captured a large share of the market, but Deutsche Telekom was able to recover, holding 46 percent of the market in late 1995 compared to Mannesman's 47 percent. In May 1994, E-Plus entered the market as the third mobile provider. In late 1995, E-Plus had 7 percent of the market. In a 1995 decision, the ministry gave mobile providers the right to construct their own transport networks.[49] Moreover, in 1997, the ministry awarded a license to Viag InterKom.

Since July 1996, existing network providers have been permitted to offer all services to the public with the exception of transmission of most voice service. As of January 1, 1998, the telecommunications market was opened completely. As a result, Deutsche Telekom's domestic market strategy is focused on positioning itself to fend off the growing number of competitors as well as ensuring that regulators do not bind it with overly burdensome requirements that restrict its ability to respond to competitive developments. This strategy is difficult to achieve in light of the formidable competition developing through combinations of domestic utilities and industrial groups aligned with such foreign giants as AT&T.

While the alliances among Deutsche Telekom's competitors appear to change frequently, Deutsche Telekom currently faces three major competitors, o.tel.o, Mannesman Arcor, and Viag Interkom. The first entity, o.tel.o, is an alliance between Veba and RWE. Veba is a German chemical and energy giant that holds a 28 percent interest in the third German mobile license (E-Plus). RWE is a leading German industrial conglomerate with a telecommunications division. The second competitor, Mannesman Arcor, is an alliance between Mannesman and the German railway telecommunications division, DBKOM. Mannesman is a large engineering company that also runs Germany's second mobile service. Mannesman has an alliance with CNI (an international network provider), Uniworld (a global telecommunications provider), and AT&T. The third entity, Viag Interkom, is an alliance between Viag, one of Germany's largest industrial groups, and British Telecom, the dominant provider in Great Britain. Each of these players either began operating a network under the narrow exceptions permitted by the telecommunications laws before 1998 or is currently planning to construct a network. As with long-distance competitors in the United States, however, they will need to access Deutsche Telekom's network to obtain access to customers' homes and to many businesses.[50]

In this increasingly active telecommunications field, two developments will have a considerable impact. The first is the implementation of the new Telecommunication Law. The second is the privatization of Deutsche Telekom.

The Telecommunications Law of 1996. The Telecommunications Law of 1996 (TKG) was sent to the parliament for approval in February 1996 and was ratified in July of that year. Consistent with the European Commission directives, the TKG established January 1, 1998, as the date on which Deutsche Telekom was required to open its networks and services to competition. Effective January 1, 1998, the TKG dismantled the Federal Ministry of Post and Telecommunications and established a new regulatory body, called the Regulatory Authority, to oversee competition in the telecommunications market. The Regulatory Authority, a branch of the Ministry of Economics, is headed by a president and is headquartered in Bonn. The president and two vice presidents are appointed by the federal government based on the recommendations of the Advisory Council. The Regulatory Authority is to operate as independently as possible, and its decisions are appealable to the courts.[51,52] Because of concerns about the presence of market dominance, the Regulatory Authority cooperates with the Antitrust Bureau to ensure that they issue consistent decisions.[53]

The TKG also established an Advisory Council to oversee the implementation of the TKG and the operation of the Regulatory Authority. The Advisory Council has 18 members, nine from the upper house of the parliament, the Bundesrat, and nine from the lower house, the Bundestag. In addition to recommending the president and vice presidents, the Advisory Council advises on regulatory decisions, including the approval of licenses and decisions concerning market dominance.

The law guarantees the provision of services to all who request them, to be provided by the market-dominant provider and funded by licensed providers with more than 4 percent of the relevant market as measured by earnings.[54] Unlike the U.S. regulations the 1996 German Act assumes that such service will be provided without the need for subsidies, unless proven otherwise. If the dominant service provider demonstrates that it can provide such services only at a loss, then the Regulatory Authority can opt to provide monetary assistance or assign the duty to another provider, who also would have the possibility of receiving monetary assistance.[55]

One section of the new law contains several provisions that apply to "market-dominant providers."[56] The definition of a market-dominant provider is taken from the Law Against Restraints of Competition and would encompass Deutsche Telekom.[57] As a market-dominant provider, Deutsche Telekom is required to file with the Regulatory Authority all rates, terms, and conditions under which transmission and voice services are provided.[58] Such rates, which must be based on efficient cost, must be filed two months before they become effective. The Regulatory Authority can accept or reject the tariffs or conditions,[59] and retains jurisdiction to revisit any approved tariff.[60] The tariffs are reviewed on a service-by-service basis or as a group, or basket, of services. Further, the TKG recognizes the importance of access to Deutsche Telekom's network and requires the market-dominant provider to allow competitors nondiscriminatory access to essential facilities in accordance with EU requirements. Failure to provide such access will support a presumption of abuse of market power.[61] Finally, as in the 1996 Act in the United States, the Regulatory Authority has responsibility for developing the specific rules governing compliance with the TKG.[62]

The Stock Offering. Deutsche Telekom's share capital, on a par value basis, is DM 10 billion.[63] The majority of this shareholding will remain with the federal government until the year 2000.[64] However, in November 1996, Deutsche Telekom placed newly issued shares in a public offering in the first of several expected tranches. The first tranche of the public offering diluted government ownership by about 25 percent.

The initial public offering (IPO) was one of the biggest in the world, and by far the biggest in Europe. By most measurements, the public offering was a tremendous success, bringing in $13.3 billion through the sale of 713 million shares of stock (representing 25 percent of Deutsche Telekom's outstanding shares).[65] The success indicates that Deutsche Telekom is regarded as a major competitor in the global telecommunications market, with a total estimated value of more than $75 billion. Deutsche Telekom can now claim to be the largest telecommunications firm in Europe, and the second in the world, behind Japan's NTT and ahead of AT&T.[66] Many important factors contributed to Deutsche Telekom's IPO success: it made large investments in its network, including approximately DM 50 billion to modernize networks in eastern Germany; Germany is Europe's largest market; and it secured several licenses to offer wireless and wire-based services in Eastern Europe and positioned itself as a global provider through its many international alliances, including its ATLAS alliance with France Telecom, the second-largest telecommunications provider in Europe, and the Global One alliance with Sprint.[67]

As Deutsche Telekom is learning, however, shareholders demand more than impressive investments—they demand impressive returns.[68] Deutsche Telekom's transition to a successful private company will require considerable further efforts. It inherited a workforce of 230,000 civil servants, a number that must be reduced if the firm is to gain the efficiencies necessary to survive in a competitive environment. Further, Deutsche Telekom has substantial debt, resulting primarily from its contribution to modernizing facilities in eastern Germany. This debt must be retired or reduced.[69] All this has to be accomplished as Deutsche Telekom fends off the future competition. Therefore, the initial success of Deutsche Telekom's public offering does not necessarily guarantee future success.

Currently, the German government is planning to transfer an additional 25 percent of its capital in Deutsche Telekom to an investment agency to be sold to commercial investors.[70] However, the remaining stock cannot be sold on the capital markets before 2000. Therefore, the German government will retain a substantial interest in Deutsche Telekom even as competition is introduced to the German market. Such an arrangement will lead many to question whether the government's priority is to promote competition or to preserve the value of Deutsche Telekom's stock until it is sold.

If the Regulatory Authority is truly independent, suspicion surrounding the government's conflict of interest may diminish. If suspicion remains, however, the Agreement on Basic Telecommunications Services negotiated through the WTO may provide a neutral forum to resolve any disputes.[71] The independence of the Regulatory Authority is likely to be tested soon, as competitors to Deutsche Telekom have filed complaints challenging the fees Deutsche Telekom proposes to charge customers when they wish to switch to competing providers (and to keep their telephone numbers in the process). While the Regulatory Authority is acting to address these complaints, the European Commission has indicated that it will intervene if the resolution of the complaints is not acceptable to it.[72]

Comparison of Telecommunications Reform in the United States and Germany

As the above discussion reflects, Germany and the United States are pursuing the same general goal of telecommunications liberalization, but have chosen somewhat different paths to get there. The United States is implementing a segmented approach to achieve full and complete competition by opening certain markets before others. Germany has experienced some incremental market openings, particularly in the equipment and mobile areas, but core service markets will open to competition simultaneously.

Despite these different approaches, both the United States and Germany will eventually see competition grow within their domestic markets. The market will be more regulated and market conditions more asymmetric in Germany, as new competitors are entering markets where the core markets—voice services and networks—are dominated by the incumbent provider. The United States, by contrast, has dominant providers, but they are limited to specific segments of the core market. Further, in the United States, each dominant provider has an incentive to provide a competitive environment within its markets—the approval to enter other market segments. Therefore, although the 1996 Act aims to create competition in all markets, it also creates competitive opportunities for all players, even the current dominant providers. In Germany existing restrictions protect Deutsche Telekom from competition without any corresponding exclusion of Deutsche Telekom from competitive opportunities.

By removing existing restrictions, Germany's approach is less dramatic than the initial opening of the U.S. long-distance market to competition. The breakup of AT&T was an extreme method of opening this market. From the current perspective, however, the U.S. approach appears to have been successful. Germany, to date, has not proposed divestiture as an option to facilitate the opening of its telecommunications markets. In light of the high probability that Deutsche Telekom will face significant competitors, divestiture may not be necessary.

Telecommunications reform in Germany has an additional element not present in the United States—the continued government ownership of the majority of the shares of the incumbent provider. The better the future performance of Deutsche Telekom, the greater the value of the government's holdings. As a result, in the United States, the independence of the FCC is presumed, whereas in Germany, the independence of the Regulatory Authority must be proved. For this reason, many future competitors advocate an ongoing supervisory role for the European Commission. The Commission, like the FCC, has only an attenuated relationship to Deutsche Telekom and other national providers and must establish rules that bind many different players facing different circumstances, and thus can be expected to act more objectively than the German government. While the Commission initially indicated that it would leave important aspects of telecommunications regulation to the member states, it has recently recognized a need to continue to oversee reform in the telecommunications field.[73] It appears that this role will continue, which should help ensure objective rule-making in Germany and other member states.

While both Germany and the United States are moving toward free and open competition in telecommunications, they will not achieve that goal in the near future. As recent developments in the United States demonstrate, historical monopolies are not penetrated easily and delays are to be expected. The benefits of a worldwide open market, which provided the incentive for the WTO agreement, should, it is hoped, likewise motivate regulatory authorities and providers alike to pursue reform as quickly as is reasonably possible.

Notes

1. See Communications Act of 1934, as amended by Communications Act of 1996, 47 U.S.C. §153.

2. Ibid.

3. See *American Regulatory Federalism, supra,* n. 2 at 47.

4. See, e.g., *Alascom, Inc. v FCC,* 727 F.2d 1212 (1984) (states challenged FCC ruling allowing carriers such as MCI to sell long-distance service on private networks).

5. *U.S. v Western Electric Co.,* 522 F. Supp. 131 (D. D.C. 1982), *aff'd sub nom., Maryland v. U.S.,* 460 U.S. 1001 (1983).

6. See *12th Annual Institute on Telecommunications, Policy and Regulation* (New York: Practicing Law Institute, 1994).

7. Communications Act of 1934 as amended by the Telecommunications Act of 1996, 47 U.S.C. §251(a).

8. Ibid. at §251(b).

9. Ibid. at §253. See also ibid. at §257 (removal of barriers to competition in all segments of telecommunications markets).

10. Ibid. at §161.

11. Ibid. at §§271–276.

12. Ibid. at §271(c)(1).

13. Ibid. at §271.

14. Ibid. at §271(d)(1).

15. Ibid. at §271(d)(2).

16. Ibid.

17. See Evaluation of the Department of Justice, In the matter of SBC Communications, Inc. Pursuant to Section 271 of Telecommunications Act of 1996 to Provide Inter-Region InterLATA Service in the State of Oklahoma, before the FCC, CC Docket No. 97–121, May 16, 1997.

18. See, e.g., Kansas Statute Annotated 66-2005 and 2008 under which the Kansas legislatures allowed Southwestern Bell Telephone, a division of SBC, to recover all monies lost due to rate rebalancing from a general fund, funded by competitors and customers, without any auditing to determine the extent of profits being subsidized through the general fund.

19. In addition, as in many of its neighbors, in Germany the responsibility for telecommunications and postal service was combined in the same ministry, which also provides banking services.

20. The United States had to push hard to get minor regulatory concessions from Germany in bilateral trade talks. See "W. Germans Announce Regulatory Concessions at Trade Meeting with U.S.," *Television Digest Inc., Communications Daily* 5, no. 241 (13 December 1985): 4.

21. See Green Paper on the development of the common market for telecommunications services and equipment (COM[87] 290, 30.06.87).

22. See *France v Commission*, Case 202/88, 91/C 96/04 (Official Journal 96), 6, 19 March 1991–Italy, Belgium, and Greece intervening; *Spain, Belgium and Italy v Commission Joined Cases*, C-271/90, 28/190, ECJ, 17 November 1992.

23. Translation: *Gesetz über Fernmeldanlagen* (FAG).

24. *Postreform I* also created two other public entities, Deutsche Bundespost Postdienst and Deutsche Bundespost Postbank, responsible for postal and banking services, respectively.

25. The transfer was implemented through subsequent ordinances. See, e.g., *Official Gazettes of the Federal Ministry of Post and Telecommunications*, 13 December 1996, p. 1887, Communication 2011/1990; Administrative Rule defining the Authority transferred to DBT voice to exercise federal sovereignty voice services monopoly on 13 July 1992.

26. Officially called Bundesministerium für Post und Telekommunikation (BMPT).

27. In consultation with the Economics Ministry.

28. See *Postreform* §1 and 1a(2); Telecommunications Ordinances (*Telekommunikations Verordnungen*—TKV).

29. See Council Directive of 28 June 1990 on the establishment of internal market for telecommunications services through the implementation of the open networks provisions (90/387/EEC).

30. See Council Resolution of 30 June 1988 (88/C 257/01; OJ C257/1, 04.10.88); Commission Directive of 28 June 1990 (90/450/EEC; OJ L230/25, 24.08.90); Council Directive of 29 April 1991 (91/263/EEC; OJL 144/45, 08.06.91).

31. See Council Resolution of 18 July 1989 (89/C 196/04; OJ C196/4, 01.08.89).

32. See Council Directive of 3 June 1991 (91/288/EEC; OJ L 144/47, 08.06.91).

33. See Guidelines on the Application of EEC Competition Rules in the Telecommunications Sector (92/C 233/02; OJ C233/2, 06.09.91).

34. The TKV was amended in September 1992.

35. See, e.g., TKV §20.

36. See TKV9(1), 6,21(1) and 24.

37. See Council Resolution on the review of the situation in the telecommunications sector and the need for further development in the market, 22 July 1993 (93/C 213/01). The Resolution provides for extensions to the deadline until the year 2000 for Ireland, Greece, Portugal, and Spain. This resolution was adopted in the Council Directive of 13 March 1996 (96/19/EC).

38. See Reorganization Act, Article 3, Law Concerning the Transformation of Deutsche Bundespost Enterprises into the Legal Structure of a Stock Corporation, §§1 and 2.

39. See Act amending the Basic Law, dated 30 August 1994.

40. See Reorganization Act, Article 7, Law Concerning the Regulation of Post and Telecommunications §4(1).

41. See Reorganization Act, Article 5, Amendment of Telecommunications Act, §1(5). To assist the ministry in carrying out its duties, the Reorganization Act set up a regulatory council.

42. See Reorganization Act, Article 5, Amendment to Telecommunications Act §28, which provides for DT's exclusive right to provide public switched voice services until 1 January 1998.

43. See FAG §3(1).

44. See FAG §3(2).

45. See FAG §3(3). In March 1995, an American CAP, Metropolitan Fiber Systems, was granted a license to construct a fiber-optic ring on behalf of the city of Frankfurt in its downtown area.

46. See Council Resolution of 22 December 1994 on the principles and the timetables for the liberalization of telecommunications infrastructures (94/C379/03). Ireland, Spain, Portugal, and Greece were granted an extension until 2003.

47. See Commission Directive of 13 March 1996, regarding the full competition in telecommunications markets (96/19/EC).

48. See, e.g., Directive 95/62/EC of the European Parliament and of the Council of 13 December 1995 on application of open network provision (ONP) to voice telephony.

49. See *Bundesgesetzblatt* Jahrgang 1995, Teil 1, s. (page) 1446, *Verordnung über Verlehungen zum Errichten und Betreiben privater Übertragungswege in öffentlichen Mobilfunknetzen vom* 23. Oktober 1995.

50. See note 37.

51. See Proposed Telecommunications Act of 1996, §65.

52. However, there is no postponement of the effect of the Regulatory Authority decision pending an appeal.

53. See Telecommunications Act of 1996, §79. The Antitrust Bureau is the Bundeskartellamt.

54. Ibid. at §§17–22.

55. Ibid.

56. Ibid. at §§24–32.

57. In general terms, the Law Against Restraints of Competition provides that a market-dominant provider is one without competition or substantial competition or one who has, relative to its competition, a highly superior market position as measured by market share, financial strength, access to supply markets, and relationship to other firms, or has erected de jure or de facto barriers to market entry with the ability to substitute its supply or demand with other products or services. Law Against Restraints of Competition (*Gesetz gegen Wettbewerbeschränkungen*), §22(1).

58. Ibid. at §25.

59. Ibid. at §§27 and 28.

60. Ibid. at §27.

61. Ibid. at §33.

62. See, e.g., ibid. at §§33, 37.

63. See Reorganization Act, Article 3, Law Concerning the Transfer of DBT into the Legal Structure of Stock Corporation, §5.

64. Ibid.

65. See James O. Jackson, "Deutsche Telekom Goes Public with a Successful Sales Blitz," *Time* (international edition), 2 December 1996.

66. This is based on telecommunications operations without revenue shares from hardware production. See Deutsche Telekom, *Working for a New Life*, K-Nr. 642 100 082, p. 20.

67. Ibid., pp. 14–55.

68. See Associated Press Worldstream, "Deutsche Telekom Stock Drops Below 30 Marks" (DT's stock plunged to its lowest level since initial offering), 15 January 1997; Reuters Financial Service, "Telekom Sours on Earning Optimism" (DT's stock price rose to a high of DM 41.95 , a 47 percent increase from issue price), 12 May 1997.

69. In December 1996, DT's debt was more than $80 billion. See Jackson, "Deutsche Telekom Goes Public," p. 46.

70. See Information Access Company, "German Government Looks for Investors in Deutsche Telekom in Bid to Raise Revenue," *Computergram International*, 30 June 1997.

71. See "U.S. Considers WTO Complaint Against Germany," *Telecommunications Alert* 14, no. 79 (22 April 1997).

72. "EC Competitors Up in Arms over Deutsche Telekom Disconnect Fines, *Telecoms Bulletin Regulator*, 18 January 1998.

73. See "EC Gets Tough on Interconnect Rates," *Communications Week*, no. 186 (2 June 1997): 1. The European Commission has decided that it will establish benchmark interconnection agreements to ensure that new entrants get similar rates and terms across Europe.

PART THREE

German Integration: Eastern Germany

Introduction:
Eastern Germany

GEOFFREY D. OLIVER

The defining event in Germany in the 1990s, perhaps even the second half of the twentieth century, has been the unification of East and West Germany.

Public reaction to unification has taken place in at least three stages. The period leading up to unification, and the first year or so after unification, were characterized by optimism regarding the economic potential of the former East Germany, but some trepidation concerning the social and political implications of unification. A year or two later, however, after the true economic condition of the new *Länder* was more fully understood, the economic costs of unification came to dominate the public perception. In recent years, issues concerning unification and the condition of the new *Länder* have faded from public view as issues relating to introduction of a European currency, further European integration, and expansion of NATO have come to dominate public debate.

The previous Bosch volume, *Dimensions of German Unification: Economic, Social, and Legal Analyses* (1995), was dedicated to the unification of Germany, and the essays contained therein analyzed specific issues relating to unification. Many of the pieces focused on the early stages of transformation of the former East Germany from an independent communist dictatorship to a part of the democratic, capitalist Federal Republic of Germany. Frederick Fucci and Mark Jrolf wrote about the activities of the Treuhandanstalt and the privatization of East German industry.[1] Angela Kurtz Mendelson analyzed dictatorship in East Germany, and Lauren Stone discussed the cultural transformation of Leipzig.[2] Several other pieces, including the speeches of Kurt Biedenkopf and Karsten Voigt, dealt with the situation of a newly unified Germany in a changed Europe.[3]

Since the publication of that volume, the German government's privatization program has largely been completed and the Treuhandanstalt has been dissolved. The political structure of Berlin and Brandenburg has been determined. The new *Länder* have completed the initial stages of transformation into parts of a unified democratic, capitalist Germany. Yet, in other ways, the situation of the new *Länder* continues to evolve. The federal and state governments struggle to balance the continuing need for economic support of the economy in eastern Germany with the desire to reduce the consequent burden on taxpayers. In the meantime, many "interim" measures continue, including substantial transfer payments from the federal government to support inefficient industries and worker training as well as investment subsidies to encourage investment in the new *Länder*. The new *Länder* continue to experiment in trying to find the optimal balance between autonomy and cooperation. Perhaps most significantly, considerable differences remain in the social outlook of the populations of eastern and western Germany.

This section continues the analysis of the new *Länder*. The chapters in this section carry the earlier discussion forward through the initial stages of integration and deal with some of the more difficult, protracted issues that remained after the completion of the initial stages of unification. Carol Kuester writes about the present degree of coordination of regional planning between the German states of Berlin and Brandenburg. As she describes, this coordination originated as a pragmatic arrangement, arising of necessity from Germany's federal structure in which the federal states were created as much by historical accident as by current political, administrative, or economic requirements. In the months leading up to unification, various schemes were proposed to rationalize the structure of the federal states in Germany. The most far-reaching proposals called for the amalgamation of certain states in western as well as eastern Germany in order to unite cities with the surrounding territories and create states with several million inhabitants. Other plans were restricted to the territories of eastern Germany and called for the creation of two or three sizable states from the territory of the former GDR and West Berlin. Almost all of these plans envisioned the combination of Berlin and Brandenburg, and perhaps additional territories as well, in a single state. These plans emphasized the administrative efficiency of such combinations. The plans, however, underestimated the popular support for the smaller, local states in eastern as well as western Germany. As a result, at the time of unification, five relatively small states in eastern Germany (based on the districts of the former GDR) were added to the eleven existing states of the former federal republic; apart from the merger of West and East Berlin, no change was made to the preexisting states in the former West Germany.

As Kuester describes, the governments of Berlin and Brandenburg engaged in increasing levels of coordination and cooperation after unification, eventually leading both governments to propose a merger of the two states. This proposal, however, was defeated in a popular referendum in 1996. Since that time, mutual suspicions between the states have grown, jeopardizing joint planning and coordination. Kuester concludes that the current lack of trust and cooperation could hinder the ability of both states to keep up with larger and wealthier German states and other regions of Europe.

Christopher Sylvester compares the investment opportunities in the new *Länder* and eastern Europe by analyzing investment conditions in the east German state of Thuringia and the Czech Republic. With the completion of western companies' initial investment plans as well as the conclusion of the German government's privatization program and the dissolution of the Treuhandanstalt, the most obvious channel for foreign investment in eastern Germany has come to an end. From now on, eastern Germany will have to win much of its foreign investment from companies seeking to invest in one of many possible locations. Sylvester identifies the factors that U.S. investors are likely to consider when selecting an investment location, including macroeconomic performance, infrastructure, the costs and quality of the labor force, corporate tax rates, the banking system, investment incentives, customer and market location, political stability, and the quality of life. After comparing the east German state of Thuringia and the Czech Republic as investment locations in light of these factors, he presents four brief case studies of U.S. investments in these regions. Sylvester concludes that eastern Germany and eastern Europe each have specific advantages and disadvantages as investment locations. Eastern Germany and eastern Europe each offer favorable investment opportunities, but a U.S. investor must be careful to evaluate the characteristics of each region in light of the investor's individual goals.

Notes

1. Frederick Fucci, "Whither the Treuhandanstalt?", and Mark Jrolf, "The Politics of Restructuring Business Enterprises in the former GDR: The case of Eko Stahl" in B. Shingleton, M. Gibbon and K. Mack, eds., *Dimemsions of German Unification: Economic, Social and Legal Analyses* (Westview Press 1995).

2. Angela Kurtz Mendelson, "A Quiet Land: Reflections on Dictatorship in East Germany," and Lauren Stone, "Slouching Towards Capitalism: Cultural Transformation in Leipzig 1993," in B. Shingleton M. Gibbon and K. Mack, eds., *Dimensions of German Unification: Economic, Social and Legal Analyses* (Westview Press 1995).

3. Kurt Biedenkopf, "Germany in a New Europe," and Karsten Voigt, "Pan-European Policy after the End of the East-West Conflict: German

Foreign Policy Needs New Concepts," in B. Shingleton, M. Gibbon, and K. Mack, eds., Dimensions of German Unification: Economic, Social and Legal Analyses (Westview Press 1995).

7

Regional Planning and Politics in Berlin and Brandenburg

CAROL KUESTER

The German states of Berlin and Brandenburg have a long and unique history. Politically separated by the iron curtain for 40 years, East and West Germany developed different cultures and experienced widely divergent approaches to economic development and land use. West Berlin, as an island within the eastern state of Brandenburg, faced unprecedented challenges and constraints. Since German unification, the Berlin/Brandenburg region has become a microcosm of the cultural, economic, and infrastructure issues and challenges facing unified Germany. The city-state of Berlin not only must work with Brandenburg toward physical, political, economic, and social reunification but also in light of the 1991 decision to make Berlin the federal capital, must prepare to be home to the German parliament, ten federal ministries, and the chancellor's office.

Almost as soon as the Berlin Wall fell in 1989, politicians throughout Germany began to envision the fusion of Berlin and Brandenburg into a single state. In June 1995, a merger contract was signed by Berlin's mayor, Eberhard Diepgen, and the minister-president of Brandenburg, Manfred Stolpe, but the voters failed to ratify the contract in a referendum held on May 5, 1996. Berlin and Brandenburg will therefore remain divided for the foreseeable future and will have to deal with their myriad challenges on a case-by-case basis. Berlin's mayor, Eberhard Diepgen, estimates that approximately 200 individual contracts will now be required to manage the relationship between the two states.[1]

In the area of land-use planning, Berlin and Brandenburg have established a contractual relationship in which the two states work together to coordinate development in the region. Urban planners have developed spatial plans to channel growth, maintaining city centers and open spaces and minimizing the environmental and transportation problems associated with development. In the coming years, urban planners will follow developments in Berlin and Brandenburg and draw lessons from this increasingly important German region.

This chapter provides an overview of regional planning in Germany; the political, economic, and physical characteristics of the Berlin/Brandenburg region; and the failed attempt in 1996 to merge the two states. It then describes the recent experience with managing development in the Berlin/Brandenburg region, with an emphasis on transportation planning challenges.

Federalism and Planning Administration in Germany

In Germany, federalism "implies that not only the country as a whole but its 16 constituent parts, the *Länder*, have some of the features of a state. Each has its own powers, though they are restricted to certain spheres, which it exercises through its own legislature, executive and judiciary."[2] The concept of federalism is politically important and has been embraced by the populace. In keeping with Germany's political commitment to federalism and the decentralization of power, regional planning takes place at the federal, state, and local levels.

At the federal level, a minister for spatial planning, development, and city building (*Minister für Raumordnung, Bauwesen und Städtebau*) is appointed by the federal chancellor. Because actual responsibility for spatial development lies with the states and cities, the federal minister acts primarily as a spokesperson for the state ministers in the international arena (e.g., the European Union) and plays a coordinating role among the states.

At the state level, spatial planning involves developing general policies and principles. States must decide whether planning at the regional level is necessary and, if so, how it should be organized. Every state in Germany (except the three city-states of Bremen, Hamburg, and Berlin) has some form of regional planning agency, although their organization differs considerably. The goal of these agencies is to implement state planning goals at the regional level. Area land-use plans (*Flächennutzungspläne*) are prepared at the regional or city level and indicate the proposed distribution of land uses according to the strategic objectives of urban development and the foreseeable needs of the community.[3] Within the parameters defined in the area land-use plan, planning for specific subareas and eventually proposals for individual projects and buildings are developed, evaluated, and approved.

Germany's long tradition of civic liberty is manifest in the fact that German cities have a high level of autonomy in evaluating and approving proposed developments. At the same time, land-use planning relies heavily on a system of checks and balances, referred to as the "countervailing procedure" (*Gegenstromverfahren*). This term refers to the fact that all spatial planning must be approved or coordinated with higher and lower levels of planning policy. Although much decisionmaking authority is delegated to the smallest units of government, each spatial plan that a city, town, or village prepares must be approved at the county level. Public participation in the planning process takes place almost entirely at the local level, a characteristic that most commentators consider positive. According to one assessment, "Local self-government gives all citizens an opportunity to play their part and have a controlling influence. They can discuss such matters as new building projects with elected councillors at town meetings and inspect budget estimates."[4]

Since 1989, the role of local government in regional planning in the five "new" (formerly eastern) states has grown considerably. German cities now have primary responsibility for approving new development, whereas previously cities in the GDR had almost no political authority: "There was no concept of independent politics, an autonomous mayor, or citizen involvement. A strong principle of hierarchy reigned. . . . Economic dependence reflected political dependence. Cities had to rely on counties and states for funding. Independent tax bases were minimal."[5]

Characteristics of the Berlin/Brandenburg Region

Historical and Political Context

Immediately after World War II ended, the Potsdam conference in August 1945 divided the city-state of Berlin into four military zones, which were occupied by the victorious Allies. The creation of the German Democratic Republic (GDR) made West Berlin into an island in the midst of East German territory. From then on, the existence of West Berlin was continually threatened, most seriously in 1948, when the city was blockaded by Soviet forces and had to be maintained by airlifted supplies. In the 1950s, Berlin became the main route for East Germans escaping to West Germany, and on August 13, 1961, the GDR began construction of a 162-kilometer wall between East and West Berlin that stood until November 1989. Throughout those 28 years, the two halves of the city developed independently.

Throughout the Cold War, East and West Berlin both served a "shopping-window function" (*Schaufensterfunktion*), or propaganda role. Each government luxuriously developed its half of the city in a competition to show off the achievements of its economic system.[6] West Berlin, protected by American, French, and British troops, was heavily subsidized by the West German government. Similarly, East Berlin, which became the capital of East Germany in 1949, was one of the GDR's model cities and was developed at the expense of other cities:

> Brandenburgers remember well how the East German capital was given preference in the centralized GDR administration. Pickles from the Spreewald were not for sale in Spreewald, but in department stores on Alexanderplatz [in East Berlin]. And in the early 1950s, when East and West Berlin competed to rebuild the ruins of Berlin, the SED [Social Einheitspartei Deutschlands, the East German communist party] took almost all the construction projects out of cities in the provinces. They fell apart and deteriorated.[7]

On November 9, 1989, the Berlin Wall fell. Less than a year later, on October 3, 1990, East Germany was incorporated into West Germany. Unification brought with it the wholesale extension of West German laws and policies to the former East German states. From one day to the next, East Germans found themselves confronted with new laws governing every sphere of life. While West Germans argued that this solution was the only politically expedient one at a time of rapid change, many East Germans believed that their laws deserved careful review rather than simply being tossed aside. Today, many East Germans still feel as if they were "occupied" by the west and are nostalgic for elements of life in the GDR. Although the Berlin Wall no longer stands, the "wall in the head" (*Mauer im Kopfkern*) of German citizens remains and indeed has become more pronounced as the euphoria of unification has dissipated. In 1996, six years after reunification, a study by the Hans Böckler Foundation found that one in every five East Germans believed that a sense of national unity was further away than it had been in 1990. Moreover, while more than one-third of East Germans still thought of themselves as former citizens of the GDR, only 17.8 percent of respondents identified themselves as citizens of the Federal Republic of Germany.[8]

Immediately after the fall of the Berlin Wall, the city governments of East and West Berlin began working together to maintain and rebuild the swiftly reunited city. Since then, Berlin and Brandenburg have made great strides in coordinating spatial planning in the city and the surrounding region. Even so, the continuing social tensions between East and West Germans have been a serious hindrance to efforts by Berlin and Brandenburg to coordinate government services.

Economic Characteristics of Berlin/Brandenburg

The legacy of a divided country and a divided city has left the citizens of Berlin and Brandenburg with some harsh economic realities. During the Cold War, West Berlin's awkward geographic location caused businesses and manufacturers to locate elsewhere in West Germany, leaving the city with an underdeveloped economic base. Since unification, many formerly state-controlled industries in Brandenburg have collapsed in the face of free-market competition or been forced to reduce their workforce considerably. As a result, unemployment in Brandenburg and in Berlin has been higher than the average in other German states. In 1996, unemployment in Brandenburg reached a high of 16.8 percent.[9]

Both Berlin and Brandenburg are net recipients of income from the process of "financial equalization" (*Länderfinanzausgleich*), in which wealthier states subsidize poorer states.[10] Berlin obtains by far the highest level of support, receiving net transfers of DM 4.1 billion per year from other German states.[11] Berlin also has a bloated public administration. To be in line with the average numbers of public-sector employees in the west German states, Berlin would need to reduce its employees by about 60,000, or one-quarter.[12] The high levels of subsidies that for years flowed to Berlin and Brandenburg, and the large number of public-sector employees in both states, have left a distinct mark on the population's attitude toward government. According to *Der Spiegel*,

> The majority of people in Brandenburg as well as in Berlin believe that the state's responsibility is not to create the optimal situation for individuals to get ahead but, rather, that it is the duty of the state to provide work and bread, like a father. But there is an increasing realization that Father State is almost broke. This is equally painful for voters in both the east and the west. In both regions, millions of people are used to receiving subsidies from their countrymen on either side of the Elbe.[13]

Physical Characteristics of Berlin/Brandenburg

Although Berlin and Brandenburg share many challenges, they could hardly be more different in terms of physical development. Berlin is a densely developed and populated metropolis, while Brandenburg is a sprawling, sparsely populated hinterland. Together Berlin and Brandenburg have a population of approximately 6 million, but of that total, 3.5 million live in Berlin and only 2.5 million in Brandenburg. Brandenburg's four largest cities, Brandenburg, Cottbus, Frankfurt-Oder, and Potsdam, have populations between 80,000 and 140,000 and hence are dwarfed by the Berlin metropolis. Moreover, 800,000 Brandenburgers live in the metropolitan area of Berlin (see Table 7.1).

Spatial Development Planning in Berlin/Brandenburg

Shortly after the fall of the Berlin Wall, Berlin and Brandenburg began working closely together to shape spatial planning in the region. With German unification, both states became concerned about controlling new

TABLE 7.1   Brandenburg/Berlin Comparative Figures

	Area (sq. km)	Population (in millions)	Gross Domestic Debt Product (millions of DM) (DM/person)		Federal Equalization Subsidy
Berlin	889.1	3.48	42,561 ($30,401)*	9,059 ($6,471)	DM 4.1 b. ($2.9b)
Brandenburg	29,481.2	2.54	25,138 ($17,956)	6,568 ($4,691)	DM .86 b. ($610m)

SOURCE: *Der Spiegel.*
*Estimate based on an exchange rate of DM 1.4 to US$1.

development in the metropolitan area around Berlin. The dramatic legal changes following unification and the need to establish new systems of local government were a major challenge for many of Brandenburg's newly elected local officials. One result of this situation was that "big-box" development, spurred on by developers eager to exploit the open spaces near Berlin, went almost unchecked in the early years after the Wall fell. The consequence was urban sprawl and the associated environmental and traffic problems, which demonstrated the need for long-term regional planning.

A first step in this direction was reform of the county structure in Brandenburg, which was implemented in 1993. According to this reform, Brandenburg went from 38 counties and 6 freestanding (*kreisfrei*) cities to 14 counties and 4 free-standing cities. Regional planners proposed a "piece of cake" model (*Tortenstückmodell*) for the development of Brandenburg's counties in which the new counties would be wedge-shaped, each encompassing a small piece of the metropolitan area of Berlin along with a larger section of the hinterlands. Planners hoped that this model would encourage a more equitable distribution of investment and resources between the heavily developed (and developing) wealthy belt (*Speckgürtel*) around Berlin and underdeveloped Brandenburg. As yet, this model has not yet been adopted because of disparate interests between the Berlin metropolitan area and the small, rural cities in Brandenburg. Regional planners remain convinced, however, that the goal of achieving similar quality-of-life standards throughout the region can be achieved only when planning interests in the metropolitan area and the rural region are linked.

In April 1995, Berlin and Brandenburg embodied their long-term planning goals in a coordinated State Development Program that included objectives for the development of the two states (*Landesentwicklungsprogramm*) and the metropolitan area encircling Berlin (*Landesentwicklungsplan für den engeren Verflechtungsraum Brandenburg/Berlin*). Since it was clear that Berlin and Brandenburg would be highly interdependent in terms of urban planning (especially transportation), economic development, education, and investment in public services such as hospitals and recreational areas, the two states officially established a Berlin/Brandenburg Regional Planning Office (*Gemeinsame Landesplanungsabteilung*, or GL) on January 1, 1996. By merging their planning functions, the two states gave up promoting their separate development in the greater interest of the region as a whole. According to Matthias Platzeck, Brandenburg's minister for environment, natural resources, and spatial planning, and Dr. Volker Hassemer, Berlin state senator for city development and environmental protection, "Instead of existing as competing neighbor states, the two states of the European region Berlin/Brandenburg will cooperate and thereby both gain advantages for success in the competition among European regions."[14]

To date, the GL is the only example of joint regional planning between German states, although the city-states of Hamburg and Bremen are also surrounded by other states and must coordinate their activities in areas like urban planning. The GL has developed plans that embody several key spatial planning concepts to benefit both states. Planners in the Berlin/Brandenburg region are pursuing a transit-oriented, decentralized form of development. As envisioned in the region's long-term planning document (*Landesentwicklungsprogramm*), fingers of development will extend out from Berlin along rail lines, and green space will be preserved between them.

In addition to the joint regional planning office with Berlin, the state of Brandenburg has founded its own regional planning agencies, which are allowed but not required by the federal spatial planning law. Brandenburg has five regional planning agencies, each covering two to three counties and freestanding cities. The regional planning agency staffs (usually five to seven employees) develop plans that are submitted to the Berlin/Brandenburg Regional Planning Office for approval and, once approved, guide development in the cities and counties (see Table 7.2).

The Failed Attempt at Berlin/Brandenburg Fusion

After German unification, politicians in Berlin and Brandenburg intended to do more than merely cooperate with each other. The unification treaty joining East and West Germany included a recommendation that Berlin and Brandenburg merge, and work began on this initiative in 1991.[15] Berlin's mayor, Diepgen, argued that cities like Berlin were no longer competitive in the global economy and that regional development had become increasingly important. In the spring of 1995, the Berlin and

TABLE 7.2   Chronology of Events Affecting Regional Planning in
Berlin/Brandenburg

November 9, 1989	Fall of the Berlin Wall.
December 15, 1989	Provisional Regional Committee for Berlin and Brandenburg established.
May 1990	Planning goals for the city of Berlin defined by the Provisional Regional Committee.
February 1992	Joint government commission resolves that a joint development plan for the region and for the metropolitan area of Berlin should be developed.
May 1993	County reform is implemented in Brandenburg.
April 1995	Joint development plan for the city of Berlin and the Brandenburg region (*Gemeinsames Landesentwicklungsprogramm*) is presented to the governments of Berlin and Branden burg.
January 1, 1996	The Berlin/Brandenburg Regional Planning office (*Gemeinsame Landesplanungsabteilung*, or GL) officially comes into existence.
May 5, 1996	Failed referendum on Berlin/Brandenburg fusion.

Brandenburg state governments negotiated and passed a contract detailing how the merger of the states would function. This contract included a requirement that the merger issue be put to a public referendum. Ratification would require approval by a majority of voters in both states, with participation by at least 25 percent of those eligible to vote. Voters also would be asked to decide whether the merger should occur in 1999 or 2002.

In their campaign for a unified Berlin/Brandenburg, Stolpe and Diepgen identified several tangible benefits of fusion, including enhanced economic development and job creation, higher efficiencies from the removal of expensive competition between the two states, a more powerful voice at the federal level and in the European Union, coordinated spatial planning, and the opportunity to act as a pilot project for other state reform efforts in Germany. In addition, the German Institute for Economic Research estimated that the two states could save approximately DM 1 billion (about $65 million) by combining their redundant bureaucracies, as foreseen in the fusion contract.[16]

As the referendum approached, however, opinion polls indicated that the population had mixed feelings about the proposed union. Although Stolpe's Social Democratic Party and Diepgen's Christian Democratic Union both supported fusion, the Party of Democratic Socialism (PDS), the successor to the East German Communist Party, spoke out against the unification contract. PDS politicians argued that they were not opposed to the merger in principle but that the provisions of the particular contract agreed to by the two states were unacceptable. Since the PDS was the only east-based German political party, its opposition to the merger worsened fears in Brandenburg about being subjected to another imposed unification on western terms. "The theme of east-west," realized Mayor Diepgen to his surprise, "outweighs all the substantive issues." Stolpe agreed, noting that the "whole disappointment of the time since reunification is attaching itself to the planned fusion."[17]

The source of the problems was not solely the anxieties of former East Germans but also the failure of proponents (notably Stolpe and Diepgen) to communicate the benefits of the merger to voters, particularly those living in east Berlin and Brandenburg. Instead of focusing on the obvious and basic efficiencies that could be realized by unifying the two states, the debate focused on more arcane issues such as how many jobs in the public sector would be lost or created, how the debt burden of the two states would be shared, and what effect the merger would have on financial support from the federal government and the European Union.

The argument that the Berlin-Brandenburg region could provide an example of positive, innovative change for Germany also fell on deaf ears. Instead, East Germans were suspicious and questioned why they, rather than the citizens of Hamburg or Bremen, should bear the brunt of experimentation. Moreover, the fears of both Berliners and Brandenburgers about being swallowed up by the other state went largely unaddressed. When the referendum finally took place on May 5, 1996, only a majority of West Berliners voted for the merger (see Table 7.3).

Implications of the Failed Merger

Although a renewed attempt at unifying the two states is conceivable, it is unlikely to occur in the foreseeable future. When it became clear that the fusion contract would not be ratified, Diepgen and Stolpe stood together and declared that the two states would increase cooperation at every level. Soon, however, the tone on both sides became more contentious. Just a few days after the failed merger vote, Diepgen announced that competition for economic resources with Brandenburg would intensify.[18] According to an article in *Der Spiegel*, "Now the hundreds of German public officials in Berlin and Brandenburg are preparing for a war between the states. The Berlin administration is working particularly hard, checking every period and comma, to see what benefits the capital city is giving to Brandenburg for free."[19] For example, 3,000 students from Brandenburg attend school in Berlin at a cost of approximately DM 33 million. Many of these services are not contractually secured because

TABLE 7.3   Berlin and Brandenburg Polling Responses

	For Fusion	Against Fusion
Berlin	53.4%	45.7%
West Berlin	58.7%	40.3%
East Berlin	44.5%	54.7%
Brandenburg	36.5%	62.8%

SOURCE: "Berlin und Brandenburg bleiben weiter getrennt," *Berliner Morgenpost*, 6 May 1996, no. 123, p. 1.

state leaders assumed that the unified state contract, had it been approved, would have made such individual contracts unnecessary.[20]

Since the failed referendum vote, policymakers in each state are asking themselves what is best for their voters rather than what is best for the region. The Berlin/Brandenburg Regional Planning Office (GL), publicly hailed as a model of interstate cooperation, is quietly being called into question. With mistrust and resentment growing between Berlin and Brandenburg, the GL, which is simultaneously responsible to both states, will have even less political direction and support than it has had to date. Although the office's existence has not technically been affected by the failed merger and is contractually bound to remain in existence until 1999, the success of the GL requires a spirit of trust and cooperation that seems to be receding. In a political climate in which policymakers in both Berlin and Brandenburg rely increasingly on advice from their own staffs, it is unlikely that the GL will play a decisive or leading role in interstate cooperation, further weakening the case for its existence. Indeed, the agency's personnel, 80 from the state of Brandenburg and 20 from Berlin, are in some cases reluctant to work together.

Interstate Transportation Projects

Work on interstate issues, most significantly transportation projects, will certainly suffer in the wake of the failed attempt at fusion. The clearest example of cumbersome interstate coordination involves the dispute over the location of a new Berlin/Brandenburg International Airport. Berlin supports expanding the existing Schönefeld Airport just south of the city, whereas Brandenburg argues for building a new airport in Speerenberg, near the state capital of Potsdam. The protracted debate over the location of the airport is harming the entire region, since in the meantime other airports are building up experience and markets. Yet the common interest in building a new airport for the region has been over shadowed by the goal of securing its benefits primarily for either Berlin or Brandenburg.

A similar point of conflict between the two states involves Transrapid, a high-speed magnetic levitation train planned to connect Hamburg and Berlin. This highly politicized pilot project offers clear benefits for both cities, since it will be funded entirely by a combination of private-sector and federal contributions. However, the states through which the train line will pass (Schleswig-Holstein, Mecklenburg-Vorpommern, and Brandenburg) will bear the brunt of the Transrapid infrastructure while receiving few benefits from the high-speed rail service. Mecklenburg-Vorpommern has successfully argued for a station in Schwerin, the state capital, and hopes to provide workers for the construction of the elevated rail line. If Brandenburg begins pressuring for similar benefits, the already troubled project could face even more political difficulties. Brandenburg may seek a Transrapid terminal south of Berlin, which would complicate Berlin's effort to site the terminal at Lehrter Bahnhof in the city center, the future site of Germany's federal government offices. Each point of contention at the regional level creates more frustration on the part of the federal government and Transrapid investors.

On a more hopeful note, an interstate agency, the Berlin/Brandenburg Transit Coordinating Council (*Verkehrsverbund Berlin-Brandenburg*), will continue its work to coordinate transit service throughout the region. Despite the failed political union between the two states, the *Verkehrsverbund* was officially founded on December 30, 1996. The goal of the council is to reduce the number of trips taken by automobile (which increased dramatically in the region after 1989) by providing higher-quality and better coordinated public transit service. In Berlin and Brandenburg, several regional transit agencies and the Deutsche Bahn AG (national rail service) operate simultaneously (see Table 7.4).

New European Union regulations require that transit providers throughout Europe be allowed to bid on providing public transit service in Germany.[21] In addition, states and cities with political and financial responsibility for transit services must be clearly separate from the companies that provide such services. A 1996 German law also specifies that the organization of public transit service is the responsibility of the German states, which can delegate authority to cities or transit coordinating councils.[22] The *Verkehrsverbund* will assume responsibility for all contracts with transit agencies providing regionally significant service, thereby coordinating transit service in the region. The council also will establish a uniform system of fares and fare instruments, service standards, and marketing.

The process of establishing the *Verkehrsverbund* and the agency's day-to-day work have been tougher than expected.[23] The substantive work of the council has been complicated by political tensions lingering from the

TABLE 7.4   Total Transit Trips in the Berlin/Brandenburg Region

	Berlin	Brandenburg
Trips per day	3.7 million	1.3 million
Trips per year	1.1 billion	0.4 billion

Averag Length of Passenger Trips in the Berlin/Brandenburg Region

Mode of Travel	Average Length of Passenger Trips
Regional Train (Regionalbahn)	36.0 km
Urban Train (S-Bahn)	1.5 km
Subway (U-Bahn)	5.6 km
Urban Bus (Stadtbus)	3.8 km
Regional Bus (Regionalbus)	8.0 km

Source: Konrad Lorenzen, "Der neue Verkehrsverbund für Berlin und Brandenburg," *Der Nahverkehr*, 3/97, pp. 18–21.

failed merger of Berlin and Brandenburg. Serious challenges to transit coordination include the need to unify state-specific transit requirements, including differing fare and financing systems. For example, Brandenburg supports transit providers by using federal-designated money to purchase transit equipment. Berlin, in contrast, uses other sources of funding to purchase equipment, allocating federal money only to expand the network of U-Bahn, S-Bahn, and streetcar service.[24]

Adding to interstate tensions is an increased nationwide emphasis on cost-effective transit service.[25] For example, the national rail-service provider, Deutsche Bahn AG, is ending service on several rail lines in Brandenburg where ridership is far too low to provide even minimal economic returns. The most utilized services, and hence those that should receive highest funding and management priority, tend to be those located entirely in, or that start or end in, Berlin. But Brandenburgers are reluctant to support a regional transit network focused on Berlin. Although agreement about the importance of regionally coordinated transit is widespread, arguments about how best to provide and finance transit service will become increasingly heated in an atmosphere in which Berlin and Brandenburg are competing for resources.

Conclusion

In contrast to the murky debates about the unification of Berlin and Brandenburg before the referendum, press coverage in the aftermath of the vote has clearly described the challenges that the continued separate existence of the two states will entail. In many respects, regional planning issues will continue to be addressed in much the same way as in the past. Battles over physical development will be fought at a local level, city by city, as each tries to capture beneficial economic growth. Controversial issues, or cases in which cities or developers attempt to bypass regional planning guidelines, will rise to a higher and more contentious political level. Regional planners, for their part, will be caught in the middle, striving to mitigate tensions and ensure that the worst development mistakes are avoided.

The biggest problem for Berlin and Brandenburg is that they will be forced to compete both with each other and with other German states for investment, new jobs, and financial support. The economic outlook for the two states is gloomy, suggesting that competition between them is only likely to increase.[26] While political coordination of services still receives much lip service, it will have almost no hope of success in an atmosphere of financial hardship and competition.

The most unfortunate outcome of the failed state fusion, however, is the conservatism and lack of innovative spirit it reflects. Instead of taking the initiative to modernize the federal system, Brandenburgers and East Berliners refused to be "guinea pigs" for the West Germans.[27] While federalism theoretically allows regional differences to thrive and creates the framework for healthy democracy, the disadvantages of the system are increasingly apparent. German states, now faced with competition from other regions in Europe, are often too small to compete effectively and can survive only through subsidies from wealthier states. Investors are frustrated when forced to deal with different regulations in every state and with the inconvenience and inefficiency that state borders can cause. According to *Der Spiegel*, "United Germany has 16 states, 16 Minister-Presidents, 157 Ministers, and 189 State Secretaries—if there was even a little more consideration for economic and political rationality, neither Saarland nor Bremen would exist."[28]

Economic and political rationality is certainly required as Germany struggles to meet the economic guidelines for a single European currency, to scale back a costly welfare state that is no longer sustainable, and to attract investors who can create employment opportunities. As one commentator pessimistically noted, "The backward development of the German republic, the gloomy economic situation and weak ability to compete—all of this has to do with the hardening and bureaucratization of our so very famous federal system."[29] Sadly, instead of leading the way to the future, Berlin and Brandenburg have shown just how detrimental the divisions among Germany's states can be, not only for the residents of those states but for the country as a whole.

Notes

1. "Berlin und Brandenburg bleiben weiter getrennt: Brandenburger lehnten ein gemeinsames Land ab, nur der West-Teil Berlins sagte 'Ja' zur Fusion," *Berliner Morgenpost*, no. 123, 6 May 1996, p. 1.

2. Arno Kappler and Adriane Grevel, eds., *Facts About Germany*, trans. Gerard Finan (Frankfurt-Main: Societäts-Verlag, 1993), p. 136.

3. Senatsverwaltung für Stadtentwicklung und Umweltschutz (Berlin), Referat Öffentlichkeitsarbeit, *Flächennutzungsplan Berlin*, 1994.

4. Kappler and Grevel, *Facts About Germany*, p. 156.

5. Heinz Sahner, "Regionale Kooperation im Verdichtungsraum Halle-Leipzig—Chancen, Probleme und Wege," *Kurzberichte aus Praxis und Forschung*, Diskussionspapier für ein gleichnamiges Forum des 27. Kongresses der Deutschen Gesellschaft für Soziologie "Gesellschaften im Umbruch," 4–7 April 1995, Universität Halle-Wittenberg.

6. Presse- und Informationsamt Berlin, *Berlin Kurzgefaßt*, 1995, p. 11.

7. "Das kleine, rote Preußen," *Der Spiegel*, no. 18, 29 April 1996, p. 52.

8. Ibid., p. 42.

9. Landesumweltamt Brandenburg, Referat Presse- und Öffentlichkeitsarbeit, *Brandenburg Regional §93*, Potsdam, 1994, p. 93.

10. Kappler and Grevel, *Facts About Germany*, p. 176.

11. "Das kleine, rote Preußen," p. 51.

12. Deutsches Institut für Wirtschaftsforschung (DIW), "Öffentliche Finanzen in Berlin-Brandenburg–Bringt ein gemeinsames Bundesland Vorteile?" *DIW Wochenbericht 38/93*, 23 September 1993, p. 522.

13. "Die haben früher auf uns geschossen," *Der Spiegel*, no. 18, 29 April 1996, p. 63.

14. Jörg Räder and Cornelia Poczka, *Berlin and Brandenburg: Planning for a Unified Future*, pamphlet distributed by the Senatsverwaltung für Stadtentwicklung und Umweltschutz, Berlin, and the Ministerium für Umwelt, Naturschutz und Raumordnung des Landes Brandenburg, 1996.

15. Ibid.

16. "Das kleine, rote Preußen," p. 44.

17. Ibid., p. 47.

18. Rüdiger Scharf, "Diepgen mahnt Brandenburg: Die Zeit des Rosinenpickens ist jetzt vorbei," *Berliner Morgenpost*, no. 125, 8 May 1996.

19. "Rundum vernünftig," *Der Spiegel*, no. 18, 29 April 1996, p. 50.

20. "Das Isses," *Der Spiegel*, no. 20, 13 May 1996, p. 93.

21. Editor's note: See Andrew Johnson, "Economic Reform: Restructuring the German Railway System," Chapter 5 of this volume.

22. VVG Gesellschaft zur Vorbereitung des Verkehrsverbundes Berlin/Brandenburg mbH, *Der Verkehrsverbund für Berlin und Brandenburg*, 2. Entwurf des Beirates in korrigierter Fassung, 5 December 1995, pp. 4–5.

23. Konrad Lorenzen, "Der neue Verkehrsbund für Berlin und Brandenburg," *Der Nahverkehr*, March 1997, pp. 18–21.

24. Klaus Kurpjuweit, "Verkehrsverbund wichtiger als Fusion: Auch bei zwei Ländern würde es weiter einen Fahrschein in Berlin und dem Umland geben," *Der Tagesspiegel*, no. 15612, 2 May 1996, p. 1.

25. Editor's note: See Johnson, Chapter 5, this volume.

26. "Rundum vernünftig," p. 50.

27. "Das Isses," p. 94.

28. "Das kleine, rote Preußen," p. 40.

29. Robert Leicht, "Der hohe Preis der Provinzialität," *Die Zeit*, no. 20, 10 May 1996, p. 1.

8

Eastern Europe or Eastern Germany:
The Choice for American Investors

CHRISTOPHER SYLVESTER

The ability to attract investment from outside Germany will be crucial in eastern Germany's efforts to promote economic growth and integrate successfully into Germany and the European Union. American investors, respected for their business sense and technological know-how as well as their substantial capital, can play a significant role in the economic development of eastern Germany. East European countries, however, also have recognized the importance of foreign direct investment to their goals of economic development and closer ties with western Europe. Because of the relatively small size of the economies of eastern Germany and the countries of eastern Europe as well as the prospect of open trade and future economic integration, many U.S. companies choose to invest in a single location in eastern Europe, some of which have proved adept at attracting U.S. investment. As a result, cities and regions in eastern Germany must make a considerable effort to convince U.S. businesses that they offer the ideal location for the investors' future activities.

This chapter examines the factors that lead U.S. businesses to choose to invest in eastern Germany or elsewhere in eastern Europe. To analyze more closely the broad issues that influence American investment decisions, this chapter presents a case study of two regions within eastern Germany and eastern Europe: the eastern German state of Thuringia, as a representative region of eastern Germany, and its toughest nearby competing region in eastern Europe, the Czech Republic. Obviously, investment conditions differ significantly between Thuringia and elsewhere in eastern Germany and between the Czech Republic and other east European countries; those differences are not addressed here. However, in general, the framework and conclusions of this comparative analysis and the lessons learned from the practical experiences of American investors can be applied effectively to both eastern Germany as a whole and larger regions of eastern Europe.

This chapter evaluates the advantages and disadvantages of investing in Thuringia versus the Czech Republic by analyzing nine key factors frequently considered by investors in selecting an investment location: macroeconomic stability, infrastructure, characteristics of the labor force, corporate tax rates, the banking system, investment incentives, market location, political stability, and the quality of life. In addition to analyzing these factors, this chapter includes interviews with managers of American firms that have chosen to invest in one or both of the areas under consideration. These interviews convincingly demonstrate various regional elements that provide advantages for particular types of investment. The resulting conclusion summarizes each area's comparative strengths and weaknesses in each of the nine categories listed above as well as the opportunities and problems experienced by these selected American companies.

Analysis of Key Investment Factors
Frequently Considered by U.S. Investors

Macroeconomic Performance

The first factor commonly considered by U.S. investors is macroeconomic performance, including rates of growth, inflation, and unemployment as well as the government budget and balance of imports and exports. Generally, both Thuringia and the Czech Republic have shown an unexpectedly strong macroeconomic performance.

Thuringia's gross domestic product (GDP) grew 11.8 percent in 1994, but then slowed to 3 percent in 1996. The initial rapid growth occurred largely because of crucial transfers from western Germany that helped struggling companies and increased personal consumption. Initial growth also was boosted because a substantial number of companies made wise use of government-provided investment incentives. However, western Germany's transfer of approximately 5 percent of its GDP to eastern Germany caused the region's domestic demand to exceed its production by up to 100 percent. This occurred because a large portion of the transfer payments took the form of health and unemployment insurance, training, wage subsidies, subsidized loans, pension funds, and spending on infrastructure.[1] Although the amount of western transfers is declining, this striking economic dependency is still detrimental to the region's overall economic health.

As in all of eastern Germany, unemployment in Thuringia remains high. The official unemployment rate of 18.1 percent in June 1997 does not take into account forced early retirement and retraining programs, which affect an additional 10–15 percent of the working population. Unemployment persists at high rates for many reasons. First, the privatization scheme of the Treuhand (the German government agency charged with privatizing and restructuring the former GDR state-owned enterprises) was not ultimately as successful as had been hoped, as some large state-owned industries proved impossible to sell or revitalize at any price. Second, the full-employment policy of the GDR ensured many superfluous jobs that were not sustainable after the integration into a competitive economy. Third, Chancellor Helmut Kohl's generous election-year promises in 1990 produced mixed results for the region's economy. For example, the immediate convertibility of East German marks into deutsche marks at a ratio of one-to-one for many accounts and at two-to-one for the remainder caused inevitable damage; a more realistic figure would have been five-to-one. The guarantee of wage rates at a level of 70–80 percent of West German rates, with the promise of parity in the near future, ensured that wage levels would exceed productivity and caused the loss of many jobs in the short term. These past actions are still keenly felt in Thuringia and the rest of eastern Germany. In addition, as addressed in the section on labor issues, Thuringia and eastern Germany's workers remain expensive to hire and maintain because of their comprehensive social benefits and shorter working hours.

In terms of inflation, the German central bank (Bundesbank) has ensured price stability throughout Germany. Thuringia and the rest of Germany enjoyed a modest inflation rate of 1.7 percent in 1996, and this rate is projected to remain steady. In addition, Thuringia's state budget has improved from a debilitating DM 20 billion deficit in 1994 to a manageable deficit of DM 2.5 billion in 1996.

After stunningly successful macroeconomic results in the first years of its transition, the Czech Republic has recently lost considerable ground in comparison to eastern Germany and other eastern European countries. Conditions have changed since late 1994, when Karl Dyba, the Czech minister of economics, confidently commented, "We are listed among the emerging markets. Forget it. . . . We have already emerged."[2] However, the government appears to have grasped the necessity of imposing needed structural changes and reforming regulation over the capital markets in order to stabilize the situation. In addition, the Czech Republic's overall performance since 1993 has still been solid and should not be discounted despite the earlier economic difficulties. It is not yet clear whether the Czech Republic's economic difficulties in the mid-1990s are temporary or whether they will continue.

The Czech economic situation deteriorated largely because of the lack of thorough structural reform of industry, government inefficiency and corruption, and the lack of needed reforms in the capital markets. As a result of declining economic performance and diminished investor confidence, the Czech government was forced to devalue its currency, the crown, and introduce austerity measures. Structural inefficiencies led to lower labor productivity and unemployment rose from 3.5 percent in 1996 to 3.8 percent in 1997 and was expected to increase further. The growth of GDP was expected to decline to 2–3 percent in 1997 from 4.4 percent in 1996.

The Czech Republic's federal budget, after running a surplus in 1995, fell into a deficit of 9.4 billion crowns (equivalent to approximately $300 million) in May 1997.[3] The budget surplus through 1995 was largely due to the "velvet divorce" with Slovakia. Slovakia, a less developed and heavily subsidized region of the former Czechoslovakia, provided a market for goods produced in the Czech region but was a considerable drain on the government's financial resources.[4]

Among these discouraging statistics, there also are some grounds for optimism. For example, the inflation rate declined steadily from its peak of 20.8 percent in 1993 to 8.0 percent in 1997. Because of the devaluation of the crown and the implementation of reforms, the Czech Republic's trade and current account deficits were forecast to shrink in 1998, while industrial output was forecast to rise. The federal budget deficit also was expected to decline. Under increasing pressure from concerned citizens, the government was expected to take tougher measures to restructure the economy and regulate capital markets. It remains to be seen, however, whether these measures will put the Czech Republic on the road to recovery.

Thus, both Thuringia and the Czech Republic have their strengths and weaknesses in terms of macroeconomic performance. Thuringia has avoided the volatility of the Czech economic performance, and current data and recent trends in Thuringia project a possible long-term improvement in macroeconomic performance. The current trend is less clear in the Czech Republic, despite its remarkable success in the early 1990s. Investors must decide which macroeconomic conditions are the most suitable for the particular business in question.

Infrastructure

The second factor concerns available infrastructure, including utilities, transport, and communications. With respect to infrastructure, both regions have shown remarkable improvement since 1989.

Thuringia has a reliable, federally supported energy system that provides energy at approximately twice the cost of energy in the United States. The high cost results mainly from poor natural resources and the political reluctance to use nuclear power because of antinuclear sentiment among the German population. In the Czech Republic, energy costs are regulated by the state agency Cez, which has kept overall costs reasonable, although corporations must pay higher rates than residents.[5] The Czech Republic, not burdened with political opposition to nuclear power, is building a new nuclear facility to complement the plant currently operating in southern Moravia.[6]

Thuringia's transportation infrastructure has benefited from investment of more than DM 60 billion by the federal government for the development of the transportation network of the new German states.[7] This has allowed the modernization of an already efficient train system and the construction and expansion of federal highways linking Thuringia with all of Europe. Thuringia's dense network of roads is already approaching West German standards, with construction and renovation of highways continuing. The high-speed Intercity Express (ICE) train routes will soon reduce travel time from Thuringia's capital city, Erfurt, to either Berlin or Munich to two hours and even less for the westward route to Frankfurt. In addition, a logistics and distribution center is being constructed to the east of Erfurt, designed to support the combined supply traffic of rail and road with an on-site freight center and haulage park. A leading American package delivery service, United Parcel Service (UPS), has established a branch office in the nearby city of Arnstadt to take advantage of this developing infrastructure. Thuringia's main airport at Erfurt is being expanded to accommodate jets of all sizes. It is used by charter airlines primarily for vacation excursions and by Lufthansa and other carriers for business connections with the larger cities of western Germany. Even after its expansion is completed, it will continue to serve primarily as a connecting airport to larger hubs.

In comparison to Thuringia's rapid improvement of its transport infrastructure, the Czech Republic is lacking in railway and airport facilities. Although the Czech Republic has a high railway density, Thuringia's system is more comprehensive and already capable of higher speeds. For example, only 22 percent of the routes in the Czech Republic's rail network can support trains traveling at 120 kilometers per hour (kph). A few selected international routes are likely to be able to support speeds up to 160 kph by the year 2000.[8] By comparison, the ICE trains in Thuringia will be able to reach speeds of up to 250 kph. The Czech Republic has four international airports, but their technical base is characterized as "adequate but lagging behind European standards, particularly in facilities available in the terminal and commercial infrastructure."[9] The

Prague airport is a notable exception after a 1997 expansion that has enabled it to accommodate nearly 5 million passengers a year. In the area of ground transport, the Czech Republic's existing road network is classified as "adequate in density but not in quality."[10] In an effort to counteract this weakness, the Czech government approved a comprehensive program to accelerate highway construction in November 1993. This 12-year program will provide for the completion of 987 kilometers of new highways linked to major European networks.[11] Despite these ambitious plans, the Czech Republic cannot compete with Thuringia's highly developed and rapidly expanding rail and road network in terms of density or quality.

Both Thuringia and the Czech Republic require vast improvement with respect to telecommunications infrastructure. Once again, heavy spending by the German government has given Thuringia an advantage over the Czech Republic. From 1990 to 1997, the German Post Office (Deutsche Bundespost) invested more than DM 70 billion in the new states, mainly through its formerly wholly owned telecommunications company, Deutsche Telekom. This successful program, called "Telekom 2000," has already resulted in the installation of more than 5 million new telephones, thus providing more than 350 telephones for every 1,000 inhabitants. This figure is rapidly nearing the West German level of 500 telephones per 1,000 inhabitants. With the ongoing installation of fiber-optic cables and the digitalization of the system, Deutsche Telekom is laying the groundwork for future advances such as visual telecommunications and high-definition television (HDTV).[12] Patricia Ames, director of foreign investments at the Economic Development Corporation of Thuringia, notes that this recent investment is leading to an interesting "imbalance in quality" favoring eastern Germany over western Germany. "If this trend continues," she adds, "the newly rebuilt eastern territories will quickly outpace all of western Europe's antiquated telecommunications systems."[13] In light of the current investment rate of almost DM 9 billion per year in telecommunications improvements as well as the recent privatization of Deutsche Telekom, Thuringia will soon have a technologically advanced telecommunications infrastructure offering increasingly affordable rates.

The Czech Republic also has invested in the future of its telecommunications network, although on a significantly smaller scale. Efforts have been hampered by the past practice of transferring telecommunications revenues to the general state budget rather than investing in further technological development. As a result, many telephone exchanges are seriously outdated, and a complete overhaul of the entire telecommunications system is necessary. In order to achieve a level of telecommunications infrastructure on a par with OECD members, the present density of lines will need to be increased from 17 to more than 35 per 100 people. The projected cost of this effort will be at least $ 4.5 billion. To accomplish these goals, the government hopes to duplicate the success of its general privatization program, which involved the distribution of vouchers among the population, with a similar effort involving the establishment of the SPT Telecom Company.[14] SPT Telecom's goal is to increase the number of telephone installations by 35–40 percent, with 75 percent of the network digitized, and to add 70,000 data stations and 170,000 public radio telephone stations. This effort received a substantial boost with the acquisition of a share of SPT Telecom by a Dutch/Swiss consortium in July 1995. This group is expected to invest approximately $131 million through 2000 in an effort to modernize the Czech telecommunications system. Bolstered by this significant new partner, SPT Telecom plans to install about 1.5 million new telephone lines through 1998 with a targeted penetration of 370 lines per 1,000 inhabitants.[15]

Despite the Czech Republic's efforts, Thuringia's infrastructure is, on average, more modern and dependable. Thuringia owes this great advantage to the substantial level of financial support from western Germany. The Czech Republic does, however, have one large advantage in terms of more affordable energy costs. Furthermore, while not on a par with the infrastructure in Thuringia, the Czech Republic's infrastructure is superior to that of other eastern European countries.

Labor Costs and Quality

The third factor concerns the labor force in general, including labor issues such as wage rates, indirect labor costs, worker training and quality, and labor productivity.

The general labor force in Thuringia has many qualities. An extensive apprentice and training system, considered among the world's finest, ensures that workers receive exhaustive schooling in both the theoretical and practical aspects of a position before they are fully employed. In Thuringia, 66 percent of the overall workforce are considered skilled workers, with 15 percent possessing a technical or university degree. The myth of East German workers' poor work ethic and unwillingness to take initiative is belied by the experience of western managers when seeking to retrain these workers. Many comment that a substantial number of East German workers already have the basic skills needed to operate machinery and perform related responsibilities and were able to quickly adapt to the use of more high-tech machinery. Their innovation was shaped by years of working with a shortage of replacement parts and technologically unsophisticated equipment, thus forcing them to find other ways to accomplish tasks. In addition, the East German workers quickly became members in the large western-based unions, ensuring stable labor relations albeit at the cost of high wage and benefit rates. The productivity of the average Thuringian worker is still at a lower level than the average West German worker, although it is steadily rising.

Thuringia's labor force also is characterized by the negative aspects of German labor in general, including high wages (although still only 70–80 percent of West German wage rates) and indirect labor costs. In January 1997, the monthly per-capita wage rate for industry in Thuringia was DM 17,300 (approximately $10,000). However, wages are still high compared to worker productivity, causing high per-unit labor costs. In addition, workers generally enjoy relatively short workweeks (on average, 37.5 to 40 hours) and long vacation and holiday periods (39 days as compared to 30 in the Czech Republic).[16] As a consequence of this imbalance, some firms have endured heavy losses and have been forced to lay off overpriced workers.[17]

The Czech Republic also can boast a highly educated and skilled workforce ranked among the best in eastern Europe. As Kathy Kriger, acting commercial attaché at the U.S. embassy in Prague, accurately describes it, the Czech Republic is "a nation of engineers" with more than 50 percent of university graduates receiving degrees in engineering.[18] Trade unions are generally cooperative with management, with only a minimum of working days lost to labor strikes each year. In addition, a Coopers & Lybrand study found high levels of motivation among the Czech workforce. In contrast to the short German workweek, Coopers & Lybrand found that professional and upper management consistently worked more than 50 hours, sales representatives and technicians averaged 50–70 hours, and in-house support staff averaged 45–55 hours a week.[19] In the Czech Republic, as in Thuringia, there are many ambitious programs designed to enhance technical, management, and English-language skills. In a comparison of apprentice and training programs, however, the Czech system cannot yet compete with Thuringia's western-tested system.

The average Czech worker costs only a fraction of the average worker in Thuringia. At the present average monthly wage of $374, even considering indirect labor costs, Czech workers cost on average less than 10 percent of the typical Thuringian worker.[20] While Thuringia's labor costs are fairly predictable, however, the future of such expenses in the Czech Republic is less certain. Since its establishment, the Czech government has been able to maintain a high level of employment through state support of inefficient industries and an implied social agreement to keep living costs low as long as the unions do not demand higher wages.[21] The initial generous government support of these industries is expected to end as it becomes too costly to maintain. This factor, combined with the increasing demand for more expensive western goods, is likely to lead to an increase in wage levels. The unanswerable question for potential investors is how far and how quickly the Czech Republic's wage levels will rise. Despite relatively low productivity and the short workweek, the quality of labor is still higher in Thuringia. The much admired apprentice program is still reaping many benefits for the local economy. The Thuringian worker is becoming steadily more productive, while proving willing to adapt and capable of operating the highest technology at West German levels. The Czech Republic can boast skilled workers who work longer hours but cannot achieve the same level of quality, especially in some high-tech fields. The lower average quality of Czech workers is offset to a considerable extent by the lower average wage rate; furthermore, the workmanship of the Czech labor force is improving steadily.

Corporate Tax Rates

A fourth factor considered by investors is applicable taxes, including the amount and structure of corporate taxes. Both Thuringia and the Czech Republic have corporate tax rates that are higher than U.S. rates (as do most other European jurisdictions). The German government passed the Business Location Improvement Act in 1993 in an effort to reform a tax system that has discouraged foreign investment. This legislation reduced the tax rate on retained corporate earnings from 50 percent to 45 percent and the rate on taxable income of foreign-owned companies from 46 percent to 42 percent.[22] This rate was later increased by 0.5 percent to cover *Pflegeversicherung*, which provides nursing insurance for the elderly and assistance for handicapped workers.[23] In comparison, the Czech Republic's corporate income tax was reduced from 45 percent in 1992 to 39 percent in 1997 and is expected to be reduced further to 30 percent by 2000.[24] Investors in both Thuringia and the Czech Republic also must factor in the costs of social benefits for workers, which Erik Best of the American Chamber of Commerce in Prague, describes as "the tax nobody wants to talk about."[25] As explained in the discussion of the labor force, the cost of social benefits in Thuringia is higher than in the Czech Republic. Overall, the Czech Republic thus offers a more favorable tax climate than Thuringia.

Banking System

A fifth factor considered by foreign investors is the local banking system. Thuringia has adopted the banking system of western Germany with all its corresponding strengths and weaknesses. The German system distinguishes itself from its American counterpart in the banks' level of participation in the management of the companies to which they lend. Ideally, bank participation on the supervisory board of a company permits the bank to assess the borrowing firm on the basis of more individual factors. This in turn has caused banks to lend proportionately higher amounts than in other countries, resulting in greater reliance by German companies on debt than equity to meet their financial requirements, as well as banks' greater interest in the long-term success of their corporate clients. This model developed in contrast to the liberal Anglo-American system traditionally characterized by impersonal, short-term financing.[26] The benefits of the German system are clear: An emphasis on long-term development and a loose partnership between borrower and lender have assured large firms of funding for long-term projects. The system, however, also encourages banks to concentrate on their larger, well-established customers. The participation of bank officials in the supervisory boards of companies can lead to "sweetheart" financing agreements that Americans might consider unethical conflicts of interest. Moreover, such participation can result in negligent oversight of loan terms and insufficient review of a favored customer's accounting and business practices. Small and medium-sized companies often find it difficult to obtain credit from risk-averse banks, which remain committed and secure with their giant corporate partners. German banks have proved particularly cautious in granting credit to East German entrepreneurs and companies. Even larger, well-known East German companies have had difficulty in securing funding because of pressure placed on banks by their western corporate customers, who want to thwart the development of future competition in East Germany.[27] This tight credit has stifled innovation not only in Thuringia but throughout Germany, by limiting overall research and development outlays and hindering the actions of creative but underfunded small and medium-sized companies.

The German banking system has come under increasing pressure for reform since the Schneider real estate scandal, which involved an allegedly fraudulent bankruptcy in 1994.[28] This scandal highlighted the potential for a disastrous outcome when banks do not scrutinize a favored customer's business operations with sufficient care. The opposition Social Democrats introduced legislation to limit banks' shareholdings in key industrial companies to 5 percent of total equity to prevent conflicts of interest. In addition, a large amount of foreign capital is required to finance the huge privatizations of Deutsche Telekom and other formerly state-owned firms. To attract this needed outside investment, banks are being pressured to adopt more Anglo-American-style transparent accounting approaches and corporate governance techniques, in contrast to the secretive ties that currently exist between large corporations and their financial institutions.[29] At present, however, it is impossible to say when reform might occur and how extensive such reform might be.

In summary, large, well-established American companies will find little difficulty obtaining credit in Germany. However, smaller companies with higher inherent risks will find serious impediments to securing sufficient credit.

The banking system in the Czech Republic is still developing. It has been dominated thus far by foreign banks, which can offer more efficient and secure services than can domestic banks. The development of a domestic banking industry was delayed by the bankruptcy of three large domestic banks in 1994, which prompted the Czech National Bank (CNB) to suspend issuance of new licenses while it audited the entire system.[30] Czech banks also have impeded investment by their flawed lending practices. Overly cautious because of past bad loans, many Czech banks have fixed wide spreads between their borrowing and lending rates and have been hesitant to approve new long-term loans. These actions have caused investors to borrow from foreign banks, which has resulted in an inflow of foreign capital. Borrowing from a foreign bank, however, leaves an investor particularly exposed to inflation or exchange-rate fluctuations, which could make exports more costly and thus reduce the investor's foreign currency earnings.[31]

The Czech banking system also is beset by other institutional problems. For example, the biggest Czech banks control the largest investment funds, which in turn hold substantial equity positions in various companies as a result of the voucher privatization campaign. This dominance by the banks has caused the stock market to develop slowly and with little market regulation, and could lead to conflicts of interest similar to those experienced in Germany. Richard Salzman, the chairman of the largest Czech bank, Komercni Banka, and director of the Prague stock exchange, sums it up as follows: "We speak English, we take advice from Americans, but look at the map. We are going towards the German system."[32]

Thus, the banking systems in both Thuringia and the Czech Republic present impediments to obtaining local sources of capital. The Thuringian banking system, despite its problems, is probably better understood and is moving toward reform. The Czech Republic's banking system has the advantages and disadvantages of novelty, but it seems to be developing many of the same problems that hamper the German system. Therefore, the German banking system, while presenting difficulties for small and medium-sized American businesses, also may offer investors more reason for long-term optimism.

Investment Incentives

An important factor considered by foreign investors is investment incentives, including direct subsidies, loans on favorable terms, tax breaks, and other inducements to investment. The Czech Republic offers no incentive packages to either domestic or foreign investors. Václav Raska of CzechInvest explained that the "area's political and economic stability are incentive enough" for investors.[33]

In contrast, American firms investing in Thuringia can take advantage of a variety of incentives from state and federal sources. The federal government and all East German states offer generous incentive packages to manufacturing firms that will create employment. For example, the federal government offers a promotional program that provides for a grant of 20 percent or more of the initial investment in the East German states. If the number of employment positions created is substantial, this figure can be raised. Under certain circumstances, a further "enlarged investment bonus" can cover up to 10 percent of expenditures on the purchase of new equipment (movable assets) and buildings. In addition, it may be possible to qualify for a separate 15 percent bonus grant for the renovation of old factories if it will lead to a corresponding increase in employment. Investment in Thuringia and the other new states also is promoted by a special depreciation allowance, which allows for a 50 percent tax write-off on the purchase and production costs of new equipment within the first five years of investment. As a result, although the Commission of the European Communities generally limits investment subsidies to a total of 35 percent of the total investment,[34] under certain circumstances these grant and tax savings can amount to as much as 40–50 percent of the original investment.

In addition to these incentives, various loan programs offer inexpensive credit. Interest rates for the European Recovery Program (ERP) and the Kreditanstalt für Wiederaufbau (Reconstruction Loan Corporation) funds at this writing were 6 percent a year within a twenty-year time frame. The credits for the ERP program offer a five-year grace period and an overall payback time of up to twenty years. These conditions are specifically designed to assist small companies. The ERP program, which consists of the remnants of the original $1.5 billion in Marshall Plan aid given to West Germany after World War II, compounded over forty years, has provided more than $26 billion in credit to investors since 1990 and continues to spur the economic recovery of the area. Various other state-supported incentives for R&D exist, and the hiring of women, the disabled, and apprentices is encouraged. Patricia Ames stresses that this generous incentive system provides the investor "with more financial assistance than anywhere else within the European Union." She explains further that the added benefits of a stable currency and political system combined with this state support result in "an investment area with a one-two punch unparalleled in Europe."[35]

Despite the benefits of this extensive incentive system, there also is a negative side. The sheer number of separate programs available (roughly 670 programs of all types, at last count) can lead to confusion. Extensive subsidies can lead to too much dependency on the state and federal governments for financial assistance. Moreover, some of the more generous programs for investment in the new states have been extended, but there is uncertainty as to how long the federal and state governments will continue to supply such largess. Although generous incentives greater than those offered in western Germany should remain, the level of extra support for the new state of Thuringia has already peaked.

Customer and Market Location

An important consideration is location of a proposed investment with respect to the customers and markets to be served. Positioned in the geographic center of Europe, both Thuringia and the Czech Republic offer favorable locations for an American company. Both regions maintain extensive sales networks and contacts with the former members of the Council for Mutual Economic Assistance (CMEA) in eastern Europe and, most importantly, the former Soviet Union. Inhabitants of both areas have an impressive level of Russian-language ability, which can prove an important asset for companies desiring to gain access to this large market.

Thuringia, however, also offers the important advantage of being located in a member of the 15-member European Union (EU)—which offers guaranteed access to a European customer base of more than 300 million relatively wealthy consumers. The Czech Republic has a free-trade agreement with the EU and may be admitted to the EU in the near future, but this cannot be assumed. Because Thuringia is a part of an EU member and has east European connections, it has certain advantages over the Czech Republic with respect to investment location.

Political Stability

While political stability is of greater concern in other parts of the world, investors in Thuringia and the Czech Republic must nevertheless still consider this factor in making investment decisions.

Few countries in the world have proved as politically stable as the Federal Republic of Germany. Forty years of relative economic prosperity in West Germany before unification taught important lessons about the need to preserve a democratic system designed to temper extremism and to provide the basis for a successful capitalist system. The years since unification have seen a marginal increase in political instability in both eastern and western Germany, with the largest destabilizing factor being the complex process of integrating the two parts of the country. Despite some loss of confidence in the political system caused by the strains of unification, Germany as a whole is in no danger of reverting to political extremism in either direction. Thuringia is no exception, as indicated by the more than 40 percent vote for the business-friendly Christian Democratic Union in the federal and state elections in October 1994. The voter participation rate was 75 percent, demonstrating the seriousness with which Thuringian residents take their new democratic system.

Since its establishment on January 1, 1993, the Czech Republic has been led by democratic reformers. Prime Minister Václav Klaus's Civic Democratic Party captured 30 percent of the parliamentary seats in the January 1996 election. His political allies, the Christian Democrats and Civic Democratic Alliance, form the rest of the governing coalition.[36] President Václav Havel, a former playwright and dissident, is the country's moral leader. The country has left-wing parties in opposition, although a resurrection of Socialist parties (as occurred in Poland) does not appear likely. The economic climate in the Czech Republic has made Klaus's hold on power less certain. In any case, the pro-business environment of the country appears secure regardless of which party is in power.

Possible complications could arise if Russia becomes more unstable or if other political crises arise. The Czech Republic has been preliminarily accepted into NATO, which helps ensure its security. Unlike eastern Germany, however, it does not have experienced democratic institutions to fallback on in case of any future domestic or foreign political turmoil. For these reasons, although the Czech Republic is functioning admirably as a democratic entity, Thuringia still has an advantage with respect to present and future political stability.

Quality of Life

Depending on the extent to which a U.S. investor intends to send U.S. personnel to manage or operate its foreign investment, the local quality of life can be an important consideration. Residing in either Thuringia or the Czech Republic would require some adjustment by American managers, since both regions lag behind western Europe in the use of English as a lingua franca.

Prague is a notable exception—this beautiful baroque city has already become a popular tourist destination. Prague also has a large, youthful American contingent (estimated at 40,000) that has enhanced the entertainment scene and improved the overall level of English-language ability. In addition, Prague offers world-class cultural offerings (opera, theater, museums, etc.) at substantially lower prices than Thuringia. It also offers all the consumer conveniences of Thuringia with more reasonable store hours. Thuringia's cities of Weimar, Jena, and Erfurt offer art and culture, but not on a comparable level with Prague. The areas outside Prague and the main population centers of Thuringia are not as appealing in cultural terms, although there is much natural beauty to be found in both regions. The main cities of Thuringia resemble western Germany with respect to providing an ample variety of consumer product offerings. Housing, however, is an important aspect of quality of life, and both regions are weak: The housing selection is limited and expensive. Both areas also have higher personal taxes overall than in the United States. In general, the overall standard of living is higher in Thuringia than in the Czech Republic, although many Americans find Prague superior in most aspects of quality of life.

Analysis of Specific Investments in Thuringia and the Czech Republic

In evaluating the location of a potential investment, a U.S. company must engage in a complex analysis specific to the planned activities and goals of the investment. These criteria serve as important reference guidelines but cannot address every company-specific detail that goes into a firm's project formulation. The investor must assign individual weights to each category according to the company's requirements and then make a company-specific decision. To demonstrate this process in practice, the following section presents a practical view of the decisionmaking process for investment locations by American companies doing business in either Thuringia or the Czech Republic, or both. By examining their decisionmaking process and the results of their respective ventures, other investors can gain better insight into which area might better meet their own business needs.

The experiences of four American companies that have recently invested in these regions provide concrete examples of the application of these criteria. Their experiences confirm the importance of defining carefully the specific objectives of any investment in the region and evaluating comparative investment conditions in light of those objectives.

The Case of Ralston-Bateria a.s.

In May 1991, the Eveready Battery Division of Ralston Purina Company formed a joint venture with the Czech battery manufacturer Bateria Slany a.s., creating a new company, Ralston-Bateria a.s., to produce plastic batteries for distribution in the central European market. Located in Slany, the Czech Republic, Ralston-Bateria a.s. is owned 66 percent by Eveready and 34 percent by Bateria Slany. Ralston-Bateria a.s. has more than 360 employees and annual sales revenues of $10 million. Eveready has invested more than $10 million to modernize the plant's equipment. Laurent Claizergues of Ralston Purina's European operations office in Geneva explained that Eveready's main reason for investing in the Czech Republic was that the best east European battery manufacturer, Bateria Slany, was located there.[37] Eveready sought entry into the classic alkaline battery market in central Europe, where customers still overwhelmingly use this type of battery.

Eveready has found the infrastructure satisfactory; it has been satisfied with energy costs and transport, but has been disappointed with the telecommunications infrastructure. It has been generally impressed with the quality of labor and low production costs, but has identified a considerable deficit in managerial skills, especially with respect to marketing and services. It has been surprised by the lack of labor mobility, particularly in management; not being located in Prague has hurt the firm's ability to recruit from the national talent pool. Claizergues called the Czech Republic's lack of government incentives "not very realistic" and described this shortcoming as a likely impediment to attracting future investment. Because of its partnership with the experienced management of Bateria Slany, Eveready did not encounter any major problems with the government bureaucracy or regulations. The company has had difficulties with the Czech Republic's confusing tax system, however, and local and federal officials cannot agree on the proper amount of taxes owed. The high tax rates and confusing regulations are likely to become more of a burden in the future. Eveready does not rely on the local banking system, preferring instead to obtain 95 percent of the necessary financing from foreign banks. The housing situation for foreign managers was described simply as a "nightmare."

Claizergues stressed the importance to potential investors of having a good internal organization, especially talented marketing staff, and remarked on the lack of trained local personnel. Although the joint venture has been relatively successful, Claizergues recommended that investors consider an outright acquisition. Eveready experienced confusion when it tried to reach decisions jointly with its local partner because of Bateria Slany's unclear ownership and management structure (including the degree of control exercised by investment funds that hold a portion of the outstanding shares). He concluded that Thuringia would be a preferable location if a company desired to establish a plant to supply the entire European market. On the other hand, if a company is seeking to use a local company's existing distribution network to focus on central Europe, it would be better served by investing in a facility in the Czech Republic.

The Case of Ivax Corporation

In July 1994, the Miami-based Ivax Corporation, a large multinational corporation involved in the pharmaceutical industry, spent $12 million to acquire 66 percent of the shares of Galena a.s., a 110-year-old pharmaceutical company in Opava, the Czech Republic. Stephen Lukas, vice president of business development for Ivax Corporation in eastern Europe, stated that in forming a joint venture in the Czech Republic, Ivax was looking for "a door into the former COMECON [CMEA] area."[38] He explained that Ivax has benefitted from the product recognition and distribution network of Galena a.s. Since its original investment in 1994, Ivax has invested over $35 million in Galena's infrastructure and operations and has increased its ownership stake to 74 percent.

Interestingly, Ivax, through its subsidiary Norton Gelkaps Gelatine Kapsel Produktion GmbH, also has taken advantage of low real estate prices, government incentives, and a good central location to build a new plant in Falkenhagen, a town in the eastern German state of Brandenburg, for the production of soft gelatin capsules. According to Mr. Lukas, Claus Winkler, the managing director of Gelkaps, summed up the benefits of the firm's location in Falkenhagen in a company statement reporting, "Our customers—the European pharmaceutical industry—are well within reach, logistics are great, and the government has rolled out the red carpet for us. We received our building permit very quickly and in a non-bureaucratic way, and the land price is very competitive considering that everything is at an ultramodern level." Gelkaps' state-of-the-art facility will supply the German and west European market with this special pharmaceutical product.

Lukas said that Ivax has been pleased with its operations in both the Czech Republic and eastern Germany. Transportation infrastructure has been good at both locations, although the telecommunications system has been problematic in Brandenburg and worse in Prague. He characterized the energy costs in Brandenburg as excessive. Ivax considers the tax rates in both locations high, although such rates were expected. Both locations are financed primarily internally through parent company resources. Ivax has been pleased with the quality of labor in both locations. Although Lukas noted that Ivax's labor costs in Prague are only 10 percent of those in Brandenburg, he estimates that labor costs are increasing 15–20 percent a year in the Czech Republic and will be roughly even by 2003. He also stressed the importance of training managers in Western business management; Ivax's schooling takes place mostly in the United States, Britain, and Ireland, and is considered invaluable for educating eastern German and Czech managers.

The Case of Carpenter GmbH

In January 1994, Carpenter GmbH, a wholly owned subsidiary of the Richmond, Virginia–based Carpenter Company, a manufacturer of polyurethane products, began construction of a new polyurethane factory in Thuringia. Rolf Poetzsch, president of Carpenter GmbH, lists geographic location, a growing marketplace, and government incentives as the main reasons for Carpenter's decision to build a factory there.[39] Because of Carpenter's desire to supply the robust German market and the fact that the company distributes 70 percent of its product by costly air transport, the firm determined it was necessary to build a well-situated factory in Germany. More of Carpenter's important customers in the furniture, mattress, and other related industries are located in Germany than in central Europe at present. If this changed, however, Carpenter would be prepared to "go to the customer" and build a factory in central or eastern Europe as well. Poetzsch noted that this scenario may well occur in the future for Carpenter, since companies seem able to start with far less capital investment in the Czech Republic and produce a similar product at a lower cost.

In nearly every investment criterion, Carpenter's top management has found Thuringia predictable, and Carpenter has generally been satisfied with Thuringia as a business location. Poetzsch emphasized that high tax rates and high labor and operational costs are a trade-off that a company must accept to gain the other benefits of investing in Thuringia. Carpenter's chief executives have been pleased with the labor force with the exception of middle management, which is still weak in marketing and other management skills. Poetzsch noted that Carpenter does not have any American employees at its plant and that much of the top and middle management is composed of local recruits. This has inevitably caused growing pains, but it also has allowed the company to benefit from local experience and connections while increasing the overall pride of the workforce.

The Case of Lear Seating GmbH Co & KG

Lear Seating GmbH, a subsidiary of the Southfield, Michigan–based Lear Seating Corporation, a producer of seats for the automobile industry, invested $17.5 million in a greenfield investment in 1992 to build a seat-making factory in Eisenach, Thuringia. Ulrich Gante, controller of the Eisenach plant, cited several reasons for Lear Seating's investment: Their main customer, Opel, had established a large-scale operation there; the region offered a skilled labor pool with experience in the automotive industry; and federal and state sources offered excellent investment incentives. In his words, these subsidies "helped sway the decision" to build the plant in Thuringia.[40]

Gante has few complaints concerning Thuringia as an investment location. Lear Seating's management has been pleased with the skilled labor and good infrastructure of the region, as well as the steady business from Opel and other automotive producers. Since the plant must be close to its customers to be able to offer "just in time" deliveries, Lear Seating never seriously considered establishing a factory in the Czech Republic. Gante noted that transport costs from the Czech Republic to customers in Eisenach would offset any savings in labor costs. Carpenter's management regards Thuringia's labor costs as high, but says that the wage gap between Germany and eastern Europe is closing rapidly. Using experienced West German managers, Lear Seating has had no trouble obtaining sufficient financing, nor has the firm been impeded by the German bureaucracy. On the negative side, Gante identified the high tax rates in Germany as one of the biggest drawbacks to Lear Seating's investment. He concluded that both Thuringia and the Czech Republic offered investors benefits. He suggested that labor-intensive industries in particular could still thrive in the Czech Republic, whereas investors in high-tech industries such as microelectronics, optics, and automotive production would most likely be attracted by Thuringia's skilled labor pool.

Conclusion

As these investment examples illustrate, American investors can succeed in eastern Germany as well as in eastern Europe. Eastern Germany and eastern Europe are characterized by differing conditions, however, and each investor must evaluate the relative importance of various factors in deciding where to invest.

Eastern Germany has the advantage over the Czech Republic in terms of macroeconomics and political stability, although high unemployment is a major problem and growth has slowed. The Czech Republic has begun to lose some of its edge over its eastern European competitors in these areas, but its initial macroeconomic success and attention to its problems must also be considered by investors trying to discern overall trends. The quality of life is comparable in these two regions, although again other parts of eastern Europe may have somewhat lower standards. Labor skills may be somewhat higher in eastern Germany; labor costs are clearly much lower in eastern European countries, although the difference in labor costs appears to be narrowing. Trained and experienced management remains scarce in both regions. Corporate tax rates are perceived as high in both regions, especially in eastern Germany. The banking systems of Germany and eastern Europe are not attractive to small and medium-sized companies, and many investors rely on their own funds or foreign sources of financing.

Eastern Germany's generous investment incentives have played a significant role in winning American investors and give it an advantage over the Czech Republic. Other eastern European countries come closer to matching the generous investment incentives available in eastern Germany. In addition, eastern Germany's infrastructure grants, supported largely by funds from the federal government, give this region another advantage. The Czech Republic's infrastructure, while not up to East German standards, nevertheless is improving rapidly, but infrastructure development lags behind in other parts of eastern Europe.

The location of customers and markets has proved the most important factor in investment decisions. Many U.S. investors in eastern Germany have established wholly owned facilities there, often to supply local customers or markets. In contrast, many investors in the Czech Republic and elsewhere in eastern Europe have formed joint ventures with formerly state-owned companies that already possess established distribution networks there. Interestingly, although many companies initially invested in eastern Europe to gain entry into the former CMEA market there, investors appear to attach considerable importance to the prospect that these countries will eventually join the EU. The Czech Republic, Poland, and Hungary appear to be likely future members of the EU, although they may have to wait several years for admission. Other countries in eastern Europe probably will have a longer wait.

Thus, both eastern Germany and eastern Europe offer American investors a variety of profitable opportunities. As the experienced managers interviewed stressed, companies should be aware of the specific disadvantages of investing in these regions. Problems such as the lack of trained management present challenges for U.S. investors. However, thorough preparation and a solid investment plan suited to the advantages of either area increase considerably the chances for success. Although there are no guarantees in foreign business ventures, the results of the companies described here demonstrate clearly that well-planned investment projects can succeed in eastern Germany as well as eastern Europe.

Notes

1. Gene Epstein, "Inefficiency, Low Productivity Still Plague Subsidized East German Economy," *Barrons*, 14 March 1994, 43.

2. "The New Bohemians," *The Economist*, 22 October 1994, 23.

3. "Indicators of Monetary and Economic Developments in the Czech Republic," *Czech National Bank Monthly Bulletin*, May 1997.

4. Richard C. Morris, "Hong Kong of Europe," *Forbes*, 20 June , 1994, 70.

5. Interview with Erik Best, representative of American Chamber of Commerce in Prague, 10 June, 1995.

6. "Czech Republic Infrastructure," *CzechInvest Information Series*, no. 11/3 (30 July 1994).

7. *Rebuilding Eastern Germany: The Second Half of the Way* (Bonn: Press and Public Relations Office of the Federal Ministry of Economics, 1995), Annex 8.

8. *Doing Business in the Czech Republic* (Prague: PP Agency, Ministry of Industry & Trade of the Czech Republic, 1994), 118.

9. Ibid., 119.

10. Ibid.

11. "Czech Republic Infrastructure."

12. *Rebuilding Eastern Germany*.

13. Interview with Patricia Ames, director of foreign investments at the Economic Development Corporation, Thuringia, 15 July 1995.

14. *Doing Business in the Czech Republic*, 45.

15. "Czech Republic Country Profile," *CzechInvest Information Series*, no. 10/4 (May 1997).

16. Michael Zumwinkle, "Standort Deutschland: Can a Changing Germany Compete in the Changing World Market?" in A. Bradley Shingleton, Marian J. Gibbon, and Kathryn S. Mack, eds., *Dimensions of German Unification: Economic, Social and Legal Analysis* (Boulder: Westview Press, 1995), 77.

17. Epstein, "Inefficiency, Low Productivity," 43.

18. Interview with Kathy Kriger, acting commercial attaché at the U.S. Embassy to the Czech Republic, 10 May 1995.

19. "Labour and Social Policy," *CzechInvest Information Series*, no. 10/3 (29 June 1994).

20. Czech law states that all foreign companies have to pay 35 percent of their Czech employees' gross salaries into social security and health insurance funds. "Czech Republic Country Profile," *CzechInvest Information Series*, Factsheet no. 13 (January 1997).

21. "The New Bohemians," 24.

22. Zumwinkle, "Standort Deutschland," 78.

23. Dieter Lau, "German Taxes Are Approaching the Limit," *Wall Street Journal Europe*, 12 January 1995, 6.

24. "Czech Republic Country Profile."

25. Best interview.

26. Adam Posen, "Less Than a Universe of Difference: Evaluating the Reality of German Finance," in *Dimensions of German Unification*, 44, 50.

27. Ibid., 53.

28. Jürgen Schneider was one of the largest real estate investors in Germany in the early 1990s. Through the use of front companies and false information, he fraudulently overvalued certain real estate properties in order to obtain inflated loans on the properties. Deutsche Bank and other creditors ultimately lost approximately $4 billion due to these schemes. Schneider fled to the United States

after the fraud was discovered in 1994, but was extradited to Germany in 1995 to stand trial.

29. John Templeman, "Suddenly, Germans Love to Hate Their Banks," *Business Week*, 20 February,1995, 56.

30. "Licensed to Fail," *The Economist*, 9 July 1994, 80.

31. "The New Bohemians," 27.

32. Ibid.

33. Interview with Václav Raska, Joint Ventures Department of CzechInvest, 14 April 1995.

34. Commission of the European Communities, *XXIst Report on Competition Policy 1991*, at 170, 283 (1992).

35. Ames interview.

36. "Czech Republic Country Profile."

37. Information in this section was obtained from an interview with Laurent Claizergues from Ralston's European Operations Office in Geneva, 10 May, 1995.

38. Information in this section was obtained from an interview with Stephen Lukas, vice president of business development, Eastern Europe, for IVAX Corporation, 12 June, 1995.

39. Information in this section was obtained from an interview with Rolf Poetzsch, president of Carpenter GmbH, 17 July, 1995.

40. Information in this section was obtained from an interview with Ulrich Gante, controller of the Lear Seating Eisenach plant, 1 August, 1995.

PART FOUR

Germany in Transition:
Minority Rights in Germany

Introduction:
Minority Rights in Germany

JONATHAN B. TUCKER

Among the most contentious domestic policy issues in Germany today is the status of immigrants and residents of non-German ethnicity. Such individuals are generally referred to as "foreigners" (*Ausländer*) even if they have lived in Germany for generations. Although individuals of non-German ancestry number about 7.4 million, accounting for one in twelve people living in Germany and one in five babies born each year, the country's laws and political culture have not yet caught up with this demographic reality.

At the root of the problem is the fact that German citizenship law, unlike that of the United States, is based on ethnicity rather than place of birth. A "German" is defined legally not as someone born in Germany but, rather, someone born to ethnic German parents anywhere in the world. No routine procedure is available for non-Germans to become permanent residents and ultimately citizens. As a result, second- and third-generation "foreigners" who were born in Germany, speak fluent German, and identify themselves as German are denied the right to vote and exposed to pervasive discrimination.

Recruitment of "Guest Workers"

The current status of "foreigners" in Germany has its origins in the postwar economic boom that was accompanied by nearly full employment, creating a labor shortage for low-paying, undesirable jobs. This deficit was met by recruiting "guest workers" (*Gastarbeiter*) from poorer countries such as Italy, Spain, Greece, Turkey, Morocco, Portugal, Tunisia, and Yugoslavia. At the time, West German policymakers assumed that the foreign laborers would complete short-term contracts, save some money, and return home. Should additional manpower be required, new recruits would replace the departing ones.

The Federal Republic never translated this plan into law, however, and economic factors ultimately worked at cross-purposes. Businesses, which required dependable workers and sought to minimize the costs of retraining, ignored the government's return policy. German labor unions also preferred long-term contracts for foreign workers to avoid the creation of a two-tiered labor system. Thus, over the years, many *Gastarbeiter* became unintended immigrants. It was not until the economic downturn of 1973 that the German government moved to halt the influx of foreign labor. Even so, the existing *Gastarbeiter* were allowed to bring their families to Germany and put down economic and emotional roots.

Meanwhile, the expansion of the European Community (EC) to less developed countries such as Spain and Portugal transformed the composition of West Germany's immigrant population. Opportunities created by increased economic growth in EC member-states gave migrants from these countries an incentive to return home, so the number of Italian, Greek, and Spanish immigrants declined sharply. At the same time, the migrant communities from nonmembers of the EC, such as Turkey and Yugoslavia, continued to grow. Today, more than 2 million Turkish citizens live in Germany and their birthrate exceeds that of the native population.

Permanent "Foreigners"

Whereas immigrants to the United States typically become naturalized citizens and go on to raise assimilated American families, the descendants of migrant laborers who settled in Germany have remained—in both legal and social terms—permanent outsiders in their adopted home. More than 50 percent of the roughly 7.4 million non-native residents have lived in Germany for more than 15 years and include first-, second-, or third-generation offspring of *Gastarbeiter*. These individuals pay taxes and often identify themselves culturally as Germans, yet they can become German citizens only with great difficulty and cannot hold dual citizenship. The fact that Germany's restrictive naturalization policies prevent the vast majority of non-native residents from voting or participating in electoral politics constitutes a serious moral and political deficit for a democratic country.

At the same time that the German government has resisted granting citizenship to non-native residents, it has permitted a major influx of ethnic-German immigrants from eastern Europe and the former Soviet Union seeking to escape economic hardship and persecution because of their minority status. Many of the new immigrants are descendants of people who left Germany hundreds of years ago and have no German cultural identity except for a German name, yet they have been able to obtain residence permits and citizenship with relative ease. The dramatic contrast between the government's treatment of new ethnic-German immigrants and long-term "foreign" residents has sharpened the political debate over immigration and naturalization policy.

Miriam Aukerman argues in this section that Germany has become a de facto multicultural and multiethnic society even if it refuses to perceive itself as such and that the government's failure to develop an effective naturalization policy has deprived the German-born children and grandchildren of *Gastarbeiter* of the basic rights guaranteed to German citizens. The absence of a naturalization policy also has contributed to social intolerance and tension. Aukerman notes that when the state treats some members of the community as second-class residents, such as when police respond inadequately to harassment of "foreigners," this behavior tends to legitimate discriminatory behavior by others. Although a large majority of Germans oppose right-wing violence against immigrants, she writes, "the same people who are appalled by the torching of asylum seekers' hostels can accept or themselves engage in less violent forms of discrimination." Redefining Germanness by place of birth rather than blood, Aukerman contends, would encourage ordinary Germans to be more tolerant of minorities and reduce discrimination.

Similarly, Caroline Fredrickson points out that long-term "foreign" residents who lack German citizenship are often victims of discrimination in employment, a problem for which German law does not provide adequate remedies. Historically, German courts have declined to protect women and minorities from job discrimination by invoking the doctrine of "freedom of contract," which holds that people should be free to choose their contracting partners and determine the content of an agreement. Fredrickson shows, however, that this principle has been applied inconsistently. Indeed, German judges and legislators have abrogated "freedom of contract" in every area of labor law except an employer's right to refuse to hire women or minorities.

Fredrickson concludes that legal principle plays a minimal role in guiding German government intervention in the employment relationship and that lack of political power provides a better explanation for job discrimination. "Women are a weak interest group and minorities are rarely citizens in Germany and hence cannot vote," she contends, "whereas unions and working people have vigorous and powerful political organizations." Fredrickson's analysis suggests that only when foreign residents become citizens and acquire some political clout will they have a chance of overcoming discriminatory hiring practices.

The Naturalization Debate

Before the German federal elections in September 1998, proposals to reform the country's outdated citizenship law, which dates from 1913, sparked heated debates in the German parliament. The Social Democratic Party (SPD) and the Free Democratic Party (FDP) proposed that the criterion for German citizenship be changed from the "law of blood" to the "law of soil" to permit *Ausländer* born in Germany to be naturalized and foreigners who have lived in Germany for eight years or are married to a German national to be granted dual citizenship. Yet the two dominant parties in the ruling coalition, the Christian Democratic Union (CDU) and the Bavarian-based Christian Social Union (CSU), opposed these reforms on the grounds that Germany is not a "country of immigrants." Right-wing parties such as the Republicans (*Die Republikaner*) and the German People's Party (*Deutsche Volkspartei*) went further, insisting that Germany is and must remain an "ethnic German state."

Prospects for a fundamental reform of the citizenship law improved with the election in September 1998 of an SPD-Green Party coalition government led by Chancellor Gerhard Schröder. The new government promised to grant automatic citizenship rights to all children born in Germany, as long as one parent is German-born or arrived before the age of 14 and has a residence permit. Other "foreigners" would be allowed to apply for German citizenship after eight years of residence rather that 15, and dual citizenship would be tolerated but not encouraged. In late February 1999, faced with a petition against citizenship reform signed by more than one million people and a defeat to the CDU in a state election, Schröder dropped his proposal for dual citizenship, but plans for a new immigration law remain.

Even if the German citizenship law is reformed, members of minority groups may still experience discrimination, and additional legal remedies will be required. Aukman discusses two approaches to protecting minority rights. The "Anglo-American model" exemplified in U.S. and British civil-rights legislation aims to provide equal treatment to individuals regardless of their particular distinguishing characteristics. In contrast, the "east European model" of legislation guarantees positive rights for minority groups that wish to preserve their distinctive identity, such as support for minority schools and cultural activities. Aukerman concludes that a hybrid approach is most suitable for Germany. Anti-discrimination legislation is needed to protect the basic rights of all persons, whether or not they belong to a recognized minority. But since descendants of immigrants may not have the option of assimilating into the dominant national culture, they may require positive minority rights as well.

9

Discrimination in Germany: A Call for Minority Rights

MIRIAM J. AUKERMAN

German society has yet to come to terms with two important social realities.[1] First, Germany is a multicultural society, even if it refuses to recognize itself as such. Second, people of different cultures living in Germany are subject to systematic discrimination. This chapter argues that the current situation is untenable and discusses the applicability of two different models for protecting minority rights in Germany.

The Language of the Debate

Immigration and discrimination are a reality in the Federal Republic of Germany, yet both issues are taboo. Chancellor Helmut Kohl epitomizes a widespread tendency when he refuses to term Germany a "country of immigration" (*Einwanderungsland*).[2] Yet Germany has in fact absorbed and largely assimilated large numbers of immigrants in its past, despite the myth that Germany was ethnically homogenous until the postwar arrival of "guest workers" (*Gastarbeiter*) in the west and the much smaller number of "contract workers" (*Vertragsarbeitnehmer*) in the east. By 1995, Germany had a foreign population of more than 7 million, or 8.8 percent of the population.[3] These numbers do not include those persons who are commonly called and treated as "foreigners" (*Ausländer*) because of their skin color or foreign heritage but who nevertheless have German citizenship. Including immigrants, ethnic German refugees, and deportees who fled eastern Europe and, before 1989, from the German Democratic Republic, scholars estimate that approximately one-quarter to one-third of the Federal Republic's current population are immigrants.[4]

The original assumption that *Gastarbeiter* were a temporary addition to the labor market in certain important areas (such as mining, steel, foundries, textiles, and the service industry) and would return home after several years is no longer valid. But the "illusion of return to the country of origin" (*Rückkehrillusion*) makes it more difficult to address the actual situation, not only for Germans but for *Ausländer* as well. Approximately 60 percent of *Ausländer* have lived in Germany for 10 years or more, and 25 percent for more than 20 years. For persons from the traditional countries of origin (*Anwerbeländer*), an average period of residence of 10 years or more is even higher: 66 percent of Turks, 72 percent of Italians, 76 percent of persons from the former Yugoslavia, and 87 percent of Spaniards.[5] Furthermore, approximately 70 percent of the children of *Ausländer* were born in Germany.[6]

Even conservatives such as Kohl, who in the past have exploited antiforeign sentiment with comments about the need to reduce the number of foreign "neighbors" (*Mitbürger*) and who continue to describe these persons as "those who have come" (*Zugewanderte*) as opposed to "those who have immigrated" (*Eingewanderte*), now admit that the former guest workers "belong as part of us."[7] While such statements implicitly recognize the permanent resettlement of the former *Gastarbeiter*, the term "immigration" (*Einwanderung*) nonetheless remains taboo. Legislation recognizing this de facto immigration, such as more liberal citizenship legislation or general immigration legislation that would provide a routine method for foreigners to become permanent residents and ultimately citizens, has yet to be passed. Although Germany has the highest level of inward-migration of any major European country, it has had the lowest naturalization rate.[8] Modest changes have been made to Germany's citizenship law in recent years, but the law (enacted in 1913) continues to be based on the *jus sanguinis* principle, in which citizenship is determined by German ethnicity. Although one in five babies is born to non-Germans, these children are not entitled to German citizenship even if their parents were themselves born in Germany.[9] While German citizenship can be obtained under certain circumstances through naturalization, this process is extraordinarily arduous and lengthy and hence is not widely used.

The percentage of the German population that is of non-German heritage will continue to grow. Politically and economically motivated migration from southern and eastern Europe (and beyond) will not stop until these areas become democratically stable and economically viable—developments that are not likely to occur in the near future. Moreover, the higher birthrates of *Ausländer* relative to ethnic Germans mean that an increasing percentage of the younger generation will have a non-German background.

That the debate about immigration, and the cultural plurality produced by it, lags behind social reality also can be seen in the inadequacies of the German language to describe the present situation. German lacks a word to describe German citizens or permanent residents of a different ethnic origin. The term "minority" (*Minderheit*), which in English describes all nondominant ethnic groups, is used by Germans only to describe Germany's recognized ethnic *Minderheiten*: Serbs, Danes, and Friesians. Because of the political imperative to restrict *Minderheit* status and the rights it entails to these groups, the government has carefully defined the term to exclude non-German minorities.[10]

Almost all persons of nondominant ethnicity, whether citizens, refugees, or longtime resident aliens, are described in popular usage as *Ausländer*, a term that properly connotes noncitizen or foreigner. The term is not typically applied to aliens from countries such as the United States or Japan, but is used in common parlance to include German citizens of a different ethnic origin. This usage of the term *Ausländer* reinforces the conceptual link between German ethnicity and German citizenship—the *jus sanguinis* principle—and denies the legitimacy of immigration by those who are not ethnically German. In contrast, the legitimacy of immigration or in German government terminology, "repatriation" of ethnic Germans from eastern Europe and the former Soviet Union (*Aussiedler*) is accepted, even though such persons may not speak German and often have a much poorer understanding of German society than *Ausländer*, a large number of whom have been born in Germany, speak fluent German, and have attended German schools.[11]

The terms used to describe individual ethnic groups also are instructive. In the United States, which has long considered itself a country of immigrants, individuals of a particular ethnicity or race frequently assume "hyphenated" or bicultural identities (e.g., German-American, African-American). In contrast, with the exception of the term "black-German" (*Schwarze-Deutsche*), which is used by Germans of African heritage to describe themselves, German terms refer exclusively to the ethnic group or country of origin (e.g., "*Türken*," not "*Deutsch-Türken*"). In contrast, ethnic-German *Aussiedler* have a hyphenated identity, such as "Russo-Germans" (*Rußland-Deutsche*), which recognizes their ties to two cultures simultaneously.

Discrimination as a Problem

In the current debate within Germany about increased legal protection for *Ausländer*, opponents employ three main arguments: (1) that the current legal regulation is adequate; (2) that discrimination is not a serious problem; and (3) that laws cannot be effective in combating discrimination. Each of these points is addressed below in turn.

The first argument—that the existing legal structure already prevents discrimination—rests primarily on provisions of the Basic Law, the constitutional framework of the Federal Republic:

> The dignity of man shall be inviolable. To respect and protect it shall be the duty of all state authority. (Article 1, para. 1)
> No one may be prejudiced or favored because of his sex, his parentage, his race, his language, his homeland and origin, his faith or his religious or political opinions. (Article 3, para. 3)[12]

While these articles in the Basic Law are of fundamental importance, they are limited in several crucial respects. First, neither article has been interpreted to apply to interactions between individuals and third parties, and both are typically limited to interactions between the individual and the state. Second, Article 3.3 has been interpreted to prohibit intentional discrimination by the state, but not de facto or indirect discrimination—as when state regulations unintentionally compromise religious observances. Third, while Article 3.3 forbids discrimination against foreigners because of their sex, parentage, race, language, homeland or origin, faith, or religious or political opinions, it does not prohibit discrimination against foreigners because they are not German citizens. Since most of those discriminated against do not have German citizenship, it can be difficult to prove that discrimination occurred on account of the individual's ethnicity or race as opposed to his or her foreign status.[13]

The second argument by opponents of increased legal protection for ethnic minorities is that discrimination is not a major problem in Germany. Substantive discussion of the issue is clouded by the attention paid by all sides in the debate to a single piece of evidence. While those seeking to prove the reality of discrimination point primarily to right-wing violence, those who deny the existence of a problem stress the low level of public support for such extremism, as well as the decline of xenophobic violence in recent years. Discrimination and violence are indeed linked to the extent that anti-*Ausländer* violence draws strength from the day-to-day treatment of *Ausländer* as second-class residents. Yet right-wing extremist violence should not be used reflexively as a measure of discrimination, even though such violence displays in its most brutal form the disrespect toward the human dignity of others that is the essence of discrimination.

The vast majority of Germans deplore the assaults on *Ausländer*, and hundreds of thousands of Germans have marched in demonstrations against extremist violence. Nevertheless, a considerable portion of this majority agrees that *Ausländer* represent a problem that needs to be solved, albeit by other means. In surveys taken in September 1991, 38 percent of western Germans and 21 percent of eastern Germans—34 percent of all Germans—could express understanding (*Verständnis*) for right-wing extremist activities. Positive responses dropped to 24 percent in a December 1991 repetition of the poll after the escalation of right-wing violence in October and November of that year, demonstrating that the majority of Germans were not endorsing violent methods of dealing with the *Ausländer* issue.[14] Yet measuring day-to-day discrimination by tracking right-wing violence is misleading because the same people who are appalled by the torching of asylum-seekers' hostels can accept or themselves engage in less violent forms of discrimination.

The link between discrimination and extremism is debilitating in political terms because it allows politicians to assume that measures against right-wing extremism, such as providing police with equipment and leadership training or organizing antiviolence programs for German youth, are a sufficient response to broader problems of discrimination. The October 1993 speech by Federal Minister Angela Merkel to B'nai B'rith is representative of such an elision. Merkel acknowledged the existence of "hostility to foreigners" (*Fremdenfeindlichkeit*) and right-wing extremist organizations and claimed that the government was taking a variety of steps in response. Yet all the measures she listed were designed to combat right-wing extremist organizations, not to counter discrimination.[15] Doing something against right-wing violence, which fortunately affects only a small number of persons directly, is quite different from taking measures against more insidious and widespread forms of inequity. Arguably, government measures to counter extremists are motivated more by concern about public perceptions, especially abroad, than by interest in improving the actual situation of *Ausländer*, which would require more far-reaching legislation. Whatever the motivation, Bonn's determination to stop the violence and avoid repeating the experience of Weimar is laudable. Nevertheless, as Douglas Klusmeyer has noted, "[if] we look too closely at Bonn through the lens of Weimar, we risk making Weimar the sole measure of Bonn . . . [and] all the problems facing the Federal Republic become viewed as mainly tests of its ability and resolve to preserve order at the expense of other dimensions to these problems."[16]

Instead of measuring discrimination merely in terms of antiforeign violence, one should examine more comprehensive information compiled through statistical incident recording and scientific research. Unfortunately, such information on discrimination is limited. Preliminary research and anecdotal evidence indicate that discrimination and racism are a considerable problem. One must distinguish, however, between the discrimination perpetrated by society generally and that embedded in legal and institutional structures. As noted above, Article 3.3 of the Basic Law does not permit German laws to discriminate on the basis of sex, parentage, race, language, homeland or origin, faith, or religious or political opinions, yet numerous laws distinguish on the basis of citizenship. Some important rights, such as freedom of movement, association, occupation, and speech, can be restricted when applied to foreigners.[17] As interpreted by the German Federal Constitutional Court, Article 4.1 of the Basic Law, which prohibits state interference in family life, does not prevent the state from keeping families separated by limiting the right to bring spouses, children, or parents into the Federal Republic. *Ausländer* who are not nationals of EU members, regardless of how long they have lived in Germany or whether they were born there, are required to obtain a work permit to be employed. Moreover, *Ausländer* can join the German civil service only in exceptional circumstances and have more limited rights to certain government benefits.[18]

Legal discrimination by the state reinforces and is reinforced by social discrimination. Certainly *Ausländer* themselves feel discriminated against, as shown in a 1991 study by the Cologne-based Institute for Social Research and Policy (*Institut für Sozialforschung und Gesellschaftspolitik*). Of the *Ausländer* surveyed, 70 percent reported having been " insulted or abused" (*beleidigt oder beschimpft*), 40 percent had been discriminated against in stores, and 20 percent had been physically attacked at least once. In contrast, only 12 percent reported job-related discrimination.[19] The limited research that has been done indicates that the perceptions of discrimination victims reflect real disadvantages. A 1989 study of industrial job opportunities in Berlin found that 59 percent of employers rejected equally qualified *Ausländer* in favor of German employees.[20] Similarly, unfavorable housing conditions reflect not only the lower incomes and larger families of *Ausländer* but also discrimination by landlords, many of whom openly advertise in newspapers for "Germans only." Hermann Korte notes that "all investigations establish unequivocally again and again that foreigners live under worse conditions but pay proportionately more rent than their German counterparts."[21] For example, a 1989 study showed that the average *Ausländer* had approximately half as much living space as the average German, even though for *Ausländer* the ability to bring spouses and children to Germany is conditioned on the possession of adequate living space.[22]

Discrimination by insurance companies is a particular problem. Advocates for *Ausländer* report that some companies have refused outright to provide even obligatory forms of insurance and that others exact surcharges from *Ausländer*. In one egregious 1993 case, an insurance company canceled the policy of a church group operating a home for refugees and ethnic German settlers from eastern Europe on the grounds that asylum homes presented a greater risk of arson attacks and theft.[23] Although a few antiracism advocates have tried to challenge such cases of discrimination under existing legislation, their general lack of success indicates the limits on the state's power to take measures against discrimination by nonstate parties such as private employers, restaurant owners, and landlords who discriminate on the basis of race or ethnic origin.[24]

Discrimination against and prejudice toward *Ausländer* have little to do with their actual number or their real impact on German society. Research in the East German states, where few *Ausländer* live, clearly demonstrates that foreigners are scapegoats for problems for which they are not responsible. A 1990 study by the Central Institute for Research on Youth in Leipzig found that even though only about 100,000 *Ausländer* lived in the former East Germany, 62 percent of the young men and 44 percent of the young women surveyed claimed that a reduction in the number of foreigners was an immediate necessity. When asked whom they thought of first under the term *Ausländer*, 48 percent responded "Turks," although no statistically significant number of Turks lived in the former East Germany at the time. Indeed, survey data indicate that residents of the East German state of Brandenburg believe that 30 percent of their state's population is foreign; in fact only 1.2 percent is.[25]

The third argument against stronger antidiscrimination legislation is that laws cannot be effective against racism. A further extension of this view is that the state not only cannot but should not tell people what to think. In fact, the experience of other countries shows that although laws do not stop discrimination completely, they sanction inappropriate behavior and can lead over time to profound changes in patterns of social and institutional relations. Minority protection laws do not criminalize thoughts but actions. At the same time, by expressing societal condemnation and requiring people to live in societies with less overt racism, laws can change opinions. Personal experience with integrated schools, workplaces, and neighborhoods often challenges old fears and prejudices. It is appropriate for governments to seek to influence public views, and indeed they cannot avoid doing so. The question is: what standards should a government promote?

The Necessity of Change

The present situation—widespread discrimination coupled with inadequate legal remedies—is economically, legally, and politically untenable over the long term, a fact increasingly recognized by German business and union leaders, civic activists, and politicians. Economically, Germany needs the workers of non-German backgrounds who are already there and will need even more such workers in the future. According to the calculations of the Rheinland-Westfalen Institute for Economic Research in Essen, foreign workers now contribute approximately DM 90 billion to Germany's gross national product and constitute a large portion of the workforce in certain critical industries.[26] *Ausländer* pay DM 57 billion a year in taxes and social security contributions while receiving only DM 16 billion in direct services.[27] Even more important, the high percentage of *Ausländer* in the labor force improves the demographic balance between those paying into the German pension system and those receiving benefits—a number that is increasing because of Germany's aging population and low birthrate. The roughly 616,000 Turkish workers greatly outnumber the 57,000 Turkish pensioners.[28] Furthermore, as an export-oriented country, Germany earns one-third of its income abroad and therefore has an economic incentive to maintain a positive image in foreign markets, which are increasingly prepared to evaluate products in terms of not only quality and price but perceptions of the society that produces them.

Legally and politically, the current system is being challenged. In a 1993 report, the United Nations committee overseeing the Convention on the Elimination of All Forms of Racial Discrimination expressed

> serious concern at the manifestations of xenophobia, anti-Semitism, racial discrimination and racial violence that have recently occurred in Germany. In spite of the Government's efforts to counteract and to prevent them, it appears that those manifestations are increasing and that the German political system has in many instances failed to provide effective protection to victims and potential victims of xenophobia and racial discrimination, as required by the Convention. . . . [T]aking into account that practices of racial discrimination in such areas as access to employment, housing and other rights . . . are not always effectively dealt with, the German authorities should give serious consideration to the enactment of a comprehensive antidiscrimination law.[29]

At a meeting in March 1997, the committee praised efforts by the German government to reduce right-wing violence and prevent discrimination but once again called for the enactment of a comprehensive antidiscrimination law. The committee also recommended that Germany consider ways in which benefits extended to traditional *Minderheiten* could be granted to all ethnic groups in the Federal Republic.[30]

Effects of European Integration

European integration will have far-reaching consequences for German immigration and citizenship law, with respect not only to citizens of the European Union (EU) but also to third-country nationals. Since Germany has accepted a disproportionate share of asylum-seekers, it has had an interest in developing common EU policies on some asylum issues, which are linked to questions of immigration. Consequently, Chancellor Kohl agreed at the Maastricht conference that not only asylum but also immigration are matters of common concern for EU members.[31] Furthermore, as Alan Philip points out, nondiscrimination among citizens of EU members in economic and employment matters and free movement of workers within the EU—both central to the concept of a modern EU—"cannot easily be separated from immigration policy." While there is still "no truly common EU immigration policy, nor yet a common citizenship policy," he writes, "the EU is acquiring authority and competence in aspects of immigration policy, even if there is no coherent strategy to bring this about, and even if the institutional responsibility is shared and mainly intergovernmental."[32] Increasing EU competence in these issues will affect German policies toward those *Ausländer* who are EU nationals, since EU law mandates equal treatment by host states in economic and social life.[33] The Maastricht treaty also expanded the rights of EU nationals to include some political rights, such as limited voting rights across the EU and access to consular facilities in third countries.

In principle, EU law applies only to EU nationals and their family members. Non-EU nationals resident in EU members are not automatically entitled to the legal and social rights conferred on EU nationals, nor do they automatically have the right to move to other EU members.[34] Nevertheless, European integration has important implications for the standing of non-EU *Ausländer* in Germany. Especially given the removal of internal frontiers within the EU, the policies of member states toward third-country nationals clearly have an impact on the Union as a whole. Perhaps not surprisingly, then, the Maastricht treaty lists among matters of common interest the "conditions of residence by nationals of third countries on the territory of Member States, including family reunion and access to employment."[35] As the immigration and citizenship policies of EU members begin to converge, Germany's immigration and citizenship laws are likely to undergo greater scrutiny, and pressure on Germany to reform these laws is likely to increase. Already, the European Commission has adopted a report that advocates granting the same rights and freedoms to legal immigrants as to EU citizens and encourages member states to speed up the process of granting such immigrants full citizenship.[36] More explicitly, the committee responsible for supervision of the European Social Charter has repeatedly charged Germany with violating the charter with respect to the family reunification of migrants.[37]

As European integration proceeds, pressure within Germany for immigration reform will continue to increase. One-quarter of *Ausländer* are nationals of other EU members (such as Greece, Italy, Portugal, and Spain) and, under EU law, have the right to work and reside in Germany. Thus, a two-tier system is developing in which *Ausländer* who are EU nationals—many of whom arrived as *Gastarbeiter* just like most non-EU *Ausländer*—have more rights than non-EU *Ausländer* such as Turks and people from the former Yugoslavia. Since Turks make up Germany's largest immigrant population, the distinction between EU and non-EU *Ausländer* is likely to exacerbate social tensions. It also will raise questions about why Germany grants more rights to an EU *Ausländer* who has just arrived in Germany than to a non-EU *Ausländer* who was born and raised there.

Limitations on the political rights of non-EU *Ausländer*, especially those who are long-term residents of Germany, deserve special mention. Certain political rights, most notably the franchise, are restricted to German citizens (and at the communal level, to German citizens and EU citizens who have been resident for six months), exposing a serious flaw in the democratic legitimacy of the German political system.[38] It is morally unacceptable and politically untenable that in a modern democratic society, one-quarter of the population, as is the case in some German cities, does not have the right to vote.[39]

Germany cannot return to a mythical time of ethnic homogeneity. Instead, it must accept that many *Ausländer* are de facto immigrants and that foreigners will continue to come to Germany, both because of violence and poverty in their own countries and because the German economy needs them. The question is not whether Germany should become a multicultural society—it already is—but how it should best manage this diversity to ensure social stability and democratic values.

The remainder of the chapter examines two basic models for cultural pluralism: antidiscrimination legislation ("the Anglo-American model") and positive minority rights ("the East European model"). These models do not eliminate conflicts between ethnic groups but provide a framework of equality within which such conflicts can be managed. As a result, they are more likely to promote long-term social stability than the continued enforcement of a two-tier society.

Citizenship and Discrimination

Whether or not members of a minority group must have state citizenship to benefit from antidiscrimination legislation or positive minority protections is a complex issue. Antidiscrimination legislation can, in principle, protect noncitizens. In the absence of more liberal citizenship laws, however, such legislation is not a promising solution for Germany because the foreigner status of *Ausländer* has subjected them to legally and institutionally sanctioned discrimination. Of course, all states differentiate between the rights and responsibilities of citizens and noncitizens, and in this regard Germany is not unusual. Yet given that German citizenship is still very difficult to obtain, that citizenship is closely linked to ethnicity, and that many *Ausländer* are really *"Inländer"* with foreign citizenship, the application of the standard distinction between citizen and noncitizen is problematic in the German case.[40]

Scholars dispute whether noncitizens are or should be entitled to positive minority-rights protections under international law. Historically, states have used the "citizenship requirement" to protect themselves from the claims of minorities, going so far as to revoke the citizenship of entire groups. Several of the most widely cited definitions of "minority" exclude noncitizens.[41] However, the UN Human Rights Committee, in an April 1994 commentary on Article 27 of the International Covenant on Civil and Political Rights (the article covering minority rights), stated that individuals need not be citizens to be protected. Similarly, the November 1994 Council of Europe Framework Convention for the Protection of National Minorities did not specify citizenship as a precondition of protection, since the governments concerned could not agree on such a proposal.[42]

While citizenship may not be a precondition of antidiscrimination legislation or positive minority-rights protections, citizenship facilitates the process of protecting minorities and also helps integrate them into the larger political and social community. Citizenship is clearly an important step toward equal treatment for *Ausländer* in Germany. There is growing political pressure to recognize the reality of de facto immigration: the number of second- and third-generation *Ausländer* in Germany is increasing; the emphasis on greater uniformity among EU members on issues of immigration and citizenship will intensify; and, within Germany itself, unions, political parties of the left, and even certain elements of the center-right are calling for more liberal citizenship laws.

Discrimination does not end with citizenship, however; ethnic minorities are subjected to discrimination on the basis of characteristics such as skin color, national origin, language, or religion. The experience of other countries shows that discrimination by private parties can be difficult to control and requires comprehensive legislation and enforcement mechanisms. Furthermore, the likelihood of unabated refugee flows suggests that Germany's population will continue to include considerable numbers of noncitizens whose rights should be protected. Simply relaxing citizenship rules, in other words, will not eliminate discrimination.

The "Anglo-American" and "East European" Models

Germany can draw upon two different approaches to the legal protection of minorities. The "Anglo-American approach," exemplified in U.S. and British civil rights legislation, aims to provide equal treatment (whether conceived of as equality of opportunity or equality of result) to individuals irrespective of particular distinguishing characteristics. As Christopher McCrudden notes, "Contemporary anti-discrimination law is largely a product of domestic jurisdictions after the Second World War and, for a considerable period of time, of the domestic law of one country in particular: the United States of America." U.S. antidiscrimination legislation was developed on three levels: (1) standards against government-sponsored discrimination; (2) nondiscrimination requirements for those contracting with the government; and (3) measures prohibiting discrimination in employment, education, voting, housing, and so forth. In addition, independent commissions were established to oversee enforcement of the legislation. This antidiscrimination approach was adopted by other countries, notably Great Britain. Hence, the term "Anglo-American model."[43] Although originally developed as a way to fight racial discrimination, the Anglo-American model has increasingly been used to combat discrimination based on such attributes as sex, ethnic or national origin, age, sexual orientation, religion, disability, and marital status.

In contrast, the "east European model" was developed primarily in international law during the nineteenth and early twentieth centuries, culminating in the minority guarantees imposed on east European countries after World War I. This model assumes that nondominant groups wish to preserve their identity, which may necessitate differential treatment by the state. The effective protection of minority rights may require the state to go beyond equal protection under the law by adopting special measures on behalf of the minority. Such measures may include support for minority schools and cultural activities and provisions for the use of minority languages in courts and state administration. Positive minority rights are not designed as privileges but, rather, are intended to make up for structural inequalities affecting the minority. For example, these provisions recognize that members of the majority implicitly enjoy the right to be educated in their mother tongue. Minorities are given rights that compensate for the advantages enjoyed by the majority.

To contrast the east European and Anglo-American models as a group-rights approach versus an individual-rights approach, as is frequently done, is overly simplistic. In practice, it is difficult to distinguish sharply between individual rights and group rights. Some individual rights imply group rights: the right to family life, an individual right, includes the right to communicate in one's own language, a group right. Similarly, the promotion of individual rights often requires the implementation of collective rights. Individual freedom of worship is usually impossible without the collective right to sustain religious institutions.[44] Hurst Hannum comments that "arguments over whether legal formulations should be expressed in terms of the group rights of minorities or only the rights of persons belonging to minorities are really procedural or jurisdictional debates. What is important to recognize is that group interests are involved, and that balancing the legitimate interests of society against the rights of the lone individual may be an incomplete approach to the problem of resolving conflicting demands."[45]

The distinction between the Anglo-American and east European models should therefore not be overdrawn. As Patrick Thornberry writes, "classical" minority protection treaties (the east European model) "almost invariably included measures of non-discrimination as a preliminary to differential rules."[46] Similarly, the Anglo-American approach incorporates some elements of the east European model. While the Anglo-American approach does not obligate the state to take positive steps to preserve a minority's identity, it may require the state to differentiate on the basis of race or ethnicity to ensure equal treatment—for example, by means of "affirmative action." Nor does the Anglo-American approach necessarily assume a "melting pot" in which differences will disappear. Fundamentally, the difference between the Anglo-American and east European models is not about process but goals. The former aims for equality of treatment, the latter for the preservation of a minority's identity.

Both models have their limitations. When minorities wish to preserve their distinctive characteristics—and this is not always the case—the Anglo-American model does not adequately address this aspiration. Conversely, the east European approach does not protect individuals who are not, or choose not to be, members of a recognized minority. For practical and financial reasons, states cannot offer positive protections to small minorities, much less to individuals, and must make decisions about which groups constitute minorities warranting protection. When a state does grant positive rights to a minority, it must ensure that the minority's rights do not too sharply limit the rights of individuals. This danger can be checked by ensuring that individuals have the right to decide whether they belong to a minority[47] and by providing basic protections to all persons, minority or not, through antidiscrimination legislation.

Which Model for Germany

In terms of integrating *Ausländer*, Germany has until now pursued neither the east European ideal—a society in which the state helps to preserve cultures of both dominant and nondominant groups—nor the
Anglo-American ideal—a society in which individuals are treated
equally regardless of their race or ethnicity. Which model is more appropriate for Germany?

Psychologically, Germany has drawn on both the Anglo-American and
east European approaches. On the one hand, the modern Federal Republic places a strong emphasis on individual rights. Although Article 3.3 of
the Basic Law does not adequately protect *Ausländer*, it does demonstrate
a fundamental commitment to the principles of nondiscrimination and
equal treatment. One option would be for Germany's immigrants to become minorities in the east European sense, entitled to positive minority-
rights protections. Even if some immigrant groups obtain this status,
however, those immigrant groups and individuals who cannot or do not
wish to be part of an officially recognized minority also must find a place
in German society. Antidiscrimination legislation under the Anglo-
American model is clearly needed to protect the basic rights and human
dignity of all persons, whether or not they belong to a recognized minority.

On the other hand, the question of whether Germany should adopt
positive minority-rights provisions for major immigrant groups in addition to antidiscrimination legislation is a complex issue related in part to
the ways in which German identity is anchored in "east European" con-
ceptions of statehood and minority rights. The German concept of statehood—the *Kulturnation*—has greater affinities with east European ideas
of the ethnically defined nation than with west European and American
models of state-citizenship. Because the German state, like many in central and eastern Europe, is strongly linked to a particular national culture, equality of treatment for minorities who wish to preserve their cultural identity will likely require positive minority rights—a fact that
Germany has already acknowledged through the recognition of certain
ethnic-German minority groups.

It is disputed whether immigrant communities can develop into minorities in the east European sense.[48] Some scholars argue that immigrants are not entitled to minority status because they lack a permanent
connection to the state over many years, while others suggest that such a
connection can develop over time—perhaps in as little as one generation.[49] Another argument against the transformation of immigrant communities into protected minorities is the idea that minority status can be
claimed only by a group of people who have been "transferred *en bloc*,

without a chance to express their will freely, to a state with a population most of whom differed from them in race, language or religion."[50] The concept is that immigrants choose freely to move to a state in which they are not the majority, whereas "traditional minorities" become minorities through no choice of their own. But this distinction ignores the fact that in states such as Germany, where society and laws discriminate against nondominant groups, the descendants of immigrants do not have the option of assimilating into the dominant national culture and thus remain minorities through no choice of their own. Historically, the minority identity of many recognized minority groups, including some ethnic-German minorities residing in eastern Europe, evolved out of the migration and intermingling of peoples and not solely as the result of changes in international borders. With the passage of time, immigrants who retained a sense of group identity were recognized as minorities.

As was affirmed at the 1990 Copenhagen meeting of the Conference on the Human Dimension of the Conference on Security and Cooperation in Europe (CSCE), it is "a matter of a person's individual choice to belong to a minority," though this "subjective decision is inseparably linked to objective criteria relevant to the person's identity."[51] Accordingly, some scholars have suggested that where a large number of individuals share certain characteristics and consider themselves members of a minority, that minority should be considered to exist. In other words, for a minority to exist, it must possess not only distinguishing characteristics but also an awareness of and desire to preserve these characteristics.[52] Here, J. A. Laponce makes a useful distinction between "minorities of force"— groups that desire assimilation but are denied equality by the dominant group—and "minorities of will"—groups that want to retain their distinctiveness and therefore seek treatment different from the dominant group.[53] Positive minority rights in the east European sense apply to "minorities of will."

Thoughtful debate about the future of immigrant communities in Germany and the appropriateness of protecting their cultures through positive minority rights is long overdue. In considering this issue, several points should be borne in mind. First, the appropriateness of protecting minority cultures in the Federal Republic depends largely on whether minorities desire such protection, that is, whether they are "minorities of will." As Hannum notes, when a group does wish to preserve its identity, "mere abstention and even guarantees of formal equality in law may be insufficient to ensure that diversity and plurality are promoted and that equality in fact is achieved."[54] Certainly some German minorities, such as Serbs, Danes, and Friesians, are "minorities of will." So are the Roma-Sinti (gypsies), and the German government, after long refusing to recognize them as such, recently acknowledged them as an ethnic minority when signing the Council of Europe Convention on Minorities.[55] The situation of de facto immigrants is more complicated. The demands of *Ausländer* are currently focused on citizenship rights and antidiscrimination legislation—demands that must be addressed. Given that Germany has already recognized the principle of positive minority rights for certain groups, however, the question of why other groups do not enjoy those rights is likely to be asked eventually.

The degree to which immigrant communities have developed a sense of community that they wish to preserve remains to be seen. Some immigrants, especially those who belong to small immigrant groups that would not be eligible for special protection, would probably prefer integration. Many members of larger immigrant groups also may desire assimilation into German society on equal terms with ethnic-German citizens. Ironically, it has been precisely the denial of this equality, and the enforced separation from German society reflected in the development of ethnic ghettos, that has intensified the sense of solidarity within immigrant communities and led a few immigrant leaders, such as representatives of the Turkish community in Berlin, to begin calling for recognition as minorities. Not surprisingly, the degree to which a state is identified with a particular national culture and, correspondingly, the degree to which minority rights are met through antidiscrimination provisions have a profound impact on the development of minority identities. The longer Germany delays granting citizenship rights and combating discrimination, the more likely it is that some immigrant communities will effectively become "minorities of will."

A second important consideration is that Germany has a tradition of accepting and promoting minority rights according to the east European model. The 1919 Weimar constitution, for example, contained provisions guaranteeing the linguistic, educational, and cultural rights of minorities.[56] While positive minority rights have not been protected under the German Basic Law, the reaffirmation in the unification treaty of the rights of Serbs, which had been protected under the constitution of the German Democratic Republic, has in part engendered the current debate about establishing new constitutional minority-rights provisions.[57] Today, the states of Brandenburg, Sachsen, and Schleswig-Holstein have minority-rights provisions for their Serb, Danish, and Friesian inhabitants. Furthermore, the federal government's deference to regional *Länder* identities, exemplified in the principle of state independence in matters of education and culture (*Kulturhoheit*), recognizes the diversity within the Federal Republic and the need for state policies to be shaped in a way that will protect that diversity.

Germany also has recognized the need for state support to preserve the identity of ethnic minorities in other countries. Between the two world wars, Germany was the champion of minority rights in eastern Europe. Today, the Federal Republic considers as an important foreign-policy goal the achievement of linguistic, cultural, and educational rights for ethnic-German minorities living in eastern Europe and promotes the rights of minorities more generally through the Organization for Security and Cooperation in Europe (OSCE) and the Council of Europe.[58] It is important to note that the Federal Republic promotes positive rights in addition to antidiscrimination measures.[59] Germany supports such measures not only out of an interest in the human and cultural rights of minorities abroad but also out of a recognition that minority protection can be one of the most effective ways to prevent instability and ethnic tension in eastern Europe, thereby reducing the number of refugees fleeing to Germany.[60] Because ethnic Germans have the right to German citizenship, Germany has been particularly concerned about improving their living conditions and keeping them in the countries where they currently reside. If Germany continues to push for positive minority rights abroad while denying such rights to some of its minority populations at home, its position will increasingly be seen as hypocritical. Other countries may question why Germany holds them to a higher standard than that to which it holds itself.

Third, while states are not obliged to fulfill every desire of their minorities, protecting minority languages and cultures at an early stage offers real political advantages. What Chancellor Kohl has said about traditional minorities applies equally to immigrant minorities: "Only minorities who feel that their identity is respected will be loyal minorities and thereby enrich the cultural wealth of their nation."[61] Moreover, satisfying reasonable expectations of moderate groups makes it much less likely that extremist elements will gain influence. Communities that feel secure generally tend much less toward extremism than those that feel endangered. Currently, ethnic minority groups in Germany are predominantly moderate, and the German government should have an interest in keeping them that way.

Conclusions

Whereas right-wing parties are reclaiming "Germanness" as a positive value, German intellectuals and journalists, particularly on the Left, have lamented the failure of the establishment to create a positive sense of postwar German identity. The dangers of a new German identity that does not accept the multicultural reality of modern Germany—such as the nationalist, ethnic-German identity espoused by the right wing—are obvious. Unification, by bringing together two different German states that had each developed a distinct culture, offers a unique opportunity to fashion a new German identity in a pluralist and inclusive way. Much political energy has been expended since unification in an effort to make the two Germanies homogenous. Perhaps unification should be viewed instead as an opportunity to accept diversity, represented not only by the differences between eastern and western Germans but also by the differences among ethnic Germans, Germans of foreign heritage, and Germans of other national origins. Precisely because German cultural pluralism would incorporate both the Anglo-American and east European traditions, it would be pluralism of a uniquely German kind.

Notes

1. A longer version of this article appeared in *The Netherlands Quarterly of Human Rights* 13, no. 3 (1995), pp. 237–257. This version appears with the kind permission of the editors of *NQHR*. The author thanks Almuth Berger, *Ausländerbeauftragte* of the state of Brandenburg, and her staff; the Robert Bosch Stiftung; Reiner Kneifel-Haverkamp; and the editors of *NQHR*. The views expressed are the author's alone.

2. Gerd Andres, "Einwanderungsland Deutschland: Bisherige Ausländer- und Asylpolitik—Lebenssituation der ausländischen Arbeitnehmer und ihrer Familien," in *Einwanderungsland Deutschland: Bisherige Ausländer- und Asylpolitik, Vergleich mit anderen europäischen Ländern* (Forschungsinstitut der Friedrich Ebert Stiftung, Abt. Arbeits- und Sozialforschung, 1992), p. 11.

3. "The Week in Germany," German Information Center, 19 April, 1996.

4. Douglas B. Klusmeyer, "Aliens, Immigrants and Citizens: The Politics of Inclusion in the Federal Republic of Germany," *Daedalus* 122, no. 3 (Summer 1993), p. 106; Klaus J. Bade, "Immigration and Social Peace in United Germany," *Daedalus* 123, no. 1 (Winter 1994), p. 89.

5. Beauftragte der Bundesregierung für die Belange der Ausländer, "Daten und Fakten zur Ausländersituation," 13. Auflage, 1992, p. 9.

6. Andres, "Einwanderungsland," pp. 7, 28.

7. Klusmeyer, "Aliens, Immigrants and Citizens," p. 92; Helmut Kohl, "Migration und Minderheitenschutz in Europa," *Bulletin*, no. 85, Presse und Informationsamt der Bundesregierung, 13 October 1993, p. 970.

8. Axel Schulte, "Multikulturelle Gesellschaft: Zum Inhalt und Funktion eines vieldeutigen Begriffs," in *Multikulturelle Gesellschaft: Der Weg zwischen Ausgrenzung und Vereinnahmung?* (Forschungsinstitut der Friedrich Ebert Stiftung, Abt. Arbeits- und Sozialforschung, 1991), p. 32; Dietrich Thränhardt, "Ein Zuwanderungskonzept für Deutschland am Ende des Jahrhunderts," in *Einwanderungsland Deutschland: Bisherige Ausländer- und Asylpolitik ,Vergleich mit anderen europäischen Ländern* (Forschungsinstitut der Friedrich Ebert Stiftung, Abt. Arbeits- und Sozialforschung, 1992), pp. 128–129; Klusmeyer, "Aliens, Immigrants and Citizens," p. 89.

9. "Who Is German?" *The Economist*, 5 April, 1997, p. 45; Human Rights Watch/Helsinki, *"Germany for Germans": Xenophobia and Racist Violence in Germany* (New York: HRW, 1995), pp. 84–85.

10. "Zweiter Menschenrechtsbericht der Bundesregierung," Deutscher Bundestag Drucksache 12/6330, 2 December 1993, p. 8.

11. Klusmeyer, "Aliens, Immigrants and Citizens," pp. 99–100.

12. Translated in Kurt Rabl, Christoph Stoll, and Manfred Vasold, eds., *From the U.S. Constitution to the Basic Law of the Federal Republic of Germany* (Munich: Moos & Partner, 1988), pp. 189–190.

13. Institut für Migrations- und Rassismusforschung, "Comparative Assessment of the Legal Instruments in the Various Member States of the European Communities to Combat All Forms of Discrimination, Racism and Xenophobia and Incitement and Hatred and Racial Violence: National Study for the Federal Republic of Germany," Contract No. 91ETVC2007, Hamburg, 1992, pp. 3, 29–31, 40.

14. Ibid., p. 10.

15. Angela Merkel, "Individuelle Verantwortung für die Verwirklichung von Humanität und Recht in der Gesellschaft," *Bulletin*, no. 85, Presse und Informationsamt der Bundesregierung, 13 October 1993, p. 974.

16. Klusmeyer, "Aliens, Immigrants and Citizens," p. 104.

17. Klusmeyer, "Aliens, Immigrants and Citizens," p. 83; Institut für Migrations- und Rassismus Forschung, "Comparative Assessment," pp. 32–34.

18. Institut für Migrations- und Rassismus Forschung, "Comparative Assessment," pp. 33, 37, 46–49, 20–21.

19. Ibid., p. 11.

20. Andres, "Einwanderungsland," p. 43.

21. Hermann Korte, "Guestworker Question or Immigration Issue? Social Sciences and Public Debate in the Federal Republic of Germany," in Klaus J. Bade, ed., *Population, Labour and Migration in 19th- and 20th-Century Germany* (New York: Berg Publishers, 1987), p. 175.

22. Andres, "Einwanderungsland," pp. 39–40.

23. Human Rights Watch/Helsinki, *"Germany for Germans,"* pp. 30, 89–91, 101–107.

24. Institut für Migrations- und Rassismus Forschung, "Comparative Assessment," pp. 43–44, 71–72.

25. Ibid., pp. 10–11; Human Rights Watch/Helsinki, *"Germany for Germans,"* p. 19.

26. Andres, "Einwanderungsland," p. 9; Institut für Migrations- und Rassismusforschung, "Comparative Assessment," p. 2.

27. Gerd Andres, "Die politischen und sozialen Rahmenbedingungen einer multikulturellen Gesellschaft," in *Multikulturelle Gesellschaft* (Forschungsinstitut der Friedrich Ebert Stiftung, Abt. Arbeits- und Sozialforschung, 1991), p. 78.

28. Andres, "Einwanderungsland," pp. 26–27.

29. United Nations Committee on the Elimination of Racial Discrimination, "Concluding Observations of the Committee," Forty-third session, 2–20 August

1993, p. 1. See also Institut für Migrations- und Rassismusforschung, "Comparative Assessment," p. 1.

30. United Nations Committee on the Elimination of Racial Discrimination, "Concluding Observations of the Committee," Fiftieth Session, March 1997.

31. Andres, "Einwanderungsland," p. 13; Merkel, "Individuelle Verantwortung," p. 975.

32. Alan Butt Philip, "European Union Immigration Policy: Phantom, Fantasy or Fact?" *West European Politics* 17, no. 2 (April 1994), pp. 168, 188.

33. Bruno de Witte, "The European Community and Its Minorities," in Catherine Brölmann, René LeFeber, and Marjoleine Zieck, eds., *Peoples and Minorities in International Law* (Dordrecht: Martinus Nijhoff, 1993), p. 180.

34. Philip, "European Union Immigration Policy," p. 171.

35. 1991 Treaty on European Union, Art. K.1(3)b.

36. "EU Report Suggests Full Rights to Legal Immigrants in Europe," *EuroWatch* 5, no. 23, 7 March 1994.

37. Institut für Migrations- und Rassismus Forschung, "Comparative Assessment," p. 24.

38. Friedrich Heckmann, "Nationalstaat, multikulturelle Gesellschaft und ethnische Minderheitenpolitik," in *Multikulturelle Gesellschaft* (Forschungsinstitut der Friedrich Ebert Stiftung, Abt. Arbeits- und Sozialforschung, 1991), p. 49.

39. Thränhardt, "Zuwanderungskonzept für Deutschland," p. 136.

40. Institut für Migrations- und Rassismusforschung, "Comparative Assessment," pp. 2, 26.

41. Patrick Thornberry, *International Law and the Rights of Minorities* (Oxford: Clarendon, 1991), pp. 6–10; Rüdiger Wolfrum, "The Emergence of 'New Minorities' as a Result of Migration," in *Peoples and Minorities in International Law*, pp. 153–156.

42. Anders Rönquist, "The Council of Europe Framework Convention for the Protection of National Minorities," *Helsinki Monitor* 6, no. 1 (1995), pp. 40–41.

43. Christopher McCrudden, "Introduction," in McCrudden, ed., *Anti-Discrimination Law* (New York: New York University, 1991), pp. xii–xiii.

44. Yoram Dinstein, "Collective Human Rights of Peoples and Minorities," *International and Comparative Quarterly* 25 (1976), p. 103.

45. Hurst Hannum, "Introduction," in Hannum, ed., *Documents on Autonomy and Minority Rights* (Dordrecht: Martinus Nijhoff, 1993), p. xv.

46. Thornberry, *International Law*, p. 10.

47. Ibid., p. 176.

48. Rüdiger Wolfrum, "Minderheitenschutz in Europa: Die staatsrechtliche Situation am Beispiel einzelner ausgewählter Staaten," in *Minderheiten in Europa: Landtagsforum am 7. Juni 1991, Schleswig-Holsteinischen Landtag* (Lübeck: Wullenwever-Druck, 1991), p. 123.

49. "Völkisches Denken oder modernes Völkerrecht: Hans Otto Bräutigam, Justizminister in Brandenburg, zu dem Vorschlag der Gemeinsamen Verfassungskommission, die Identität von Minderheiten zu achten," *Frankfurter Rundschau*, 10 May 1994.

50. Thornberry, *International Law*, p. 154; see also Wolfrum, "The Emergence of 'New Minorities'," pp. 160–163.

51. Rönquist, "The Council of Europe Framework Convention," p. 41; see also *League of Nations Official Journal* (1927), pp. 477, 498.

52. Wolfrum, "Minderheitenschutz in Europa," pp. 122–123.

53. J. A. Laponce, *The Protection of Minorities* (Berkeley: University of California Press, 1960), p. 16.

54. Hannum, "Introduction," p. xv.

55. U.S. Department of State, "Country Report on Human Rights Practices for 1996: Germany," Bureau of Democracy, Human Rights, and Labor, 30 January, 1997.

56. Gemeinsame Verfassungskommission, "Bericht der Gemeinsamen Verfassungskommission," Deutscher Bundestag Drucksache 12/6000, pp. 72–73.

57. Reiner Hofmann, "Minderheitenschutz in Europa," *Zeitschrift für ausländ isches öffentliches Recht und Völkerrecht* 52, no. 1 (1992), p. 32; Dietrich Franke and Rainer Hofmann, "Nationale Minderheiten—ein Thema für das Grundgesetz?" *Europäische Grundrechtezeitung*, 14 September 1992, p. 13.

58. "Antwort der Bundesregierung auf die große Anfrage der Fraktion der CDU/CSU und FDP zur Unterstützung der Reformprozesse in den Staaten Mittel-, Südost- und Osteuropas (einschließlich der baltischen Staaten) sowie in den neuen unabhängigen Staaten auf dem Territorium der ehemaligen Sowjetunion," Deutscher Bundestag Drucksache 12/6162, p. 50; see also Gemeinsame Verfassungskommission, "Bericht," p. 73.

59. "Zweiter Menschenrechtsbericht der Bundesregierung," p. 7.

60. Kohl, "Migration und Minderheitenschutz," p. 970.

61. Ibid., p. 971.

10

Employment Discrimination: Germany's Lack of Legal Remedies

CAROLINE FREDRICKSON

1. *All people are equal before the law.*
2. *Men and women have equal rights.*
3. *No one may be disadvantaged or favored because of sex, parentage, race, language, homeland and origin, faith, or religious or political opinions.*

—*German Basic Law, Article 3 ("Equality")*

Although the German Basic Law (*Grundgesetz*) was originally intended as an interim constitution pending German unification, a united Germany has retained it because of its success in protecting the democratic order and guiding the Federal Republic's remarkable transformation from a fascist state to a peaceful and prosperous democratic nation. Enacted in 1949, the Basic Law contains provisions designed to prevent antidemocratic forces from subverting the new social order, including a prohibition on amendments that would erode the fundamental principles of democracy and the rule of law. Thanks in large measure to the constitutional establishment of a generous social-welfare state, the prosperity of postwar Germany has been widely distributed among the German people.

German workers in particular have benefited greatly from the new political order by gaining numerous workplace rights under the Basic Law and subsequent statutes, including safety standards, minimum vacation time, maximum work hours, and protection against arbitrary job termination. Workers also enjoy astonishingly broad rights to shape company policy. Through elected "works councils," workers exercise significant participation rights in the workplace, are guaranteed extensive information from management, and have veto power over many traditional management decisions. Workers also elect representatives to serve on the supervisory board of the employer, allowing them to influence larger issues of company strategic decisionmaking and financial planning (*Mitbestimmung*). In no other country in the world have workers acquired greater participatory rights than in Germany.

The Basic Law and its governing statutes do not, however, go so far in addressing discrimination in employment. Indeed, Germany's failure to punish such behavior is inconsistent with the fundamental guarantees of the constitutional order and, specifically, the guarantee of equality in Article 3 of the Basic Law. Quoted at the beginning of this chapter, Article 3 promises equal treatment, yet a lack of penalties for violations means that women and minorities continue to be disadvantaged in employment. Specifically, the German government has not provided adequate remedies for an employer's refusal to hire a job applicant for discriminatory reasons. In other countries, such as the United States, employers who refuse to hire a job applicant because of sex, race, or ethnicity may be required by a court to give that person a job as a remedy for the discrimination. Not so in Germany.

To justify the refusal to award a job to an applicant who would have been hired but for discrimination, German judges and scholars invoke the doctrine of "freedom of contract." Some consider this principle the bedrock of a liberal free-market society, giving people the right to choose their contracting partners, mutually determine the content of the agreement, and construct a privately negotiated penalty for noncompliance with contractual duties. Yet in Germany, as in the United States, this concept today exists more in theory than in reality. Both societies have sought to regulate the market when it is found wanting, for example, by imposing environmental controls and consumer safety measures.

To demonstrate how the ideology of freedom of contract has retained a toehold solely in the area of German antidiscrimination law, this chapter examines the history of this concept, comparing developments in the United States with those in Germany. In particular, the discussion focuses on how current German legal thought addresses contractual rights in the labor contract and whether freedom of contract has been applied consistently to the formation, content, and termination of private agreements. What soon becomes apparent is that judges and legislators have abrogated the principle of freedom of contract in almost every area of employment law, based on the perception that workers deserve protection from exploitation on the job. Yet German legal scholars argue that an employer's decision not to hire women and ethnic minorities cannot be overruled because it would interfere with their freedom of contract. In fact, freedom of contract as the basis for legal decisionmaking in Germany cannot be harmonized with the principles of the Basic Law or with statutory labor law, which intervenes in many areas of the employment relationship to address power imbalances between workers and employers.

Freedom of Contract: A Brief History

The U.S. Experience

In the United States, the nineteenth century gave birth to a strong commitment to "freedom of contract." The philosophy of economic liberalism became dominant, replacing older forms of thinking about human relationships. The conditions of one's birth, it was believed, should not play a decisive role in determining one's place in the social order. Instead, individuals should be free to enter into contractual relationships, choosing for themselves a preferred career, employer, and contract terms. Liberty of contract, according to its advocates, was both a virtue in itself and a utilitarian good, guaranteeing the most efficient creation and distribution of wealth. Unfettered bargaining was believed to safeguard liberty and invigorate the economy. In this view, the market functions most efficiently when people are able to pursue their interests without government interference, especially in the form of legal constraints on the private sector.

Adherents of this free-market philosophy believed that contract negotiations should be free of outside interference, without regard to the identity of the bargaining parties or the type of contract at issue. In view of the then high unemployment and regular influxes of immigrant labor, many employers exploited the workers' weak bargaining position by repeatedly driving down wages and maintaining dangerous and unhealthy working conditions. Although changing public opinion led to the passage of many protective labor statutes in the early twentieth century, free-market theorists continued to insist on the doctrine's applicability in all contexts. Their arguments made major inroads in legal thought, affecting judicial interpretation of the Constitution and protective statutes. Federal and state judges, referring to the due process clauses of the Fifth and Fourteenth Amendments to the U.S. Constitution[1]—which they believed gave implicit protection to the strictest form of contractual libertarianism—struck down laws prohibiting child labor, establishing maximum working hours, and setting minimum wages.[2]

One famous example of free-market ideology swaying judicial outcomes is the Supreme Court's 1908 decision in *Lochner v. New York*.[3] In this case, the Supreme Court struck down a New York law setting maximum work hours for bakers of 10 hours per day and 60 hours per week. Justice

Peckham, writing for the Court, acknowledged that the police power allows the state to impose limitations on the making of a contract, such as by forbidding agreements that have an illegal act as their objective. The Court questioned, however, whether the maximum-work-hour law was "a fair, reasonable, and appropriate exercise of the police power of the state, or . . . an unreasonable, unnecessary, and arbitrary interference with the right of the individual to his personal liberty, or to enter into those contracts in relation to labor which may seem to him appropriate or necessary for the support of himself and his family?"[5] Relying on the Fourteenth Amendment, the Court found the maximum-work-hour law unconstitutional because "[the right to purchase or sell labor is part of the liberty protected by this amendment]" and "[there is no reasonable ground for interfering with the liberty of person or the right of free contract by determining the hours of labor, in the occupation of a baker.]"[6]

The early twentieth century marked the beginning of a change in attitude among U.S. legal experts toward the employment relationship. Unwilling to accept the existing allocation of power as the natural or inevitable basis for the bargaining process, some scholars and politicians questioned whether employees could ever bargain as equals with employers.[7] Workers, they insisted, cannot exercise freedom of contract as individuals. Because of a severe inequality in bargaining power, they are compelled to accept most terms proposed by a potential employer. These commentators argued that the sale of labor is qualitatively different from the sale of commodities. Not only does the employer exercise psychological domination over the relationship stemming from hierarchical superiority, he or she also has an almost existential control over the worker, possibly determining whether an employee can afford to pay rent or buy food. According to this critique, an employer's capacity to coerce grows exponentially with an employee's proximity to hunger and homelessness. Only if workers could band together into a union would the employer face an approximate equal in bargaining power. Without the right to unionize, these scholars argued, "freedom of contract" was little more than a mechanism for the exploitation of workers.

The views of these commentators received judicial support only in the mid-1930s. Under the presidency of Franklin D. Roosevelt, the Democratic majority in Congress passed a series of protective labor laws, which the Supreme Court initially continued to strike down. In 1937, however, the Court changed course. Two landmark cases that year ushered in a new era in American jurisprudence. Rejecting a constitutional challenge, the Supreme Court upheld the National Labor Relations Act (NLRA),[8] a law enacted in 1935 to give workers the right to form unions and to require employers to bargain with the employees' chosen representative.[9] In addition, the Justices determined that minimum-wage laws could be compatible with the constitutional guarantee of liberty. In upholding a Washington State law, the Court outlined a new approach to the Fifth and Fourteenth Amendments' guarantees of due process, the Court's original basis for its theory of "freedom of contract":

> The Constitution does not speak of freedom of contract. It speaks of liberty and prohibits the deprivation of liberty without the due process of law. In prohibiting that deprivation the Constitution does not recognize an absolute and uncontrollable liberty. Liberty in each of its phases has its history and connotation. But the liberty safeguarded is liberty in a social organization which requires the protection of law against the evils which menace the health, safety, morals and welfare of the people. Liberty under the Constitution is thus necessarily subject to the restraints of due process, and regulation which is reasonable in relation to its subject and is adopted in the interests of the community is due process.[10]

Just as in *Lochner*, the Court used a balancing test to analyze whether the law under attack could be justified as protecting the "health, safety, morals and welfare of the people." While both opinions state that liberty is subject to certain constraints within a civil society, in 1937 the Court accorded much more weight to the legislative determination that the regulation was reasonable and necessary, an approach that was to remain dominant thereafter.

Once the Supreme Court had condoned the NLRA's requirement that one party (the employer) must negotiate with another (the union), freedom of contract became an increasingly rare justification for finding a law unconstitutional. In the area of racial and sexual discrimination, the Court upheld a federal law making it unlawful to refuse to enter into a contract on the basis of sex or race and compelling the completion of the contract as a remedy. In *Runyon v. McCrary*,[11] the Court relied on a federal civil rights statute[12] that prohibits discrimination in the making and enforcement of contracts to require a private school to accept black children as students. The dissenting justices argued that the Civil War–era law had not been enacted to grant a positive right to execute an agreement, but only to ensure that no person could be denied the right to enter into and enforce contracts with a willing partner. The majority countered this thesis by noting that since white children were allowed to study at the school, guaranteeing the "same right to contract" meant that black children also had the right to attend the school. This statute and a companion Civil War–era statute also have been applied to employment and housing contracts, such that an employer or landlord who refuses to enter into a contract with a job applicant or would-be tenant solely because of his or her race or sex may be forced to hire the applicant or house the tenant.[13] Similarly, the 1964 Civil Rights Act[14] proscribes discrimination in employment and provides that the discriminating employer can be compelled to enter into an employment contract with the victim.[15]

In late twentieth-century America, limitations on the market abound, ensuring that consumers have information before buying a product, landlords maintain livable dwellings, and workers enjoy safe working conditions. Many believe that such protections are necessary to level the playing field, enabling weaker parties to bargain more equitably and ensuring that they enter into contractual relations with true freedom. Nonetheless, workers do not exert significant influence over the management of the enterprise in which they are employed. While U.S. law accords substantial remedies to victims of discrimination, workers who seek to exercise or broaden their collective rights face a greater challenge and less protection against discrimination. As the discussion of German law demonstrates, this situation is the mirror-opposite of the German experience.

The German Experience

As in the United States, industrialization in Germany brought with it a changed understanding of the traditional relationship between employer and worker. Replacing the paternalistic bonds between master and servant, the liberal market economy treated the labor relationship as a pure exchange of labor for wages.[16] As elsewhere, working conditions and wages suffered under continuing pressure from new job applicants who were prepared to underbid competitors in order to feed their families.

In the nineteenth century, German lawmakers gradually began to address the abysmal conditions of working people. In 1891, a new social-insurance law gave workers some financial security in case of accidents or sickness, and the German parliament passed legislation authorizing voluntary workers' committees.[17] These reforms were more symbolic than real, however, and it was only during the Weimar Republic that the position of German workers improved substantially. Maximum-work-hour limits, restrictions on job termination, and worker representation in company management through work councils and supervisory boards were introduced at this time.[18] Although most of these laws were abrogated by the Nazis, they were reenacted quickly and augmented after World War II.[19] Germany, like the United States, felt a need to provide greater balance in the labor bargaining process, adding a little additional weight on the side of otherwise overpowered workers. As noted in an introduction to labor law published by the German government:

Historical experience teaches that without protection through labor legislation and collective bargaining agreements, the individual employee was inferior to the employer and was often exposed to unfair and inhumane working conditions, inadequate protection from workplace accidents, overly long working hours, etc. Today, the unconfined construction of the labor relationship is restricted through laws, collective bargaining agreements and works agreements.[20]

Thus, like their American counterparts, German legislators and legal commentators came to accept that freedom of contract should not automatically prevail and that other, sometimes more important principles must be considered in resolving social conflicts.

Discrimination in employment, however, remains a special case. Despite a history of protective labor legislation, Germany has not dispensed entirely with contractual libertarianism, in that the doctrine of freedom of contract limits protection against discriminatory hiring practices. Interestingly, unlike the constitutional guarantee of equal treatment in Article 3, freedom of contract is not explicitly protected by the Basic Law. Rather, German legal scholars and judges have derived this principle from Article 12 of the Basic Law, which protects the right to choose and exercise a profession.[21] They argue that the right to pursue a chosen career implicitly gives the employer the right to retain some control over the operation of his or her business, including the making of contracts.

Article 12 is not absolute, however, and may be overridden when justified by a need to protect the general welfare, provided the means chosen are narrowly tailored and necessary to serve that end and the justification outweighs the severity of the intervention.[22] This balancing test allows the German parliament considerable freedom to pursue regulatory goals in the area of employment and social relations.[23] Nevertheless, German legal commentators contend that the implicit guarantee of contractual liberty in Article 12 outweighs the explicit prohibition on discrimination in Article 3.[24] One scholar sums up the freedom accorded to employers as ensuring precisely the right to choose whom one wants to hire or not to hire. This freedom should not be constrained by applying the constitutional guarantee of equal treatment to the formation of the work relationship.[25] According to this interpretation, the law does not prevent an employer from refusing to hire minorities.[26]

Limits on Contractual Freedom in the Employment Contract

While German legal scholars invoke the principle of freedom of contract to reject hiring as a remedy for racial or sexual discrimination in employment, they do not extend their analysis to other, closely analogous employment situations. In fact, Germany has numerous statutes that encroach upon an employer's free choice in hiring, among them protections for union members, "generally binding" collective-bargaining agreements, and the compelled hiring of injured miners and apprentices who have been serving as members of the works council.[27] An examination of these legal constraints on the making of labor contracts, contract terms, and the dissolution of contracts shows that German labor law treats discrimination in employment differently, reserving the doctrine of freedom of contract for this area alone.

Discrimination Against Union Members

Article 9 of the Basic Law protects freedom of association, ensuring workers the right to join unions for mutual aid and collective bargaining and prohibiting employers from discriminating against union members in the hiring process. The Federal Law Book (*Bundesgesetzbuch* or BGB) sets forth a category of laws known as "protective laws,"[28] violations of which must be compensated by putting the victim in the position he or she would have been in had the illegal act not taken place.[29] This approach is known as "natural restitution." Under German law, union members have significant legal rights under Article 9 because the constitutional guarantee of freedom of association has been deemed a protective law, with all the remedies attendant on that designation.[30] As a result, an employer who has refused to hire an applicant solely on the basis of union membership can be required to give the worker a job, an act of natural restitution.[31] Commentators accept these remedies as essential to fulfilling Article 9's protection of association rights.[32] Thus, in a case where an employer turned down a fully qualified applicant because she refused to give up her union membership, the court held that the employer could not rely on freedom of contract to protest the forced conclusion of the employment contract.[33]

Constitutional guarantees of equal treatment and statutory anti-discrimination provisions would seem to fit the description of protective laws. For example, Article 3, paragraph 3, of the Basic Law postulates that no one shall be disadvantaged based on sex, race, speech, national origin, homeland, beliefs, or religious or political opinions, and has been described as a cardinal ordering principle of labor law.[34] Yet German judges and legal commentators have not interpreted Article 3 to mean that victims of racial or sexual discrimination in the employment process are entitled to a job as restitution. Indeed, it is unclear why they do not accord Article 3 of the Basic Law the same status of protective law as they do the Article 9 protection against antiunion discrimination, which serves a similar anti-discriminatory purpose.

German statutory laws provide additional protections against sexual discrimination that could be deemed protective laws and allow a court to award a job as a remedy for discrimination. Section 611a of the BGB,[35] derived from European Economic Community Directive 76/207,[36] forbids employers from discriminating on the grounds of sex in any matter relating to employment, including the hiring process, unless it is a necessary requirement for the job.[37] Germany translated this provision into national law in 1980, two years after the deadline for its implementation, but limited compensation to out-of-pocket expenses to the applicant of applying for the job.[38] In cases that came before the European Court, two German women argued that the failure of BGB Section 611a to provide for adequate remedies was a violation of European law.[39] The European Court determined that the purely symbolic reprimand in Section 611a did not satisfy the European Community's dictate, and Germany was instructed to rewrite the provision.[40] Initially, the German parliament failed to pass new legislation, requiring judges on the Federal Labor Court to fill the gap. These judges set a maximum recovery of one month's salary, arguing that freedom of contract prevented them from ordering a discriminatory employer from hiring the victim of the discrimination.[41]

In 1994, after Section 611a was found deficient, the German parliament enacted a law ostensibly designed to bring Germany into compliance with European law. This 1994 law set a maximum recovery of three months' salary for an individual and six months' salary to be shared among a group of individuals who were not hired because of sexual discrimination. The European Court, however, found the German ceiling incompatible with the EC's directive on equal treatment, in part because it treated sexual discrimination differently from analogous civil and labor law.[42]

A small group of critics have countered the governing theory that job applicants who suffer discrimination are not entitled to a job as a remedy. According to these legal scholars, a job contract should be a possible compensation for the injury of discrimination in hiring under current German law because Section 611a should be considered a "protective law."[43] Just as in cases of discrimination against union members, female applicants should be put in the position they would have been in without the discrimination—that is, in the job they desired.[44]

A second principle of German law should allow victims of discrimination to enter into the contract that they were denied. Discrimination in hiring should fall under the principle of "fault in contracting" (*Verschulden bei Vertragsschluss* or *culpa in contrahendo*), which enforces the duty to bargain in good faith.[45] Under this principle, courts in other contexts have seen fit to put the victim in the position he or she would have been in had the other party not committed a punishable breach during the negotiation. By rights, an employer's decision to exclude the most qualified applicant solely because of race or sex should be considered a breach of the duty to bargain in good faith, entitling the victim to the desired job as a remedy.

In practice, however, these fundamental principles have not been applied to discrimination directed at women and minorities. Neither Article 3 nor Section 611a has been given the status of protective law, nor has discrimination in hiring been seen as a breach of the duty to bargain in good faith. Commentators argue that to do so would violate freedom of contract. For example, one legal scholar contends that the natural restitution envisaged by the BGB provisions is available only if compensation for the injury were feasible in practice. But, he argues, compensation for discrimination in the form of the job or damages is not possible because, in such cases, an immense number of rejected candidates would file claims, each alleging vague and basically unprovable injuries.[46] The author provides neither empirical evidence nor a defensible theoretical basis for this assertion. Indeed, he goes on to note that freedom of association, protection of the handicapped, the law against unfair competition, and hundreds of other statutes have been deemed protective laws.[47]

One is left wondering why it is so much easier to calculate damages suffered as a result of denial of the freedom of association or the rights of the disabled than those resulting from employment discrimination based on sex or ethnicity. Remedies for a failure to hire could be as simple as requiring the employer to hire the victim of discrimination. Moreover, many laws provide analogies that would help courts calculate appropriate damages in cases where offering the victim a job as compensation is not feasible. For example, in the Termination Protection Law, when an employee is fired unjustly but cannot return to the labor relationship for personal reasons, the law foresees severance pay of up to 12 months' salary.[48]

It is possible that the German parliament may yet take the rulings of the European Court to heart and provide the same right to natural restitution for employment discrimination as is currently available for violations of other protective labor statutes. But if Germany continues to refuse women and minorities the same protection against discrimination that it accords to union members, it will remain in noncompliance with European law and will continue to see its remedial statutes struck down as failing to conform to the European Council's Directive on Equal Treatment.

"Generally Binding" Collective Bargaining Agreements

Apart from the example of forced contracting with union members discussed above, German law contains many provisions that may require the forcible conclusion of a contract as a possible remedy. The "generally binding" collective-bargaining agreement (*Allgemeinverbindlicherklärung,* or AVE) represents the most pervasive example of forced contracting, and the one that most contradicts the principle of freedom of contract. Normal collective-bargaining agreements govern the relationship between union and employer or employer association, establishing maximum-work-hour rules, vacation days, and wage classifications. The AVE, by contrast, requires companies that are not parties to the collective-bargaining agreement or members of the employer association that negotiated the contract to abide by its terms.[49] For an agreement to be declared "generally binding," one of the bargaining partners must apply to the minister of labor, the parties must have entered into a legally effective collective-bargaining agreement, members of the negotiating employer association must employ a minimum of 50 percent of the workers in that industrial sector, and the declaration of an AVE must benefit the public.[50] For example, the minister of labor may find a public benefit if the proclamation of an AVE would prevent a worsening of labor conditions that could occur if nonunion employers undercut a collective-bargaining agreement.[51] In 1979, 585 agreements were declared AVEs, affecting 4.4 million workers.[52]

The AVE interferes significantly with freedom of contract, particularly with the right not to enter into a contract. If collective agreements can be imposed on noncontracting parties, why is it not appropriate to require an employer to hire a woman or minority as a remedy for discrimination? Some might argue that there are great differences between an individual contract and the collective one. The major distinction, however, between a collective-bargaining agreement and an individual employment contract is that the terms of the former apply to more people, a difference in scope and not in kind. Indeed, a collective contract imposes more onerous contractual requirements on the employer than does an agreement with a single employee.

Miners and Apprentices as Protected Classes

German labor law includes two additional provisions requiring employers to hire certain workers: mandatory hiring of disabled miners and the requirement that apprentices who serve on the works council of a company be given permanent employment. In several German states, affirmative-action provisions require that disabled miners be given special consideration in the hiring process. In the Saarland, this consideration goes so far as to allow local authorities to force the hiring of such a miner against the will of the employer.[53] In the case of an apprentice serving on the works council, the Works Constitution Act requires the employer to hire the apprentice at the end of his or her apprenticeship.[54] Legal commentators argue that without such a provision, apprentices would never dare to serve on the works council. If they lacked a guaranteed job at the end of the training period, apprentices would have reason to fear that, by engaging in works council activity, they would diminish their chances of permanent employment.[55] Although admitting that this obligation verges on an infringement of freedom of contract, one commentator justifies its application because of the infrequent occurrence of such cases.[56] While it may be true that employers are rarely forced to hire under this situation, infrequent application is not a principled basis for drawing a legal distinction between cases where freedom of contract is violated and where it is not.

Content of Labor Contracts

The German parliament has circumscribed negotiations over the content of employment contracts by mandating a myriad of implied terms, most, if not all, of which benefit the employee. From an American perspective, the rights won by German workers are quite astonishing.[57] The Works Constitution Act ensures workers significant participation in company decisionmaking by establishing an elected works council entitled to extensive information from management and with veto power over many traditional management decisions. For example, the employer may not hire or transfer someone without the approval of the council. The council also shares decisionmaking with management on such issues as setting work times and method of payment, introduction and use of technology for worker supervision, and the administration of workplace benefits such as cafeterias and sports facilities.[58] A "conciliation committee" consisting of an equal number of works council and employer representatives and a mutually acceptable chairperson settles disagreements over these issues. Workers also participate on the supervisory board of the enterprise under the Codetermination Law,[59] with the elected worker representatives enjoying the same rights and responsibilities as the shareholder representatives.[60]

In addition to statutory participation requirements, a series of German laws and regulations provide minimum standards in the workplace, such as stringent health and safety standards, minimum vacation time, job security during parental leave or civil or military service, and generous sick pay.[61] A few examples convey the breadth of this body of law. The Parental Leave Law obliges an employer to hold a position open for up to three years while a parent is raising a newborn child.[62] Those performing military or civil service duty also retain the right to return to their job and must receive all benefits they would have received had they been working for that period of time.[63] Thus, years spent away from the job count toward salary and pension calculations. Every company must provide at least 18 workdays of paid vacation[64] and pay up to six weeks' wages to a sick employee per illness per year.[65]

It is clear even from these few examples that German legislators have mandated numerous terms of employment contracts, recognizing that workers and employers are not in a relationship of equal bargaining power and that some government intervention is required to ensure minimum safety and job security. Freedom of contract has certainly not limited the German parliament's actions in this area.

Termination of the Contract

German employers also face great restrictions on their freedom to terminate employment contracts. Under the Termination Protection Law, employers must justify to the labor court a decision to fire an employee by demonstrating that the decision was based on poor job performance or the firm's diminished need for labor.[66] In addition, the employer must provide the employee and the works council advance warning of an impending termination. If the works council opposes the dismissal, the fired employee may continue to work until the case is resolved by the court.[67] Moreover, it is practically impossible for management to dismiss any members of the works council. Only in cases of serious misbehavior will a labor court approve the firing of a works council member.[68]

Freedom of contract seems to have vanished from labor law in all areas except employment discrimination. No satisfactory explanation illuminates the reason for the different conceptual approach in this area.

Conclusion

One of the fundamental differences scholars find between civil and common law systems is that, in the former, "human dignity and personal freedom derive from the rights and duties laid down in law. Law therefore serves as a guide to freedom and right living. In the common law tradition, by contrast, freedom precedes law; freedom, after all, is the individual's natural state; judges therefore make law on a case-by-case basis as persons seek remedies for intrusions upon their freedom."[69]

Generally, this analysis correctly identifies the differences between the German social-market system and the more libertarian American system. Yet the legal systems of the two countries trade positions when it comes to discrimination. The American legal system imposes few controls on the labor relationship except for strict legal controls on discrimination. In Germany, in contrast, all aspects of the labor contract are influenced by laws, regulations, and collective-bargaining agreements, yet an employer's right to refuse to hire women or minorities remains practically immune from state regulation.

A well-respected legal commentator, discussing the guarantee of equal treatment in Article 3 of the Basic Law, summed up the position of the German legal establishment rather well:

> Here the general tense relationship between freedom and equality becomes especially clear. The farther one allows Article Three to penetrate into the realm of private law, the more private autonomy is restricted. Because the freedom to form relations in the private sphere is in any case ever more narrowed through a multiplicity of legislative rules, it has been expressly promoted that *here* the constitutional principle of freedom has priority.[70]

Thus, it is hard to see the decision of the German legal establishment to place freedom of contract above equal treatment in the hierarchy of constitutional values as anything more than arbitrary line-drawing. Much like the Supreme Court's decision in *Lochner*, German courts frequently invoke the principle of freedom of contract but do not apply it consistently or often. Perhaps this is simply a question of German domestic politics: Women represent a weak interest group and minorities are rarely citizens in Germany and hence cannot vote, whereas unions and working people have vigorous and powerful political organizations. This discrepancy in political strength may be reflected in legislative and judicial line-drawing. Certainly, legal principle plays only a limited role in determining the extent of state intervention in the labor relationship, since the doctrine of freedom of contract explains very little.

In October 1994, Article 3, paragraph 2, of the Basic Law was amended to include the following language: "The state supports the actual achievement of equal rights for men and women and works towards the elimination of existing disadvantages." This amendment was adopted in connection with the unification treaty's call to review the Basic Law for necessary changes.[71] It is to be hoped that this new language, coupled with the strictures of European law, will force German legal thinkers to reexamine their reflexive reliance on the freedom of contract to defeat attempts to address discriminatory hiring practices. If not, the rare appearance of freedom of contract in legal discourse will continue to highlight the dismissive attitude of prevailing German legal opinion with respect to the very real problem of discrimination against women and minorities in the workplace.

Notes

1. The Fifth Amendment prohibits the federal government from depriving any person of "life, liberty, or property, without due process of law"; the Fourteenth Amendment applies the requirement of due process to the states.

2. See William E. Forbath, *Law and the Shaping of the American Labor Movement* (Cambridge: Harvard University Press, 1991). Appendix A to Forbath's book contains a list of the protective labor laws struck down in the nineteenth and early twentieth centuries.

3. *Lochner v. New York*, 198 U.S. 45 (1905). See also *Adair v. United States*, 208 U.S. 161 (1908) striking down a law banning so-called yellow dog contracts. Employers used these contracts to keep unions out of their factories by forcing prospective employees to sign an employment agreement stating that they would never join a union.

4. *Lochner*, 198 U.S. at 53.

5. *Ibid.* at 56.

6. *Ibid.* at 57.

7. See Roscoe Pound, "Liberty of Contract," *Yale Law Journal* 18 (1909): 454, 481–487; Robert L. Hale, "Bargaining, Duress and Economic Liberty," *Columbia Law Review* 43 (1943): 603, 626.

8. 29 USC §§151–169 (1988).

9. *NLRB v. Jones & Laughlin Steel Corp*, 301 U.S. 1 (1937).

10. *West Coast Hotel Co. v. Parish*, 300 U.S. 379 (1937).

11. 427 U.S. 160 (1976).

12. 42 USC §1981 guarantees all citizens the same right to make and enforce contracts as white citizens. See generally Caroline Fredrickson, "The Misreading of *Patterson v. McClean Credit Union*: The Diminishing Scope of Section 1981," *Columbia Law Review* 91 (1991): 891.

13. See *Jones v. Alfred H. Mayer Co.*, 392 U.S. 409 (1968) (finding 42 USC §1982 to bar racial discrimination in the sale or rental of property by private citizens; allowing forced rental or sale as remedy).

14. 42 USC §§2000e et seq.

15. Other possible methods of compensation are damages, back pay, or reinstatement in the case of discriminatory termination. 42 USC §2000e–5(g).

16. See Reinhard Richardi, "Introduction," in *Arbeitsgesetze*, 44th ed. (1993) at x–xi.

17. On social insurance, see Gerhard A. Ritter, *Social Welfare in Germany and Britain, Origins and Development*, trans. Kim Traynor (New York: Berg Publishing, 1983), 103 ff.; Jürgen Tampke, "Bismarck's Social Legislation: A Genuine Breakthrough?" in W. J. Mommsen and Wolfgang Mock, eds., *The Emergence of the Welfare State in Britain and Germany* (London: Croom Helm, 1981), 71–83. See also Gordon A. Craig, *Germany 1866–1945* (New York: Oxford University Press, 1978), 150–152. On workers' committees, see Wolfgang Däubler, Michael Kittner, Thomas Klebe, and Wolfgang Schneider, eds., *Beitrag: Betriebsverfassungsgesetz Kommentar für die Praxis*, 3d ed. (Cologne: Bund-Verlag, 1992), 106–107. See also Clyde Summers, "Worker Participation in the United States and the Federal Re-

public: A Comparative Study from an American Perspective," *Recht der Arbeit* (1979): 257, 260.

18. See Der Bundesminister für Arbeit und Sozialordnung, ed., *Übersicht über das Recht der Arbeit* (Bonn: Bundesminister für Arbeit und Sozialordnung, 1991), 26–28; see also *BetrVG: Betriebsverfassungsgesetz Kommentar für die Praxis*, 106–107 n. 18.

19. See *Übersicht über das Recht der Arbeit*, 26–28 n. 19; see also Summers, "Worker Participation in the United States and the Federal Republic," 261 n. 18; see also Richardi, "Introduction," xi–xii n. 17.

20. *Übersicht über das Recht der Arbeit*, 53 n. 19. See also Richardi, "Introduction," xi–xiv n. 17.

21. Manfred Gubelt, in Ingo von Münch, ed., *Grundgesetz-Kommentar*, 2d ed. (Frankfurt: Athenaum Verlag, 1981), 520. See also Heribert Buchner, in Reinhard Richardi and Otfried Wlotzke, eds., *Münchner Handbuch Arbeitsrecht* (Munich: C.H. Beck, 1993), 500.

22. See Buchner, *Münchner Handbuch Arbeitsrecht*, 500 n. 22 (citing BVerfGE 81, 156 ff. vom 23. 1. 1990).

23. Ibid.

24. Gubelt, *Grundgesetz-Kommentar*, 182 n. 22. According to Gubelt, because freedom of contract trumps the constitutional and statutory guarantees of equality, employers may force employees to bargain away rights accorded under Article 3. In contrast, protections embodied in a "general labor law norm or basic principle" are absolute and cannot be bargained away. Gubelt cites here a decision by the Federal Labor Court (BAG NJW 1962, 1459), ratifying an agreement whereby a female employee gave up her right to equal pay. This decision has since become obsolete because of European Court pronouncements finding such an agreement a violation of the basic guarantee of equal treatment. *Übersicht über das Recht der Arbeit*, 117 n. 19.

25. Manfred Löwisch, *Arbeitsrecht*, 3d ed. (Heidelberg: C.F. Mueller, 1991), 59. See also Buchner, *Münchner Handbuch Arbeitsrecht*, 509 n. 22.

26. Löwisch, *Arbeitsrecht*, 385–386 n. 26.

27. Outside the employment field, other laws compel the conclusion of a contract. For example, private companies holding monopoly control over an important product are required to provide it to all comers. Insurance companies are the major target of this obligation. Moreover, quasi-public institutions such as museums and hospitals also must provide services to all. See "Comparative Assessment of the Legal Instruments in the Various Member States of the European Communities to Combat All Forms of Discrimination, Racism and Xenophobia and Incitement and Hatred and Racial Violence," *National Study for the Federal Republic of Germany* (Rapporteur: Institut für Migrations- und Rassissmusforschung, Hamburg, March 1992), Sections 3.1–3.2.

28. Section 823, para. 2, of the BGB.

29. Manfred Löwisch, in Reinhard Richardi and Otfried Wlotzke, eds., *Münchener Handbuch Arbeitsrecht* (1993), 100; see also Josephine Shaw, "Recent Developments in the Field of Labour Market Equality: Sex Discrimination Law in the Federal Republic of Germany," *Comparative Labor Law Journal* 13 (1991): 18, 30; Löwisch, in *Münchener Handbuch Arbeitsrecht*, 100.

30. Ibid., 100 n. 30.

31. BAG vom 2.6.1987, *Der Betrieb* (1987): 2312. See also Löwisch, *Arbeitsrecht*, 54, 386; Buchner, *Münchener Handbuch Arbeitsrecht*, 570 n. 22. If providing "natural restitution" in the form of a job is not an acceptable remedy because, for example, the worker no longer wants the position, then the compensation may take the form of money damages.

32. See, e.g., Löwisch, *Münchener Handbuch Arbeitsrecht*, 101 n. 30.

33. BAG vom 2.6.1987, *Der Betrieb* (1987): 2312.

34. *Übersicht über das Recht der Arbeit*, 115 n. 19.

35. *Arbeitsrechtliches EG-Anpassungsgesetz*, BGB 1 I S. 1308, also sometimes known as the *Gleichhandlungsgesetz* (Equal Treatment Law).

36. Council Directive 76/207/EEC of 10 February, 1975, *Journal of the European Community* 19, no. L 39: 40 (equal treatment).

37. For example, it is legal to refuse female applicants for male roles in a play. Some German commentators would go quite far in providing wiggle room for employers, allowing societal prejudices to justify differential treatment. See Löwisch, *Arbeitsrecht*, 56 n. 26.

38. Thus, an applicant could recover only the few marks it cost to mail a job application or to take the bus to an interview. This outcome has earned the law the nickname "the Stamp Act." See *The New York Times*, 26 November, 1995, p. 10. See also Klaus Bertelsmann and Heide M. Pfarr, "Diskriminierung von Frauen bei der Einstellung und Beförderung," *Der Betrieb* (1984): 297; Shaw, "Recent Developments in the Field of Labour Market Equality," 24 n. 30.

39. See Bertelsmann and Pfarr, "Diskriminierung von Frauen," 1297 n. 39; Shaw, "Recent Developments in the Field of Labour Market Equality," 24 n. 30.

40. Ibid.

41. Judgment of 14.3.1984, BAG 1231, *Der Betrieb* (1984): 2297; see also Shaw, "Recent Developments in the Field of Labour Market Equality," 31–32 n. 30.

42. *Draehmpaehl. v. Urania Immobilienservice ohG*, Court of Justice of European Communities, Case C-180/95 (22 April 1997).

43. See Bertelsmann and Pfarr, "Diskriminierung von Frauen," 1297 n. 39; see also Wolfgang Däubler, *Das Arbeitsrecht* 7th ed., vol. 2 (Reinbek bei Hamburg: Rowohlt, 1990): 690.

44. Ibid., 690–691 n. 44. See also Bertelsmann and Pfarr, "Diskriminierung von Frauen," 1300 n. 39. A 1993 Constitutional Court decision brings some hope that there may be a change in the judges' approach to Section 611a. That case held that Article 3, paragraph 2's equal treatment guarantee, as developed by Section 611a, applies to discriminatory actions by private individuals such as employers and does not just prevent the legislature from enacting discriminatory laws. This could be a first step toward recognition that Article 3 and Section 611a should be given the status of protective laws. See Judgment of 16 November 1993, BVerfG, 89 BVerfGE 276 (FRG).

45. Section 249 of the BGB.

46. Gubelt, *Grundgesetz-Kommentar*, 1553–1555 n. 22.

47. Ibid.

48. See Sections 9 and 10, *Kündigungsschutzgesetz* 1969 (BGB 1. I 1317) (KSchG). See also Bertelsmann and Pfarr, "Diskriminierung von Frauen," 1299–1300 n. 39.

49. Many German employers voluntarily join employers' associations that subject them to industry-wide collective bargaining agreements even if their own employees are not unionized. These collective bargaining agreements serve as instruments of national economic policy by establishing minimum standards in many areas of the labor market. See Summers, "Worker Participation in the United States and the Federal Republic," 261 n. 18.

50. See Section 5 I TVG. See also Summers, "Worker Participation in the United States and the Federal Republic," 261 n. 18.

51. Günter Schaub, *Arbeitsrecht Handbuch*, 4th ed. (Munich: Beck, 1979), 1067.

52. Ibid., 1068.

53. *Übersicht über das Recht der Arbeit*, 49 n. 19.

54. Section 78a BetrVG.

55. Buchner, *Münchener Handbuch*, 501–502 n. 22.

56. Ibid., 502.

57. See Manfred Weiss, "Labor Law and Industrial Relations in Europe 1992: A German Perspective," *Comparative Labor Law* 11 (1990): 411, 416—"It is quite possible that this body of protective law is the most comprehensive legislation of its kind in the world."

58. Section 87 Betrag. See generally Summers, "Worker Participation in the United States and the Federal Republic," 261 n. 18.

59. The supervisory board in a German corporation performs two functions primarily: It selects the managing board that handles the day-to-day management of the company; and it supervises the managing board's conduct of business. See Roland Koestler, "Codetermination in German Enterprises," in *Codetermination: Introduction into the Legal System of Worker Participation in the Federal Republic of Germany* (Hans-Böckler-Foundation pamphlet), 5.

60. Ibid., 7.

61. See Weiss, "Labor Law and Industrial Relations in Europe 1992: A German Perspective," 416 n. 58.

62. *Bundeserziehungsgeldgesetz* 1992 (BGB1. I S. 68).

63. *Arbeitsplatzschutzgesetz* 1980 (BGB1. I S. 425).

64. *Bundesurlaubsgesetz* 1963 (BGB1. I S. 2).

65. *Lohnfortzahlungsgesetz* 1969 (BGB1. I S. 946).

66. *Kündigungsschutzgesetz* 1969 (BGB 1. I 1317) (KSchG).

67. Section 102 (5) Betrag.

68. KSchG Section 15; Section 103 Betrag.

69. Donald P. Kommers, "German Constitutionalism: A Prolegomenon," *Emory Law Journal* 40 (1991): 837, 848.

70. Gubelt, *Grundgesetz-Kommentar*, 153 n. 22 (emphasis added).

71. *Gesetz zum Änderung des Grundgesetzes*, BGB1. I 3146. For discussion, see Ninon Colneric, "Making Equality Law More Effective: Lessons from the German Experience," *Cardozo Women's Law Journal* v3 (1996): 229, 231.

PART FIVE

Germany in Transition:
Alumni Conference Speeches

11

Germany and the United States in Multilateral Institutions

KARL TH. PASCHKE

I am honored and pleased that you have invited me to be your keynote speaker this year. This clearly indicates the advancement of my professional career because the last time I addressed the Robert Bosch Alumni Association, in 1988, it was only to introduce another keynote speaker, Horst Teltschik. I have always valued highly the role played by the association in relations between Germany and the United States. The German Robert Bosch Foundation had an excellent idea when it decided to bring young American leaders across the Atlantic to learn about my country and become familiar with its political, societal, and economic structures. But it was an *American* initiative by the first alumni of this program to create this Association, which actually reinforces, extends, and perpetuates the linkage that each and every one of you has established with Germany and the Germans while a Bosch fellow.

Since you are all so thoroughly conversant in things German—that goes without saying—as well as in the major factors of American foreign policy, I hope you will find it appropriate for me to offer a few thoughts about the role of Germany and the United States in multilateral institutions.

Our world, on the eve of the millennium, is becoming more and more interdependent. President Clinton, in his address to the UN General Assembly on 24 September 1997, expressed this as follows: "Now we find ourselves at a turning point in human history. The blocs and barriers that long defined the world are giving way to an age of remarkable possibility. . . . The challenge before us is twofold: to seize the new opportunities for more people to enjoy peace, freedom, security, and prosperity, and to move strongly and swiftly against the dangers change has produced."

Let me quote briefly from another speech, offered in the UN General Assembly at the same time, this one by German foreign minister Klaus Kinkel: "We must look beyond our national borders and think and act accordingly. . . . We [Europeans] stand for a policy of international cooperation among equals, a global partnership for development and the environment in the twenty-first century. New opportunities for such a partnership derive from the globalization of industry and technology."

Germany, perhaps more than most other nations, has always been mindful of its political and economic dependence on the outside world, for historical and geographic reasons. After the disaster of 1945, the strong belief in multilateralism even became an *Ersatz* (substitute) for shattered national pride. The Germans were the first to embrace the idea of a united Europe and today are still the motor of the European Union. Our visible efforts over the past four decades to re-establish Germany as a reliable team player on the international scene—in the European Community, in the context of the Organization for Security and Cooperation in Europe, in the United Nations—resulted in a capital of trust and estimation that we badly needed when the East suddenly crumbled and we were faced with the chance for reunification. I am convinced the foreign policy aspects of the unification process would not have been so easy to address, and our neighbors would not have been as supportive as they were during those dramatic months when two German states merged into one, had the Federal Republic of Germany not proved a trustworthy and multilaterally inclined partner in the preceding decades.

This pronounced, firm, and unshakable belief in multilateralism as an overriding foreign policy principle also has characterized Germany's attitude toward the United Nations.

Although Germany, along with Japan, was public enemy number. 1 in 1945, at the time of the creation of the world organization and when the UN charter made specific reference to this, the Federal Republic of Germany began to become actively involved in the work of the world body very soon after its inception. However, it was not until 1973 that both Germanies—the FRG and GDR—were admitted as full members of the United Nations. This was, of course, one of the significant results of the so-called *Entspannungspolitik* (policy of détente). It is interesting to note that, while the two Germanies were members, there were very few instances where their ideological and political differences played out in the different UN forums. What the French used to call *les querelles allemandes* (the intra-German haggling) almost never became an issue in the United Nations. As a matter of fact, the two delegations, although belonging to different regional groupings, more often than not developed common ground on multilateral issues—an illustration of the potential real advantages of a multilateral environment.

In the early 1980s, when Hans-Dietrich Genscher was foreign minister, his annual UN program in New York for the opening sessions in September always featured a meeting over lunch with his East German counterpart to discuss mutually interesting multilateral questions. In 1990, when, as a consequence of the fundamental shakeup of Eastern Europe, the GDR disappeared, the united German role in the United Nations obviously changed, too. In fact, Germany became the third-largest contributor to the UN budget after the United States and Japan. Germany's increased political weight on the international scene also translated into wider responsibilities in the UN context.

It took some time for Germany to adjust to this larger role. The German government faced specific problems with regard to the constitution (the Basic Law) as well as to public opinion when it began to fully embrace those increased responsibilities in the field of peace-keeping.

But, by and large, a UN-friendly German foreign policy has always been strongly supported by all responsible political parties in Germany and I trust that this will continue to be the case. It also can be said that German UN policy has always been characterized by a balanced and realistic understanding of the function of the world organization. Bonn perceives the United Nations as the one political forum where all the countries of the world, on the basis of legal equality, conduct a continuous dialogue with the aim of seeking consensus on global issues. Bonn believes in the increasing importance of the United Nations now that the East-West conflict is over and the blockage of the organization by Cold War superpower confrontations has vanished. Bonn also understands that the majority of the global issues haunting the international community, which will continue to dominate the agenda in the decades to come, are basically North-South issues. Therefore, Bonn handles UN matters primarily under the umbrella of fostering stable, nonconfrontational relations between the industrialized countries and the third world, while trying to be a team player in the European and Atlantic context in this effort.

It appears that Bonn has been successful in its UN policy so far, as indicated by the fact that there is almost no opposition *to*, and a lot of support *for*, Bonn's request to be given a permanent seat on the UN Security Council. Only the Italians, for reasons of their own, are openly contesting this claim. Yet this question will probably remain open for some time because reshaping the Security Council to reflect more closely the political realities of the 1990s will take more than just adding the Germans (and, for that matter, the Japanese). Incidentally, the United States has from the start been very supportive of the German candidacy for a permanent seat on the Security Council.

While the German position towards the United Nations might be described as continuously supportive and mindful of the intricacies and constraints of multilateralism, the American attitude towards the world organization and other international, multilateral bodies is more of a roller-coaster story. One could say that the United States, the only remaining superpower, has the same problems with international organizations that Dan Marino would have if he had to quarterback a high school football team.

Let me remind you that the U.S. Congress shot down President Woodrow Wilson's high-flying League of Nations plans in 1919—a first indication of America's uneasiness with international organizations. At the end of World War II, however, the United States, obviously shaken by this global catastrophe and captured by the idealistic thought that this had been the "war to end all wars," became the first and foremost backer of the new world organization called the United Nations. It was no accident that the founding conference took place in San Francisco and the organization chose New York City as its first headquarters. In fact, the United Nations became very much an organization with an American design. The Americans agreed to incur 40 percent of the cost of the United Nations and the Rockefellers donated the land on which the impressive buildings for the General Assembly and the Secretariat were to be erected.

But in the day-to-day multilateral business, the United States soon came to view the world body as a rather complex, awkward, and not terribly helpful mechanism. The antagonism between the United States and the Soviet Union began to unfold in the Security Council. The veto power given to each member of the Security Council prevented it from becoming a forum for effective crisis management.

The third world grew into a more and more significant factor in the United Nations. Washington, which had set out as the mentor and—to use the metaphor again—the quarterback of the United Nations, increasingly found itself the target of harsh criticism for "imperialism, capitalism, and neocolonialism." The enthusiasm in the United States for the world organization gave way to disappointment.

At this point a few rather general observations about American foreign policy are in order. First, this country traditionally wavers between shouldering all the burdens of the world and negating international obligations that stem from being a superpower. Spells of isolationism not only are quite frequent in public opinion but flare up in Congress and occasionally even in government actions. The rejection of U.S. involvement in the League of Nations was only one example of that line of thinking: Why should this huge, self-sufficient country bother with the problems of the outside world? What business does it have in faraway places like Africa?

Admittedly, only people who do not know or do not want to know how complex and interdependent today's world is can take this isolationist attitude. But there are more subtle forms of isolationism that translate into a strong and emotional disbelief in the role of, and an animosity toward, the United Nations.

A recent article in *Foreign Affairs* contended that it is not the job of the United Nations to meet the needs of 5.5 billion people, but the job of nation-states. Elsewhere in the same article, its author comments that when every local/regional problem becomes global, the buck stops nowhere. Furthermore, he maintains that in making every issue global, the UN is trying to create a nonexistent world. The author of the article is Senator Jesse Helms (R-NC), chairman of the Foreign Relations Committee of the U.S. Senate.

Much more prevalent in U.S. foreign policy, however, is the notion that the country must get involved abroad, that it is indeed in keeping with a noble American tradition not to close one's eyes to problems or to human suffering wherever they occur. Remember Somalia: When the images of starving children entered living rooms across the country as broadcast on CNN, President George Bush immediately felt the pressure to do something about it. In Europe, the reaction would have been: We must request some joint action under the auspices of the United Nations. In the United States, the reaction is: Send in the Marines. Don't bother with the United Nations—it will only complicate and slow down the necessary measures. We must move strongly and swiftly—and that means unilaterally.

Here, in a nutshell, you have America's major difficulty with multilateralism. Multilateralism means slow and cumbersome decisionmaking processes, consensus-seeking, and readiness to accept a compromise that falls short of one's original goals and aspirations. And if one feature is obviously lacking in U.S. foreign policy, it is patience. Either it is in your national character, or it comes automatically with superpower status: the desire to tackle problems aggressively and to achieve solutions right away, along with the disinclination to be tied down by others who do not possess the same amount of power.

Bob Dole once commented in a speech that America must be in the driver's seat of the United Nations. The problem with multilateralism is that all participating countries wish to have a hand on the steering wheel of the organization—and legitimately so. I must admit that this makes the United Nations a rather slow-moving and, at times, erratic vehicle.

On the other hand, I can assure you that the community of nations has always been more than willing to accept America's *leading* role in the United Nations as well as in other multilateral institutions. This is reflected in the sizable number of Americans in top positions in multilateral institutions, from the World Bank to certain UN agencies, funds, and programs, as well as in the weight that American positions and interventions carry in all these bodies. To paraphrase an old commercial slogan: When the United States talks, multilateral institutions listen.

Recently, however, Washington's partners have been very uneasy with the obvious discrepancy between attempts by the United States to throw its weight around in the United Nations, especially on reform issues, and the U.S. Congress's unilateral refusal to pay the U.S. membership dues, which has resulted in the huge arrearage of $1.2 billion. I heard someone say that if the United States wants to be in the driver's seat, it also has to pay for the gas. I believe that this congressional refusal has not strengthened but actually weakened American leverage and leadership within the United Nations. So people in the Secretariat of the United Nations were encouraged when President Clinton, in his General Assembly speech, said, "We are paying our dues and we are committed to paying off our accrued obligations soon."

Let me conclude with one last thought about the financial contributions the United States makes to the United Nations. The assumption is widespread that the United States is paying enormous sums of money for foreign aid in general and for the United Nations in particular and that it is not really getting anything tangible in return. The truth is that every American citizen pays only $1.25 per year into the regular UN budget. U.S. dues to the United Nations are only a tiny fraction of 1 percent of the U.S. government's budget. In return, the United States has enjoyed the political, economic, and financial benefits of relatively stable North-South relations for the past 50 years.

What would otherwise have degenerated into a stormy, hostile, and probably belligerent antagonism between North and South, between rich and poor, is today a multilateral dialogue, not always friendly, but civilized, and an honest, if imperfect, exercise in grappling jointly with global issues. The number and dimension of these global issues will grow, and no country—certainly not Germany, and not even the United States—will be able to cope with these challenges single-handedly. Therefore both Germany and the United States need the United Nations, and the United Nations needs these two key members.

Notes

Speech delivered to Robert Bosch Foundation Alumni Association annual conference, Washington, D.C., 5 October, 1996.

12

The Superpower
and the Soft Hegemon

JOSEF JOFFE

In June of this year, we celebrated 50 years of the Marshall Plan. We might just as easily have commemorated 50 years of German-American ... what? Reconciliation, partnership, alliance? I would rather call it the "beginning of a wonderful friendship," to borrow from the most famous line of the most beloved movie of my generation, *Casablanca*.

A propos "beloved." That's how I decided to get serious about the Hamburg lady who is now my wife. I gave her, as was then my somewhat outlandish habit, the "Casablanca test" composed of three questions.

First, the easy one: What was never said in the movie? "Play it again, Sam." Right. Ingrid Bergman merely said: "Play it, Sam." A bit more difficult: What did the old German emigré couple say to each other when practicing their English? "How much watch, mein Liebchen?"—"Ten watch"—"Such watch?" She got that one right, too. On to the third question. What did Carl, the waiter, say when Rick asked him to give Major Strasser the best table in the house? "Oh, Mr. Rick, I already gave him the best table. Since he is a German, I knew he would take it anyway." At that point, I started thinking engagement.

And we are still married.

So are, as it were, the United States and Germany—after 50 years. That feat is extraordinary in the history of nations where, as Palmerston taught us, there are neither permanent enmities nor friendships, only permanent interests.

We'll come to the interests later. Let's first talk about emotions, and that is where the Marshall Plan, announced at Harvard 50 years ago, played such an extraordinary role. The Marshall Plan was not much by today's standards. All told, the aid package—grants, loans, real stuff like food and fuel—came to $12.5 billion over three years. Make that $80 billion in current dollars, more or less the same sum western Germany has been plowing into eastern Germany *annually* since reunification in 1990.

And yet the symbolism mattered much more than the substance in a story that ranks among the finest moments in the annals of American diplomacy. Try to picture Germany's position in 1947. Germany was the most hated nation on the planet. Hitler's heirs were still expecting revenge and retribution without end—Versailles cubed, as it were. But instead, there were the four "F's": food, fuel, fiber, and fertilizer "Made in the U.S.A." The psychological impact was phenomenal.

Back at Versailles in 1919, the Germans had been branded like Cain; they alone bore the guilt for World War I. Their lands were amputated, their industries dismantled. They were to pay backbreaking reparations until kingdom come. And now? Along with the other West Europeans, the Germans were handed the Marshall Plan. In money terms, it was not that much. West Germany received only one-tenth of the total—a meager $19 per capita—as compared to one-fourth for Britain and one-fifth for France.

But the real pay-off is still impossible to quantify. What was it worth for a pariah suddenly to be part of the club? What price tag can you attach to respectability and community when you thought that you were off to prison forever?

The Marshall Plan was so much more than the four "F's." Instead of exacting reparations, as after 1919, it offered precious start-up capital. Instead of imposing discrimination, it offered rehabilitation. And let us not forget what is always ignored. While extending aid, the Americans not only opened their vast market but also relentlessly pressed the Europeans to resist their protectionist instincts in favor of freer trade among themselves.

This, too, offers a benign contrast to the aftermath of World War I, when competitive devaluation and rising trade barriers regularly nipped recovery in the bud. If Germany today is an exemplary democracy—the very opposite of the doomed Weimar experiment—we have the Marshall Plan (and what followed) to thank for it. And why? Because this time, German democracy was associated with prosperity and security, and that made all the difference.

Roots of U.S.-German Friendship

In the beginning, there were feelings—of relief and gratitude—mixed with chewing gum and CARE packages. But it is not emotions that bind nations together. This "wonderful friendship," more accurately this ultra-stable relationship, had three roots: solid interest; cultural affinities; and, compatible, rather than clashing, historical memories. Let us discuss these in reverse order.

1. *Memories*. In stark contrast to France or Russia, the United States had no historic traumas standing between it and Germany. Sure, the United States had twice in this century gone to war against Germany. But because of a benign geography, no "arch enmity" had ever poisoned that relationship, as happened with France.

Separated from Germany by an ocean, the United States had never been directly threatened, let alone occupied, by Germany. There had been neither imperial rivalries, as with England, nor hegemonial conflicts, as with France—memories that extend back to the Thirty Years' War. Psychologically, the slate was fairly clean between the United States and Germany at the threshold of the "wonderful friendship" that began to blossom 50 years ago.

2. *Cultural Affinities*. According to legend, the young American republic almost adopted German as its official language. Nice, but wrong. Nonetheless, America's cultural ties to Germany have always been thicker than those to, say, France. Germans, after the English and Irish, are the largest group with which Americans identify their ancestry.

Although Harvard started out as a British-type divinity school, Johns Hopkins was founded on the German model. After 1933, flight and expulsion constituted an enormous cultural transfer from Germany to the United States. Think about Albert Einstein and Henry Kissinger, think about the faculties of America's top universities after World War II. Take my own experience: My four most important professors at Harvard all came from Central Europe.

Then think about the postwar "Americanization" of Germany. Not about the triumph of American pop culture from Disney to Levis—though the company's founder, Levi Strauss, also was a German immigrant. My point is the enormous acculturation of the West Germans under American auspices. Nowhere was the soil more fertile for modernity and "Made in U.S.A." as it was in postwar Germany.

Germany in 1945 was a bit like America in the eighteenth century: a kind of *tabula rasa*. The kaiser was gone; the aristocracy had lost its power; the Nazis were destroyed. With all pre-or anti-democratic structures demolished, the grounds were flattened and plowed, so to speak, waiting for the right seed. And the seed corn came from the United States: liberal democracy, an open society, decentralization of power, and market economics.

On the virtually virgin soil of postwar Germany, these implants could flourish much more luxuriantly than in the tradition-bound societies of France and Britain. Sure, democracy came on the back of tanks driven by the U.S. occupiers, but the West Germans grabbed these gifts and ran with them, especially since this time democracy was associated not with humiliation but with rehabilitation and prosperity.

3. *The Bonds of Shared Interests.* Memories and affinities were the emotional cement of this "wonderful friendship." But the steel core of this construction was complementary interests that continue to hold up even after 50 years. In the beginning there was an obvious deal. The United States delivered security, capital, and respectability. The West Germans delivered themselves, so to speak—their strategic territory and the largest supply of European arms in NATO.

A "Special Relationship"?

So each gave to the other what it needed most, and that set the tone: an enduring complementarity of interests. The comparison with Britain and France is quite instructive. Into the 1960s, the "special relationship" between the United States and Britain was not special at all. There was the silent duel for the mantle of empire, which the United States won in the face of bitter British resentment.

Worse was the unending struggle with France. The Franco-American rivalry in Europe has never stopped—all the way to today's Kulturkampf over films, language, and TV. On French radio, I am told, deejays have to be called *disque-tourneurs.* They have to announce the hit parade as *parade de frappe,* with a band like the "Spice Girls" being called *Les Filles d'Epices.*

Now compare this to the crises between Bonn and Washington. If I listed those of the 1950s, 1960s, and 1970s, you would probably listen in puzzled bemusement—and rightly so. Yesterday's clashes over the Radford Plan, the Multilateral Force, or the International Access Authority for West Berlin ring hollow, if they ring at all. They are, at best, the stuff of dissertations.

There was only one serious clash of interests, which unfolded in the early 1980s. The period began with the Soviet invasion of Afghanistan and America's decision to meet the Soviet challenge across the board. The United States would always ask the Europeans for proofs of loyalty to the Atlantic alliance: Do not go to the Moscow Olympics, do not build the Ural gas pipeline, withhold credits from the Evil Empire, take our nuclear missiles.

For the first time since 1945, the German-American relationship was seriously strained. Why? Because this time, there was a serious collision. While the United States was declaring Cold War II, the Germans wanted to protect their separate détente with the Soviet Union and East Germany. This was the time of rampant anti-Americanism among the young and of sullen sentiment among their elders, at least on the Left.

Nonetheless, even this crisis makes my point, as it soon dramatized not the frailty but the solidity of the relationship. The Great Euromissile War over Pershings and cruise missiles ended with the electoral victories in 1983 and 1987 of Helmut Kohl, who had staked his political fate on the American connection. But the United States delivered, too. In its second term, the Reagan administration also understood that alliances do not flourish when principals do not take care of their junior partners' interests. And so ranks closed again.

Why? Because Bonn and Washington never lost sight of their larger and enduring interests. Both were, and continue to be, partners bound by complementary rather than competitive interests. For the Federal Republic, the most vulnerable actor on the Cold War stage, the United States was the one and only credible guarantor of security vis-à-vis the Soviet Union. For the United States, the Federal Republic was its "continental sword" par excellence—a critical strategic *glacis* and the largest military power on the continent.

But there is more than these complementary interests. Germany and United States also share many domestic similarities. Both are federal, rather than centralized, constructions. Both are open societies and open markets—though the German economy suffers from a good deal of neo-corporatist rigidities. Compared to other large continentals, Germany is the most "American" in the sense that it absorbs rather than defies whatever cultural and economic impulses come across the Atlantic. Hence, German deejays can safely say "hit parade" rather than "*Schlagermarsch.*"

Economically, the United States and Germany share similar preferences for free trade—and for the occasional protectionist deviation. Free trade is not a matter of mere ideological instinct but also of economic strength. It is far easier for Germany, the export engine of Europe, to preach free trade than it is for France or Spain.

Above all, the United States and Germany do not see each other as rivals for primacy in Europe, let alone beyond Europe, in the Middle East. One evident explanation is Germany's dual defeat in this century; that has been a sobering and enduring experience. Germany, once ultrachauvinist, is today the least nationalist nation in Europe, and for good reason. Germany—liberal, democratic, and well managed—now enjoys what panzers and jackboots could never achieve. It has a specific kind of hegemony, what I would call a "soft hegemony." Its "soft hegemony" does not rest on the *Wehrmacht* but on the deutsche mark. It feeds off the strength of the German economy and the attraction of its socioeconomic arrangements.

What is the "German model"? Let's call it "corporatist capitalism." It is defined by consensual conflict management, which ensures that no group must pay the entire price of change and adaptation. It is further defined by a large government sector, which takes in more than 50 percent of the gross domestic product and cushions everyone against the harsh verdicts of the market.

Inasmuch as this model continues to secure both economic growth and social peace, it remains more attractive in Europe, especially in the East, than the statism of France or the half-hearted Thatcherism of Britain. Above all, though, the Germans have learned that their "soft hegemony," muted further by a strong dose of self-containment, has been all the more successful as it has remained "soft." "Soft power"—call it "Kohlism"—has proved far more profitable than Wilhelmism.

A Division of Labor

To repeat the point, America's and Germany's positions in the international system favor a division of labor and roles with low friction and high cooperation. Why? Their visions of themselves and the world do not collide. To illustrate the point, let us examine the recent past and the two countries' policies in Europe.

Towards Russia, Bonn and Washington essentially pursue parallel policies. They are trying to socialize Russia and to puncture Russian fears of neocontainment. At the same time, they have been prudently trying to integrate Eastern Europe into the West.

When it comes to the European Union (EU), both countries scrupulously avoid pushing each other too far. Although the United States cannot be completely happy about Europe's bloc-building tendencies, it will never try to alienate Bonn from its European partners. On the other side, Germany will take care to soften the worst French reflexes that would turn the EU into a Fortress Europe. For Germany, the United States remains what it has always been: not just a power in Europe, but a *European* power.

Reunification is a typical example of this enduring complementarity. Remember 1989–1990. As France and Britain tried to brake, if not stop, the process, Washington moved to the vanguard. Two weeks before the Berlin Wall collapsed, President George Bush set the tone when he said, "I do not share the worry other European nations might have about reunification." That clinched it. Thereafter, Washington ran interference for Bonn all the way to October 3, 1990—reunification day.

Who knows whether reunification would have proceeded so smoothly if the United States had not diligently cleared one stumbling block after another? No wonder Helmut Kohl said afterwards, "Stronger support could not have been wished for." He "would never forget this."

In those nine months that shook the world, all the elements of complementarity that have carried the relationship forward for 50 years came together. Unhindered by bitter historical memories, the United States could think strategically; hence, Washington understood immediately that a united Germany would constitute a strategic gain vis-à-vis its old rival Russia. So the United States never worried about a loss of status and power, as did France and Britain.

A united Germany easily fit into the overall framework of American interests—provided that all of Germany would be in the West. Hence, the United States was practically predestined to turn Germany's interests into its own. Indeed, 1990 recalled the logic of the early 1950s, when it was the United States that pushed for German rearmament and integration into the North Atlantic alliance. As it was then, so it was again in 1990. Once more, the United States thought it was better to have the strongest continental power as a friend—that a strong Germany inside the tent was better than a weak, alienated Germany outside.

Conclusion

Let me conclude. What about the future? Yogi Berra once said, "I never make predictions, and least about the future." But it is hard to think up scenarios where this basic complementarity of interests would pale. Will the Germans turn into protectionists, pulling up the EU's draw-bridge with the French? Will this Germany ever play a Rapallo-like game with Russia, or challenge the United States globally?

To be sure, after reunification, the Federal Republic shed a lot of those dependencies that used to tie it to the United States—above all, in matters of security. But, ironically, a main pillar of continuity has not crumbled at all. As in the past half-century, the United States continues to play the vital role of both buffer and legitimator of German power. Recall the 1950s, when the other Europeans worried more about a rearmed Germany than about Stalinist pressure.

Without America's pledge to keep a permanent military presence in Europe, those old "archenemies" France and Germany hardly would have joined hands in friendship and community. They could do so because, for the first time in history, there was a player in the game who was stronger than each and who could thus reassure both. With America as protector and pacifier, rivalry and security fears could at last be dispatched in favor of cooperation and integration.

That American role continues to work its blessings. Though Germany is a "soft hegemon," it is Europe's No. 1 again. So, it is nice to have America in the game. This superpower shortens the shadow of German might. Thus, the U.S. is the soft counterweight to the "soft hegemon" that is Germany.

This is good for Germany and for Europe. For the first time, Europe need not worry about a united Germany, and Germany need not share the fears of its neighbors. Just by being there, the United States removes the sting from German power. So, for the first time in German history, Germany is encircled only by friends. In this respect, the 1990s resemble the 1950s. This is why the "wonderful friendship" between victors and vanquished has blossomed into a "natural partnership" between the global No. 1 and The regional No. 1.

In the beginning I spoke about emotions, affinities, and interests. Sentiments and cultural similarities alone have never provided an enduring cement among nations. In the end, it is the permanence of congruent interests that carries the day. That is the secret of this "wonderful friendship," and it is difficult to foresee what could rend it asunder in the next 50 years.

No German today would say, "go home." Instead, they plead, *"Don't go home."* That is quite a feat in the annals of international politics, and it all began with the Marshall Plan 50 years ago. What will happen in the next 50 years? Like Yogi Berra, I do not want to make any predictions. But I do have one piece of advice for Americans who might think that they could safely leave the European game. Let me misquote *Casablanca* and say, "Play it again, Uncle Sam."

Notes

Speech given to the Robert Bosch Foundation Alumni Association annual conference in Washington, D.C., November 1997.

13

German Foreign Policy Beyond the East-West Conflict: A New Foreign Policy Framework

KARSTEN D. VOIGT

From the debris of the Berlin Wall emerged a new world, but one that caught us unawares and unprepared and whose new shape is still evolving. From the standpoint of foreign policy, however, one thing is clear: This new world is less simple and less manageable than the one that existed before 1989. Between the conclusion of World War II in 1945 and the implosion of the Eastern Bloc in 1989, all foreign and security policy questions in Germany had to be viewed and judged in terms of the East-West conflict. Whether it was German rearmament or detente, the need for western integration, or the NATO dual-track decision, the East-West conflict invariably furnished the backdrop for the political decisions to be taken. The link between foreign policy issues and the literally life-threatening East-West conflict also explains why foreign and security policy not only provided topics for discussion by political and intellectual elites but moved ordinary people to take to the streets.

The simple standoffs in the East-West conflict were reflected in the lines of dispute that marked foreign policy debates in Germany. Here we had *détente*, there anti-communism—such buzzwords sufficed to establish the identity of Left and Right. Even today, some people still miss that good old polarization option. During the Persian Gulf War, for example, attempts were made to polarize opponents' views along traditional lines. But by the time of the dispute between the "pacifists" and the "warmongers," new arguments were evolving that no longer fit neatly on either side of the familiar demarcation lines separating Left and Right. A further attempt made at the time of the hostilities in the former Yugoslavia to conduct a debate on the militarization of German foreign policy based on traditional patterns was doomed to failure. The attempt failed not only in Germany's Social Democratic Party but also among the Greens. At the other end of the political spectrum, Christian Democrats could no longer always seek their electoral salvation in the 1950s slogan, "All Socialist roads lead to Moscow." Since we have no polarization option, we are not surprised to find greater agreement in certain areas of policy among members of different parties than among different members of the same party.

It is not easy to fully grasp what has changed for our foreign and security policy since the revolution of 1989–1990, and it will take some time before we really come to terms with the changes. When Hans-Dietrich Genscher, in connection with negotiations on German unity in 1990, affirmed that there would be unbroken continuity in German foreign policy after German unity, I pointed out that the only value in such a statement was that it built confidence among our neighbors. After all, Germany's neighbors, too, had their problems assessing the significance of the revolutionary events of 1989–1990, so they, too, were hoping that Germany would go on pursuing its pre-1989 policies, which had been based on the simple standoff positions of the East-West conflict. However, as soon as our neighbors themselves began to grasp the impact of the changes then beginning, they looked behind the undifferentiated professions of continuity in German foreign policy and were compelled to infer either some secret foreign policy agenda or an incapacity to grasp the facts of the new situation. As an analytical statement, therefore, Genscher's statement was inaccurate. The change in the underlying conditions of foreign and security policy in the years 1989–1990 was greater for Germany than for any other country. This change concerns the 45 years since the conclusion of World War II. German partition ended on October 3, 1990, and Germany is no longer subject to the constraints placed on its sovereignty by the occupation laws. But the changes go much deeper and concern a period that covers centuries. Germany is surrounded by states that are well disposed toward it. Never since the first German disaster of the Thirty Years' War has the country found itself in such a favorable foreign policy situation. Quite unlike the political environment after the Peace of Westphalia in 1648, the Congress of Vienna in 1815, the Treaty of Versailles in 1919, and the Potsdam agreement in 1945, the situation in 1990 for a reunified Germany with a federal form of government was such that it was no longer regarded as a threat by its European neighbors.

Interests and Perspectives

To reiterate, identifying Germany's foreign and security policy interests before 1989–1990 was an easy matter, much easier than defining interests in a new situation under constantly changing conditions, as has been the case since 1989. One consequence is that our discussions of foreign policy contain more about responsibility and values and less about interests. But Germany does have interests, of course, and a lack of clarity in defining them can lead to a lack of clarity in laying down priorities.

Germany has an interest in preserving and extending peace and democracy, promoting its economic prosperity, and improving social and ecological conditions. Such goals are best achieved in an international community dedicated to democracy and human rights. In this respect, the current regional and global environment is more and more tightly knit than ever before. So we must translate our interests into foreign policy.

Viewed against this background, German foreign policy has the following priorities:

- deepening European integration;
- renewal of, and extensions to, Euro-Atlantic links;
- stabilization in East Central and Eastern Europe as well as Southern Europe through integration and cooperation with democratic states;
- stabilization, economic cooperation, and the defusing of security risks in the states of the Middle East; and
- solving global problems of economics and ecology, some associated with security issues, some with the United Nations, some with the World Trade Organization, and some calling for new institutions and rules for dealing with globally oriented economics and ecological questions.

The Task of European Integration

Germany is interested in further European integration for two reasons: to preserve peace and to maintain economic growth.

By itself, the German market is too small for the needs of an economy geared to external trade, so the country has an interest in cultivating trading relations set in an economic environment that is as open as possible and, in its immediate vicinity, in having the largest possible integrated common market with a common currency. This means that Germany not only must press ahead with the integration process but also must open the European Union (EU) to those states in East Central and Eastern Europe that are already in a position to participate in the integration process.

The big role played by the peace policy idea can be seen in the ongoing danger of destabilization from the struggle for influence among European states. If Germany's political discussions repeatedly refer to Germany bearing sole responsibility for its policies, such responsibility can be discharged politically only if it is backed by influence. Although Germany seldom stresses the concept of political influence, this concept is based in reality, as confirmed by the example of Bosnia. So it is not merely a question of whether a state has influence but of how it uses that influence. In view of Germany's size relative to its neighbors, its influence is tolerable for them only if it is balanced by multilateral integration. Using that influence within an integration setting is something that Germany still has to learn, however. Without integration, coalitions will arise around foreign and economic policy to offset Germany's power. Even if these coalitions are not based on defense policy, they will evoke fears among Germans of being fenced in. The only way out of this dilemma is to resolve the problem of Germany's influence constructively within a European context by pursuing a process of integration into common institutions with Germany's neighbors. Hence, integration is an instrument for avoiding the possibly adverse consequences of a situation in which states feel in a weaker position in their bilateral relations with Germany.

Only a Germany integrated into multilateral institutions is compelled to take account of its neighbors' concerns when defining its own foreign policy interests. The same also is true of our neighbors. Otherwise, none of them would ever be able to promote their interests. But it also means that relations between Germany and its neighbors no longer depend on German intentions. Any German policy that failed to take adequate account of its neighbors' interests would come to grief in the intricacies of multilateral integration. This being so, the positive effects of multilateral integration are in line with properly understood German interests: For Germany's neighbors, this alleviates the problematical consequences of growing influence.

The Euro-Atlantic Task

The closeness of Euro-Atlantic relations can no longer be taken for granted because North America and Europe are no longer linked by the need to face a common and strong adversary. Extensions to the Euro-Atlantic stability axis, nevertheless, continue to be one of the main themes in German foreign and security policy. In the future, however, military dependence on the United States and the protection offered by a nuclear umbrella will link partners across the Atlantic much less than in the past. Future transatlantic relations will enjoy long-term stability only if they are balanced. For that reason, too, it is important to have a strong European Union that is able to act, which is why it also is sensible to build a strong European pillar within NATO. With U.S. troop reductions and the reintegration of France and Spain into NATO, and after the eventual integration of East Central European countries such as the Czech

Republic, Poland, and Hungary, the United States can no longer expect to claim and fill all command structures as in the past. The United States will have to surrender positions to a more independent European partner.

In principle, the rules governing Euro-Atlantic trading relations also will have to be clarified. The Helms-Burton Act passed by the U.S. Congress, which imposes sanctions against companies profiting from U.S. property nationalized by the Cubans is one example of how carelessness in dealing with questions affecting both Europe and the United States can create long-term harmful friction. All too often, the two sides fail to ensure adequate consultation about issues or conflicts outside the North Atlantic. In such talks, not only is it possible for one partner to be incorporated into the strategy of the other but jointly agreed global strategies might even be the result.

Fundamentally, the need to increase Euro-Atlantic consultation covers all areas, including security policy. In the future, as a consequence of the end of the East-West conflict, Germany, too, must play its part in discussions about out-of-area military operations. This demand is new in German politics and one that—in view of its defense policy philosophy, which has been confined to the national level and NATO ever since the Federal Republic was established—is difficult for us to process both psychologically and politically.

Official Euro-Atlantic cooperation is not enough. In the past, semi- and non-official exchanges also took place on a large scale. Euro-Atlantic relations would benefit from an extension of these exchanges and from the inclusion of the new democracies in East Central and Eastern Europe.

The Tasks in East Central and Eastern Europe

In the past, European integration was confined to the western end of the region, and its continuation in an easterly direction also is in the forefront of German interests in foreign and security policy. The economic aspect of this interest is obvious: Moves to enlarge a successful common market to include new members enhance the options for profitable trade and economic growth in the entire region. German interest goes beyond the economic aspect, however.

Germany's neighbors to both its east and its west would view matters with some suspicion if Germany were to make separate, bilateral efforts to shape its relations with its East Central and East European neighbors. That might introduce a risk of one state being played off against another, of one gaining advantages that the others do not have, of smaller groups of states ganging up on others. The result would be a potential for conflict and a risk of distrust generating differences of opinion and actual conflicts. On the other hand, a bilateralization of policy by Germany and other EU members is unavoidable if Germany's eastern neighbors are not integrated multilaterally into the EU and NATO. We are already aware of how much these states wish to have closer ties and more trade with the West as well as closer security relations with their western neighbors. That is why they repeatedly call on the major states in Western Europe, and Germany in particular, to cooperate more closely with them at the bilateral level as well. Such a development is one that Western Europe can ignore only at its peril. Poland, for example, whose biggest trading partner is Germany, wants more German investment but less dependence on Germany. These two goals can be reached simultaneously only if Poland, like Germany, is embedded multilaterally in the EU and in NATO. Bilateral dependence on Germany would then be a relative affair. This is precisely what is needed to have stable relations, so it also is an interest reflected in German policy.

On top of this, we have the special factor of Germany's relations with Russia. Russia is not a world power in the way the Soviet Union was, but it continues to be a major power and an important political and economic partner for Germany and for the entire EU. This is reason enough for Germany, the EU, and NATO to have an interest of their own in agreeing on constructive relations with Russia. As we have seen, however, Russia's own interest in having good relations with the West is so great that, in spite of its opposition to an opening of NATO, it would like to cooperate with that organization, mainly because most NATO members are, at the same time, members of the EU. Russia's trade with the EU is greater today than its trade with all other members of the Commonwealth of Independent States (CIS) combined. Germany's investment in Russia is roughly at the level of its involvement in Slovakia. All the same, Germany is one of the biggest investors in Russia and, after Ukraine, Russia's biggest trading partner.

Russia's opposition to any opening up of NATO has resulted from its obsolete interest in maintaining Russian spheres of influence and buffer zones. It is precisely such Russian aspirations that the states of East Central and Eastern Europe fear. For this reason alone it was not possible for Germany and the West to reject, out of consideration for Russia, an opening up of NATO to the states of East Central Europe—nervousness would have made barometers rise there! Although Russia's opposition was understandable, Moscow came to realize in time that it has more important, differently structured interests. Under the terms of the Founding Act resolved between NATO and Russia in 1997 in the face of NATO enlargement, Russia was not given any decisionmaking or veto rights in NATO, but it does have a right to information on NATO planning and decisionmaking on a reciprocal basis. Even on missions like the one in

Bosnia, Russia will in the future be involved not only in the mandating process through the OSCE and the United Nations, but also in planning and implementation. Hence, the Founding Act is a constructive forward-looking step because it demonstrates that Germany—like its Western partners—is interested in closer cooperation with Russia. It also demonstrates Russia's interest in improving cooperation with the West. For this reason, too, we must welcome the declaration of Foreign Minister Yevgeny Primakov that Russia will be making long-term efforts to work towards integration into the EU. The examples of Spain and Portugal have shown how long it can take for states that have not yet reached the level of development of EU members to become full members. It is easy to imagine, then, how long it will take East Central European states, since they are well below the level that Spain and Portugal had reached when they started their entry negotiations. This is why Russia's EU membership will not be decided until the twenty-first century. The first major step will be for Russia to form a free-trade area with the EU. Nonetheless, Russia's resolve to achieve membership and Primakov's assurance are important indicators of the western orientation of a democratic Russia.

One problem that is especially difficult to solve conceptually concerns those countries that wish to join NATO but are unable to do so, either at present or at all, in particular, the Baltic states. Even if the West assures them that Russia does not constitute a danger, their memories tell them a different story. And in view of the stances adopted by the Russian Duma, the subjective security interests of these states are greater than they appear when observed from Western Europe. But since, if only out of consideration for Russia, we cannot include these states in the first round of NATO expansion, other models must be discussed. An exchange of military observers, for example, could have some appeal. Ukraine, for its part, has no intention of joining NATO. It has expressed positive views with regard to NATO expansion, but does not wish to impair its own relations with Russia. For this reason, NATO has agreed on a separate charter with Ukraine. In some places, this document has a different, though no less significant, content from that of the Founding Act agreed between NATO and Russia.

With all the steps involved in enlarging EU and NATO, the question arises as to why new borders have to be drawn at all. The answer is that the process of extending an institution necessarily leads to new borders. The only question is whether the new borders are better than the old ones. To the extent that EU and NATO extensions advance the process of integration in Europe, they reduce existing problems. After all, there is talk of an "opening" only because the new borders will involve fewer standoffs and more bridge-building across old front lines. European integration in an easterly direction is a step-by-step process. This means that

EU and NATO membership can increase only gradually. All the same, European integration does mean solving problems and not creating new ones. The resolution adopted on the new CFE (Conventional Forces in Europe) treaty in Vienna, which will bring definite progress in disarmament in Europe, shows what positive changes in the overall situation can follow when the West is open to integration and willing to cooperate with states in the former East Bloc.

In this connection, the OSCE is often called the most comprehensive organization able to form a framework for cooperation and stabilization for the successor states of the East Bloc as well. However, this could easily be asking too much of the OSCE. Although the indivisibility of security in the OSCE area does exist on paper, the security situation in Tajikistan is different from that in Ireland. An institution like the OSCE with all its different members is indispensable if standards are to be established in the long run for inter- and intra-state conduct. When it comes to implementing such standards, however, the organization will necessarily remain weak, so, in addition to defining the standards, the OSCE's role will largely be mandating measures or conflict prevention. The idea of developing the OSCE into an alternative to NATO had no chance of success as soon as the OSCE was extended to include all successor states to the Soviet Union. Without the OSCE, however, there will be no pan-European peace order. Its set of political rules must therefore be extended and its powers gradually widened.

In the future, Europe will have different institutions with varying degrees of integration. The wider the membership of an institution, the lower the degree of possible integration. This being so, integration must always be confined to states able to engage in such a process while, at the same time, leaving room for cooperation with other states.

The Tasks in the Mediterranean

Solving the multitude of problems in relations among Europe, the Arab states, and Israel is beyond the capability of the policy options available to Germany or the EU in the short or medium term. Nevertheless, a start was made at the Barcelona conference in 1995. This conference attempted to address the problems of economic backwardness in most non-European Mediterranean states, as well as the recurrent threats emerging from political confrontation and splintering in the region and, finally, efforts to promote the intercultural understanding that has so often been lacking in Christian-Jewish-Muslim history. This is why Germany—acting in a way that is possible only in an EU setting—must support economic reforms in the non-European states of the Mediterranean; promote projects to combat poverty (if only to avoid a worsening of the problems caused by population growth and migratory pressures); and play the role of intermediary in arms control agreements, confidence-building measures, and disarmament treaties. Germany should also encourage democratization, the development of political diversity, and a respect for human rights and the importance of the civil society—especially in issues concerning the protection of women and their rights. The Israeli-Palestinian peace process is an important component in all of this.

Global Tasks

In addition to Germany's foreign trade interests are global risks, upstaged by security problems during the East-West conflict and now coming to the fore again, as are the forces of world-encompassing economic dynamism and new technologies. This being so, Germany must have an interest in comprehensive arrangements for dealing with ecological issues and in solving migration and arms proliferation problems. That is why Germany has always played an active role in global institutions and, since the time of the Social-Liberal coalition, has been advocating an international policy based on cooperation and a reconciliation of interests, dialogue, and confidence-building. Germany's interest in a permanent seat on the UN Security Council follows directly from this willingness and ability to assume global responsibility. This interest is in line with the interests of other states. The third world is interested in Germany having a seat, because Germany—as a result of the nature of its interests—is more multilateral in its stance than the United States, so it leans more towards a balance of interests between North and South.

Whether Germany can cope in the longer term with these new challenges confronting its foreign and security policy is hard to say. A country can fail even in the face of urgent challenges. However, the flexibility with which Germany has been attempting since 1990 to adapt to new and still-changing conditions in its foreign and security policy situation gives cause for optimism. Based on experience gained during the East-West conflict, Germany should be able to cope with the situation in its aftermath. Germany finds itself in a situation like the one it faced after the end of the Thirty Years' War in 1648, after the Congress of Vienna in 1815, or after the end of World War II—that is, after every upheaval in European history that redefined foreign and security policy structures. Now, as then, it must learn to come to terms with its new situation.

Notes

Speech (revised) delivered to the Robert Bosch Foundation Alumni Association conference in San Francisco, California, in November 1995.

Appendix:
Chronology of German Unification

December 1943   Tehran Conference

February 1945   Yalta Conference

7–8 May 1945   German unconditional surrender

5 June 1945   Allied Control Council: Berlin divided into four sectors: Germany divided into four zones of occupation

July-August 1945   Potsdam Conference

January 1947   "Bi-Zone" created by merger of American and British zones

1948–1948   Berlin blockade

23 May 1949   FRG founded

6 October 1949   GDR founded

25 July 1952   Entry into force of the Treaty of Paris establishing the European Coal and Steel Community

17 June 1953   GDR Uprising

23 October 1954   NATO admits FRG to membership

May 1955   Warsaw Pact established, including GDR

1 January 1958   Entry into force of the Treaty of Rome establishing the European Economic Community

13 August 1961   Berlin Wall erected

1970   Treaties by FRG with Moscow and Warsaw

1971   Quadripartite Agreement on Berlin

1972   FRG-GDR Treaty on the Basis of Relations

1 July 1987   Entry into force of the Single European Act on completion of the internal market

Summer-Fall 1989   Exodus of GDR citizens via Hungary (also via embassies in Poland and Czechoslovakia)

7 and 9 October 1989   GDR public demonstrations against SED government in Berlin and Leipzig ("Monday demonstration")

9 November 1989   Berlin Wall breached

28 November 1989   Chancellor Kohl lays out ten-point program to overcome the division of Germany and Europe

18 March 1990   First free elections in GDR

5 May 1990   "Two plus Four" talks begin; foreign ministers of Great
                      Britain, France, U.S., USSR, FRG, and GDR meet in
                      Bonn for first talks on German Unity
1 July 1990   Economic, monetary, and social union of FRG/GDR
31 August 1990   Unification Treaty between FRG and GDR signed in
                      Berlin
12 September 1990   Treaty on the Final Settlement with Respect to Germany
                      ("Two plus Four") signed
19 September 1990   GDR People's Chamber ratifies Unification Treaty
20 September 1990   Bundestag ratifies Unification Treaty
1–2 October 1990   Document to suspend Four-Power rights is signed
3 October 1990   In accord with Article 23 of the Basic Law, GDR accedes
                      to territory of the FRG and five new states are formed
2 December 1990   First Bundestag elections in unified Germany
17 June 1991   Treaty with Poland signed (guarantee of the Oder-
                      Neisse border)
21 June 1991   Bundestag vote establishing Berlin as the future capital
29 October 1993   Decision to base the European Monetary Institute
                      (precursor of the European Central Bank)
1 November 1993   Entry into force of the Maastricht Treaty establishing the
                      European Union
January 1994   German unemployment exceeds four million for the
                      first time since World War II
4 March 1994   Legislation introduced in the federal parliament to
                      dissolve the Treuhandanstalt, which had privatized
                      almost 13,000 state-owned enterprises
20 May 1994   Legislation adopted by the lower house of the federal
                      parliament establishing a fund of
                      DM 18 billion to provide compensation for
                      nationalized and expropriated property in the former
                      GDR
9 September 1994   Departure of last American troops from Berlin

About the Contributors

Miriam J. Aukerman accepted a Root-Tilden-Snow Fellowship to study public interest law at New York University. As a 1993–1994 Robert Bosch Foundation Fellow, she worked at the Central Europe desk of the German Foreign Ministry, and for the Foreigner Authority (*Ausländerbeauftragte*) of the state of Brandenburg. From 1994 to 1997 she was a consultant to the Russian and East European programs of The Ford Foundation, at both the New York and Moscow offices. In addition to her position at Ford, she served as the U.S. representative of the Gulag Museum, based on the site of the Perm–36 Gulag camp. She earned an M.Phil. in international relations from Oxford University in 1993 as a Keasbey scholar.

Lisa Creighton-Hendricks joined the law firm of Sonnenschein Nath & Rosenthal in Kansas City, where her practice includes telecommunications and litigation. She entered private practice in Kansas City and subsequently worked as an attorney for Sprint Communications Company L.P. While a 1995–1996 Robert Bosch Foundation Fellow, she worked at the federal Ministry for Postal and Telecommunication Services and at Deutsche Telekom. She earned an M.A. in political science in 1988 from Kansas State University and received a J.D. from the Washburn School of Law in 1990.

Caroline Fredrickson has worked since 1996 as legislative assistant for labor and judiciary in the office of Senator Tom Daschle, minority leader of the U.S. Senate, and she now serves as the counsel to the minority leader. She clerked with the U.S. Court of Appeals for the Second Circuit. As a 1993–1994 Robert Bosch Foundation Fellow, she worked at the Hans-Böckler-Stiftung in Düsseldorf, where she helped train worker representatives in how to exercise their legal rights, and with a labor lawyer in Berlin specializing in litigation involving works councils and terminated employees. In 1994–1996, she was an associate at Bredhoff & Kaiser. She received a J.D. from the Columbia University School of Law in 1992.

Crister S. Garrett is a transatlantic scholar based at the Monterey Institute of International Studies. In the United States, he teaches courses on the European Union, social democracy, and comparative European politics. In Europe, he lectures on U.S. foreign policy and politics. From 1997 to 1998 he was a Fulbright scholar at the Amerika Institut, University of Leipzig. As a Robert Bosch Foundation Fellow in 1994–1995, he focused on German foreign policy in the Bundestag and at the Stiftung Wissenschaft und Politik, Ebenhausen. He has published in the United States and Germany. He holds a Ph.D. from the University of California at Los Angeles in contemporary history and political science.

Molly E. Hall works as an assistant U.S. attorney for the Eastern District of Wisconsin in Milwaukee. She was a trial attorney for the Environmental Enforcement Section of the U.S. Department of Justice from 1990 to 1997. As a 1994–1995 Robert Bosch Foundation Fellow, she worked for the Environmental Ministry in Bonn in the areas of wildlife, trade, and the environment, and with the Bavarian State Environmental Ministry in Munich. She holds a J.D. from Washington and Lee University Law School.

Josef Joffe is editorial page editor/columnist for the *Süddeutsche Zeitung*, Germany, and a contributing editor to *Time* (International) and *U.S. News and World Report*. He was a Visiting Professor of Government at Harvard in 1990–1991 and at the Johns Hopkins University, as well as a scholar at the Carnegie Endowment for Peace and Woodrow Wilson Center. In addition to appearances as a talk show host on German TV and commentator on British and U.S. radio and TV, his essays and articles have been widely published in the U.S. and Europe. Joffe is the author of *The Limited Partnership: Europe, the U.S. and the Burdens of Alliance* as well as *The Future of War: Three Predictions for the 21st Century*. He holds a Ph.D. from Harvard University.

Andrew P. Johnson practices law at Orrick, Herrington & Sutcliffe in San Francisco, with an emphasis on corporate mergers and acquisitions, reorganizations, securities offerings, and venture capital transactions. In 1987–1988, he studied language, history, and international economics at the Georg August Universität, Göttingen, Germany. As a Robert Bosch Foundation Fellow in 1995–1996, he worked at the federal Transportation Ministry in Bonn and at the corporate headquarters of the Robert Bosch Company outside Stuttgart. He earned a J.D. from the University of Virginia School of Law in 1995.

Carol Kuester consults on public transportation projects in Europe and the United States with TransTec GmbH of Hanover. As a Robert Bosch Foundation Fellow in 1995–1996, she worked at the federal Transportation Ministry in Bonn and the Berlin/Brandenburg regional planning offices in Potsdam. Kuester earned an M.A. in urban planning from the University of California at Los Angeles in 1993.

John Leslie lived in Berlin, where he attended the Freie Universität and worked at the Aspen Institute from 1987 to 1990. In 1989–1990 he was a producer for NBC News in East Germany and Czechoslovakia. As a Robert Bosch Foundation Fellow in 1995–1996, he worked with the SPD Bundestag Fraktion and in the state representation of Rheinland-Pflaz in Bonn. He is a Ph.D. candidate in political science at the University of California, Berkeley, and a fellow at the Center for German and European Studies. He has been an adjunct faculty member at the University of San Diego.

Karl Th. Paschke has served as Under Secretary-General for Internal Oversight Services at the United Nations since 1994. From 1990 to 1994, he was responsible for the staff of the German Foreign Office and 200 missions abroad, and from 1987 to 1990 he was Deputy Chief of Mission at the German embassy to the United States. Other postings have included German ambassador to the United Nations and other international organizations in Vienna, spokesman for Foreign Minister Hans-Dietrich Genscher, and chief of the press department in the Foreign Ministry. Earlier in his career he held positions in the German embassy to

Zaire and as German Consul in Louisiana. He holds a J.D. from Bonn University and is an active jazz musician and composer with several CDs to his credit.

Christopher Sylvester received his M.A. in international relations at the Paul H. Nitze School of Advanced International Studies (SAIS) in 1994. As a Robert Bosch Foundation Fellow in 1994–1995, he worked in the Office of Foreign Affairs for the city of Rostock and at the Economic Development Agency for the state of Thuringia (LEG), Erfurt, Germany. After completing his fellowship, he worked as a consultant at LEG and, since August 1996, has been a policy analyst at Charles Fishman, P.C., an energy and political consulting firm in Washington, D.C.

Damon A. Terrill is currently a student at New York University School of Law, where he is editor-in-chief of the *Journal of Legislation and Public Policy*. As a Robert Bosch Foundation Fellow in 1994–1995, he worked at the German Foreign Ministry and the Ministry of Economics and European Affairs of Mecklenburg-Vorpommern. He also has held positions with the U.S. Department of State in Leipzig and with the law firms Coudert Brothers in Berlin and Rogers & Wells in Washington, D.C. He received an M.A. in international affairs from American University's School of International Service in 1995. His publications on Germany include "Tolerance Lost: Disaffection, Dissent and Revolution in the German Democratic Republic" *(East European Quarterly,* Fall 1994).

Karsten D. Voigt has been a member of the Bundestag since 1976, and serves on the Committee on Foreign Relations. He has been the SPD spokesperson for foreign policy and a member of the executive committee of the SPD Parliamentary Group. He served as vice president and, later, president of the North Atlantic Assembly, Brussels, and has been a member of the executive committee of the Union of Social Democratic Parties of the European Union. He has published widely and is known for his expertise on the United States and Russia.

About the Editors

Gale A. Mattox has been a professor of political science at the U.S. Naval Academy since 1981 and president of Women in International Security (WIIS), an international network based at the University of Maryland. She served in the U.S. State Department on the Policy Planning Staff (1994–1995) and in the Office of Strategic/Theater Nuclear Policy, and has also worked as an international affairs analyst at the Congressional Research Service. She has written on arms control and Europe, in addition to serving as co-editor of *Germany at the Crossroads* and *Germany Through American Eyes*. She holds a Ph.D. from the University of Virginia and is a former vice president of the International Studies Association, president of the Robert Bosch Alumni Association, and northeast director, Conference Group on German Politics.

Geoffrey D. Oliver recently joined the Office of Policy and Evaluation at the Federal Trade Commission. From 1985 to 1986 he served as law clerk to the Hon. Joseph L. Tauro of the U.S. District Court for the District of Massachusetts. As a Robert Bosch Foundation Fellow in 1986–1987, he held positions with the Federation of German Industries in Cologne, the Federal Cartel Office in Berlin, and the chemical firm BASF in Ludwigshafen. From 1987 to 1998, he practiced antitrust and international trade law in the Washington, D.C., and Brussels offices of O'Melveny and Myers. He received a J.D. from Cornell Law School in 1985. He has published a number of articles in the fields of antitrust and international trade law.

Jonathan B. Tucker is a research professor at the Center for Nonproliferation Studies of the Monterey Institute of International Studies. He has testified before Congress and published on a wide range of arms control and nonproliferation issues. As a 1987–1988 Robert Bosch Foundation Fellow, he worked at the NATO desk of the German Foreign Ministry in Bonn and for the aerospace firm Dornier in Friedrichshafen. Tucker has worked for the U.S. Department of State, the congressional Office of Technology Assessment, the U.S. Arms Control and Disarmament Agency, and the Presidential Advisory Committee on Gulf War Veterans' Illnesses. He received an M.A. in international relations from the University of Pennsylvania in 1982 and a Ph.D. in political science from the Massachusetts Institute of Technology in 1990.

Index